Managing Innovation in Policing

The Untapped Potential of the Middle Manager

by

William A. Geller

Associate Director
Police Executive Research Forum

Guy Swanger

Sergeant
San Diego Police Department

A Publication of the
Police Executive Research Forum
Sponsored by
The National Institute of Justice
Washington, D.C.

The research and writing of this book were supported by National Institute of Justice grant number 92-IJCXK004 to Harvard University's Kennedy School of Government, Program in Criminal Justice Policy and Management, and a subcontract to the Police Executive Research Forum. NIJ's and Harvard's support are gratefully acknowledged. Points of view in this document are those of the authors and do not necessarily represent the official position or policies of the U.S. Department of Justice, Harvard University, or the membership of PERF.

Police Executive Research Forum
1120 Connecticut Ave., N.W., Ste. 930
Washington, D.C. 20036

Library of Congress Catalog Number 95-71870

ISBN 1-878734-41-5

Cover design by Marnie Deacon

This book is dedicated to the many police middle managers across America who are doing an excellent job of implementing community policing—despite expert prognostications that middle managers are the worst obstacles to organizational change. As the great pitcher Satchel Paige observed (and great cop Chris Braiden so helpfully reminds us), "It ain't what we *don't* know that hurts us. It's what we *know* that *just ain't so*."

* * * * * * * * * * * * *

And this work is affectionately dedicated as well to Bill Geller's mentor, Norval Morris. Upon his recent retirement from full-time teaching at the University of Chicago Law School, Norval remarked what a queer experience retirement is: "I still think of myself as a promising young man," he confided. Many of us still think of you that way, too, Norval. Godspeed as you continue reaching.

Foreword

The quiet revolution that George Kelling referred to in American policing has become very noisy. We are knee-deep in this revolution that has been brewing for the past 20 years. In jurisdictions large and small, urban and rural, rich and poor, police agencies are redefining their core philosophies as they adopt community policing and problem solving.

The movement that began with a few special units and programs devoted to community involvement has now grown to where it is changing the most basic structures and philosophies of police agencies. Police departments now talk about empowering, de-layering, reengineering, and core process redesign—significant changes that make a real difference in how police respond to crime and disorder.

While much has been written about the roles of chief executives and officers in community policing, the roles of middle managers have been left out of the discussion, except for the common assumption that middle managers are roadblocks to change. In *Managing Innovation in Policing*, Bill Geller and Guy Swanger systematically examine this issue head-on and give us some encouraging food for thought. Geller is coauthor of the seminal work *Deadly Force: What We Know* and editor of the International City/County Management Association's "green bible," *Local Government Police Management*. Swanger is a street-level pioneer in the San Diego Police Department's internationally respected problem-solving efforts. Together, they lead us on a journey across the country to find examples of the new role of middle managers in American policing.

Their path takes us from the Charlotte-Mecklenburg, N.C., Police Department's Captain Kevin Wittman—who accepted the challenge of converting the training academy into an "on-line" operational support function that "does something practical to support problem solving"—to Seattle police middle manager Clark Kimerer—whose pioneering work forging problem-solving partnerships between police and previously antagonistic social service workers was inspired by the recommendation of a skid-row arrestee. The common theme in these and the other tales this book tells is that middle managers, when equipped with the tools and support they need, can *and are* making valuable contributions to community policing. Rather than finding middle managers to be obsolete, Geller and Swanger show us that middle managers have a dynamic and exciting part to play as policing moves toward the 21st century. This book serves as a guidepost, documenting the emerging role of these managers. This book may do for policing what *In Search of Excellence* has done for private-sector innovation. We are, therefore, particularly grateful to the National Institute of Justice and its director, Jeremy Travis, for providing the support and encouragement without which this volume could not have been developed.

As police agencies expand and redefine their roles in communities, they cannot afford to write off middle managers as significant resources. *Managing Innovation in Policing* shows us that middle managers have tremendous potential to be key players in community policing, encourages us to tap that potential, and shows us how to do it—all for the good of both our police organizations and the communities police serve.

Chuck Wexler, Executive Director
Police Executive Research Forum
Washington, D.C.
October 1995

Foreword

Community policing commands center stage across the Nation for law enforcement agencies of all sizes. These agencies are implementing a mode of policing that, among other objectives, encourages officers to become more active partners with the community for the purpose of jointly identifying and addressing the problems of crime and disorder facing the community. Proponents of the community policing philosophy believe that, by proactively dealing with those underlying conditions, police departments and sheriffs' offices can prevent many crimes that otherwise would have claimed substantial departmental resources, including investigations and arrests.

This new orientation to policing has its roots in a series of studies in the 1970s, including research projects sponsored by the National Institute of Justice. Those studies helped to direct the attention of police executives to unanticipated limitations of three key components of then-current policing strategy: random, preventive patrol; rapid response to calls for service; and follow-up investigation. Such studies—combined with the civil unrest of the 1960s and 1970s and the recommendations of national crime commissions—helped motivate police agencies to look beyond incident-driven, reactive crime fighting, and to add—not substitute—a proactive, preventive, problem-solving approach that forges closer ties to the community.

Community policing, a key component of the 1994 Crime Act and an area of ongoing Institute-commissioned research and evaluation, is a powerful concept offering great promise. If poorly implemented, however, even ideas of enormous potential stand little chance of surviving long enough to become incorporated into agency operations.

This book's many recommendations and insights address a key, long-neglected task in the implementation of community policing: garnering the support of middle managers and regarding them as part of the solution, not foreordained obstacles to change. Executive leadership alone is not sufficient; enthusiastic support by line officers is welcome but still falls short; as this book vividly and convincingly argues, the transformation to community policing requires the active involvement of middle managers.

It would be tragic if the potential for reform of the police function in our society foundered on the shoals of mismanaged implementation. There is too much at stake. This thoughtful book identifies middle managers as a key to successful innovation.

Jeremy Travis, Director
National Institute of Justice
Washington, D.C.
October 1995

Contents

Introduction

Organizational development experts, experienced senior managers within and outside of policing, and battle-scarred police strategic reformers widely share the perception that middle managers in hierarchical, bureaucratic organizations are likely to be among the most daunting obstacles to efficient and meaningful organizational change. Many police chiefs report that their strategic innovation directives are thwarted by obdurate middle managers (Sadd and Grinc 1994; Zhao, et al. 1995: 19-22). For instance, Cheektowaga, New York, Chief Bruce Chamberlin found that "fairly often police officers try to follow my request that they take innovative approaches to community problems, only to find that their [mid-level] superiors balk at the departure from past practices" (Chamberlin 1995b). Why so many managers and management advisors in policing and other arenas believe the middle manager is a speed bump on the road to progress we shall discuss somewhat later in this book.

Some before us have contested on theoretical and experiential grounds the conventional wisdom that most mid-level employees will staunchly resist most organizational change. They include, among others, Kanter (1982, 1983); Sayles (1993); Kelling and Bratton (1993); and Braiden (1995). If one believed that the prevailing view among the experts is correct, then it would follow logically that a good way to reduce internal opposition to police strategic change would be to thin the ranks of middle management wherever possible. Suppose for a moment that flattening police departments by eliminating such middle management ranks as lieutenants, captains or comparable level civilian employees was indeed a better way than merely reorienting middle managers' work to accelerate police operational improvements. Even so, a practical problem would arise, at least for near-term progress. For while some agencies have pruned their middle ranks, we believe they will prove to be the exceptions rather than the rule over the next decade or so. Guyot (1979) graphically characterized the challenge that reformers have encountered over the years when trying to alter the rank structures of American police departments. She called the task "bending granite" (see also Sparrow 1992: 50; compare Wycoff and Skogan 1993: 35). And Greene, et al. (1994: 93) assert: "[T]he history of police organizational change has generally favored the police organization over other institutions bent on changing it."

A number of leading advocates for police strategic innovation take the position that *some* flattening or *interim* flattening of the police hierarchy could prove beneficial. Former Edmonton Police Superintendent Chris Braiden, for instance, suggests: "If I were a chief, I'd probably cut down the number of middle managers, but I would not eliminate them." And he asks: "Are some chiefs who are great proponents of flattening organizations prepared to do more work themselves? If the tasks are important, they still need to be done by someone" (Braiden 1995). Former British police manager Malcolm Sparrow, who found refuge from practice by joining the Harvard University faculty, urges a temporary, *functional* flattening—in the sense of enabling direct communications between the chief and first-line officers—during times of "accelerated change" in the organization. But, he cautions, "This is not proposed as a permanent state of affairs, as clearly the rank structure has its own value and is not to be lightly discarded" (Sparrow 1992: 56).

Since we believe that middle managers probably *can't*, *won't*, and *shouldn't* be jettisoned from the police departments of America in our lifetimes, our mission in this small volume is to explore some of the ways that middle managers can be deployed, so long as they are employed, to help strengthen community policing implementation efforts. At the very least, one would hope for approaches that *minimize the opposition* of middle managers to strategic reforms and the concomitant infrastructural changes. Ideally, as we shall try to explore below, there will be steps that police and local government and community leaders can take to create working environments in which middle managers voluntarily, proactively, and effectively help implement community policing strategies.

Our proposals for the contributions middle managers can make to police strategic improvements are hardly exhaustive. Given the paucity of attention devoted thus far to the role of middle managers in the community policing movement (Reiner 1992: 485-86), we seek merely to advance the discussion by identifying some of the steps that are worth considering and researching further. Most of these recommendations are derived from more general suggestions about the implementation of community problem solving contained in the literature and from advice we and scores of other police practitioners and management advisors have given to and received from police change-agents over the past decade or so.

Many of those to whom we are deeply indebted for·the ideas contained in this book are quoted on the pages that follow. But many others who deserve heartfelt thanks are not singled out by name. That in no way diminishes our gratitude. With advancing years comes increasing *originality*, which, as they say, is remembering what you heard and forgetting where you heard it. We do recall, however, the police practitioners, trainers, advisors, and scholars who have been kind enough to read and make helpful suggestions for improving drafts of this book. They include Wanda Barkley, Joseph Beazley, Linda Black, Chris Braiden, Joseph Brann, Gerald Cooper, Everett Erlandson, Julie Shannon Geller, Murray Geller, Eduardo Gonzalez, Clarence Harmon, Craig Huneycutt, Sandy Kaminska, George Kelling, Nancy McPherson, Dennis Nowicki, Mary Peters, Laurie Robinson, Norman Stamper, Darrel Stephens, Jeremy Travis, Ben Tucker, Kevin Wittman, David Wray, and the alphabetically often—but substantively rarely—last Mary Ann Wycoff. We also appreciate Connie Moy's thoughtful copy editing of the final draft.

The general organization of this book is as follows:

First, what is the evolving community policing strategy that middle managers are thought to resist and which we seek their help in advancing?

Second, what generally are the traditional roles and functions of middle managers in most police departments, and should middle managers be doing what they are doing in light of the new mission?

Third, if changes in the contributions middle managers are making seem warranted, why is it that these police employees are considered by so many organizational analysts to be reluctant participants in the modifications?

Fourth, if there are strong reasons to anticipate resistance, are there also powerful reasons to hope and expect that middle managers can become willing partners in the reform movement?

And *fifth*, what ideas can we offer for ways that police departments, local government officials and other stakeholders might help position and motivate middle managers to play constructive roles in adopting and improving community policing?

I. Defining the Community Problem-Solving Strategy

Providing a foundation for exploring how police middle managers might advance community policing requires some clarity about what one wishes to advance. An increasingly common definition of community policing (popular among Justice Department funding and research agencies, police training institutes, police membership organizations, police practitioners, community organizers and your authors) is something like the following:

What it's not...
Community policing is a reorientation of policing philosophy and strategy *away from* the view that police *alone* can reduce crime, disorder and fear. The strategy is based on the view that police don't help their communities very much by placing *primary* reliance on random preventive patrolling, rapid response to calls for service irrespective of their urgency, post-incident investigations to identify and arrest offenders, and other primarily *reactive* criminal justice system tactics.

What it is...
The strategic shift is *toward* the view that police can better help redress and prevent crime, disorder, and fear problems through active, multi-faceted, consultative and collaborative relationships with diverse community groups and public and private-sector institutions. Such partnerships are established to:

- better inform the police and communities about the nature and extent of tractable public safety problems;
- better analyze how to reduce these problems;
- more effectively and efficiently take appropriate action against the identified problems;
- monitor the problems to ensure that interventions were successful, that different approaches are attempted as needed, and that preventive measures are implemented to forestall recurrences of the problem; and
- periodically review and improve the police organization's structures and systems so they facilitate more efficient, effective, and legitimate pursuit of the foregoing objectives.

In short, community policing (or community problem solving) employs the dual strategies of community engagement and problem solving to safeguard communities.

> *"[I]t is partly the ambiguity of the concept [of community policing] that is stimulating the wide pattern of experimentation we are observing. In this sense, it is important that the concept mean something, but not something too specific. The ambiguity is a virtue"* (Moore 1994: 290).

The Vera Institute of Justice, led at the time by University of Wisconsin Law Professor Michael Smith, collaborated with New York City Police Commissioner Ray Kelly on some excellent definitional materials, disseminated in problem-solving handbooks to street cops and their supervisors. In one of these manuals, the role of a traditional beat cop is analogized to that of a paramedic working an ambulance detail. "The paramedic's principal function," they noted, "is to stabilize patients until they can be delivered to a hospital for appropriate medical treatment" (Farrell, et al. 1993a: 3). By comparison, officers who are not engaged in community problem solving could, in handling a 9-1-1 emergency call, aspire only to "stabilizing the situation, preventing further harm or violation of law, and making an arrest, issuing a summons, taking a report of a past crime, or making a referral to other police commands for some follow-up action." Though these are not unimportant tasks, to be sure, there was no specialized component within the NYPD to which first-responding officers could make a referral for "follow-up service, except where serious, unsolved crime required investigation by detectives. A major thrust of the move to community policing," they explain, "is to fill that gap—by authorizing patrol officers to follow-up on the community problems they encounter, and by allowing them sufficient time to do so effectively" (Farrell, et al. 1993a: 3).

While the advocates of community policing and problem-oriented policing differ on a variety of significant and marginally important definitional issues, virtually all would concur that community problem solving is *not* intended to be a temporary "program" grafted onto conventional police structures and systems. As a St. Louis Metropolitan Police Department officer told his superiors during a let-our-hair-down brainstorming session on obstacles to implementing problem-oriented policing: "I have heard that low morale and lack of manpower are key reasons why the program won't work. I feel that the first problem is that everyone thinks of problem solving as a program and not a way of thinking."

> *"Police officers in community policing assignments are expected to be 'full-service' personnel—to serve as a resource to those living and working on the beat..., to help them forge links with service-providing agencies, to help them organize to fight the problems that beset them, to engage them in the process of setting priorities among those problems, and to help them devise and implement plans to deal with their priority problems and eliminate the conditions that give rise to them. That is a tall order. It is not what most officers now on the force were trained to do when they went through the Academy years ago, nor is it what they learned when they first hit the streets"* (Farrell, et al. 1993a: 2).

Community problem solving is variously described as a strategy, a philosophy, a style, or, in Lavrakas' helpful term, a "process" (1995: 105). "Community policing," Lavrakas suggests, "is not a specific program but can embrace varied substantive components. The promise this process holds for revolutionizing how we deploy our law enforcement resources within a comprehensive crime prevention effort is what forms its appeal."

Who is "the community" in community policing? This is one of myriad definitional questions that gets asked on a recurring basis, and it's an important one. What police strive for are energized citizen partners in the fight against particular kinds of problems. Accordingly, sometimes the "community" will refer to a geographic neighborhood, while at other times it will entail a *community of interest* (Trojanowicz 1994: 258), whose members are dispersed around the police department's entire service area. Suppose, for instance, a police department is dealing with patterns of victimization or fear that generally afflict a city's small business owners, landlords, tenants, the banking community, a public transit system, or ethnic or religious groups. In such cases, the police may enjoy the competent, highly motivated partnership of groups and institutions who already have strong working relationships among themselves despite being physically remote from one another.[1]

Bennett (1994), Osborne and Gaebler (1993), and Friedman (1994) offer three more worthy descriptions of the essence of community policing:

☐ "[T]he main elements of a community policing philosophy might be summarized in a single sentence as a belief or intention held by the police that they should consult with and take account of the wishes of the public in determining and evaluating operational policing and that they should collaborate with the public in identifying and solving local problems" (Bennett 1994: 229).

☐ "The basic idea is to make public safety a *community* responsibility, rather than simply the responsibility of the professionals—the police. It transforms the police officer from an investigator and enforcer into a catalyst in a process of community self-help" (Osborne and Gaebler 1993: 50). It transforms the police department into one "that offers customized rather than standardized services, then measures the results" (*ibid.*: 174).

☐ "'Problem-solving partnerships' captures, in a phrase, two ideas central to community policing: a focus on patterned, repetitive crime and disorder, and the need for police to have allies in solving these problems" (Friedman 1994: 263; see also Zhao, et al. 1995: 12).

The problem solutions may entail traditional police enforcement powers (arrest, etc.), but often imaginative police and community members find more effective, more enduring, and cheaper solutions by using tools other than traditional investigative and criminal justice system methods. The literature on community policing and problem-oriented policing is replete with examples of nontraditional peacekeeping techniques, and the reader unfamiliar with this strategic reform movement is referred to those materials for background.[2] In many ways, the detailed

---

[1] Sherman (1986: 180-81) raises the basic question whether the emphasis on "community" in the phrase community policing arises from

"nostalgia for small-town community life.... [I]t is possible that policing may be equally or more effective when focused on other units of analysis or on other targets for proactive efforts. Offenders, addresses, *problems*, relationships and social networks may be as important as are communities, especially with modern revolutions in life-style that make many residential neighborhoods largely empty for most of the business day" (emphasis added).

His suggestion that *problems* may be a more suitable unit of analysis and work than *communities* goes to the heart of debates that raged during the 1980s over whether "community policing" was the *umbrella concept* under which problem-solving was a *tactic* or vice versa. These debates, in our view, were partly principled and partly struggles over institutional credit, for different organizations had embraced one or the other of the two labels.

[2] The worthwhile literature includes Eck and Spelman (1987); Spelman and Eck (1987); Goldstein (1979, 1987, 1990); Moore and Stephens (1991a, 1991b); Moore (1992, 1994); Stephens (1993); Sparrow, et al. (1990); Stamper (1976); Burgreen and McPherson (1990, 1992); Trojanowicz and Bucqueroux (1990, 1992); Trojanowicz (1992, 1994); Michigan State University School of Criminal Justice (1992); Couper and Lobitz (1991); Wasserman and Moore (1988); Wilson and Kelling (1989); Behan (1986); Taft (1986); Cordner (1986, 1988); Braiden (1985, 1990a,

illustrations of community problem solving in action contained in much of this literature will be far more informative than will a succinct definition of the emerging policing strategies. Goldstein (1993: 1), acknowledging the widespread desire for "definition and simplification" and for "agreement on a pure model of community policing," nevertheless cautions against "oversimplification." That, he warns, "can be a deadly enemy to progress in policing. The field already suffers because so much in policing is oversimplified."

Though perhaps an odd notion, it may be that those in the best position to help society by furnishing accessible, succinct descriptions of community problem solving will be those *outside* the police reform field who can see the forest for the trees. For instance, Liz Schorr's (1988) descriptions of successful social service programs typically are more interesting and more illuminating even than the various summaries published by the visionaries who led the projects. It's not only writing skill that empowers Schorr, we believe, but an ability to view those projects through the eyes of the general public rather than from the perspective of project managers and advocates. It is often difficult to recognize something clearly when you are in the middle of it. As communications guru Tony Schwartz put it, "I don't know who discovered water, but it probably *wasn't* a fish."

So at the risk of violating the maxim that "everything should be made as simple as possible but no simpler," we summarize: The twin implementation objectives that middle managers might be enlisted to advance are (1) strengthening the police agency's capacity to consult productively and respectfully with the community and (2) improving its collaborative and solo problem-solving capacity. In both instances, the organizational change-agent quickly confronts not only skill deficits among some of the police employees at all ranks but numerous organizational traditions, structures, policies, procedures, and practices that, if left unchanged, will thwart the efforts of the department to engage the community for problem solving. Overcoming these and other types of implementation obstacles—solving organizational problems so the organization can solve community problems—can become a core job function for sworn and civilian police middle managers.

> *"What is community policing? Police others as you would have others police you. That really says it all"* (Braiden 1995).

1990b, series of undated papers); Hornick, et al. (1993); Leighton (1994); Portland Police Bureau (1990); Potter (1992; Lungren (1992); Wycoff (1988); Wycoff and Skogan (1993, 1994); Skogan (1990); Skogan, et al. (1995: 40-43); Kennedy (1993); McElroy, et al. (1993); Travis, et al. (1993); Farrell (1988); Farrell, et al. (1993a, 1993b); Koller (1990); Rosenbaum (1994); Hayward Police Department (1990); Brann, et al. (1992); Brann and Whalley (1992); Capowich and Roehl (1994); Williams and Sloan (1990); Brown (1985, 1989, 1991); Brown and Wycoff (1987); Bratton (1994); Davis (1985); Toch and Grant (1991); Toch (1995b); Weisel (1990, 1992); Weisel and Eck (1994); Vernon and Lasley (1992); Webber (1991, 1992); Crawford (1992); Glensor (1990); Peak, et al. (1992); Pate, et al. (1986); Sulton (1992); Alpert and Dunham (1989); Klockars (1988); Bennett (1994); Friedman (1994); Weisburd (1994); Weisburd, et al. (1988); Riechers and Roberg (1990); Chicago Police Department (1993); Bayley (1988, 1994); Skolnick and Bayley (1986, 1988); Wilkinson and Rosenbaum (1994); Lurigio and Rosenbaum (1994); Sadd and Grinc (1994); and Zhao, et al. (1995).

II. What Do Police Middle Managers Do—
And Should They Be Doing It?

To figure out in any given organization how much of a change in role for middle managers might be needed, it is helpful generally to begin by understanding the middle managers' current roles. Traditionally, lieutenants, captains and civilian middle managers are assigned to any of three functions: patrol operational management (e.g., watch commander); special unit management (e.g., narcotics or robbery/homicide unit commander or leading a short-term special project such as crowd control at a major public event); and administrative roles (e.g., heading a personnel, budget, planning, internal affairs, training or public information unit and serving in senior staff positions for the chief or other senior managers).

> *Middle managers have historically focused on control and evaluations in organizations. The leadership role, seen as more important and as a visible position, is left to the chief executive officers or frontline supervision. Middle managers traditionally don't inspire, act creatively, or lead change. They simply manage the system. Some organizations are now re-evaluating the worth of middle management. IBM, the U.S. Postal Service, and U.S. automakers have used downsizing to eliminate several thousand middle management positions. As roles and companies change to keep pace, middle managers are truly caught in the middle.*

In most of these assignments most of the time, middle managers have the responsibility, as Seattle Chief Norman Stamper (1992: 153) likes to put it, of "keeping the promises" made by higher-ups. For instance:

☐ When the chief promises to clear a neighborhood block of open-air drug marketing and prostitution, the managers of the narcotics and vice units have to develop a responsive plan and carry it off in a timely fashion. To do this, these managers have to prioritize activities and allocate resources in a way that does not harmfully neglect other important unit obligations.

☐ Or the mayor may promise to step up directed, preventive patrols in a neighborhood plagued by gang turf battles. The patrol managers need to keep this promise, but in a fashion that still leaves the patrol force ready to respond to emergency calls and able to continue carrying out other important tasks.

☐ Or suppose the chief or a city council member promises to develop the conflict management skills of first-line officers and sergeants to help reverse an escalating pattern of violent street conflict between Latino young men and young Anglo officers during field interrogations. Then the training manager and perhaps a special projects manager from the chief's office will need to explore ways to adjust the in-service and pre-service training curricula to accommodate the new topic without slighting other crucial aspects of education for effective policing.

A common thread in each example is the obligation of the manager to invest enough resources to keep the promise while conserving enough resources (that is, *responsibly withholding* them from the current task) to be able to meet continuing, legitimate demands on the agency. The police manager functioning as such a conserver of resources can easily be misconstrued as hoarding resources in order to impede the accomplishment of the latest initiative. To be sure, some middle managers do deserve this criticism. Sparrow (1992: 57-58), for instance, writes of chiefs who "may have the authority to allocate police resources as they think best, but [who] are frequently frustrated by administrators who find some bureaucratic reason for not releasing funds for particular purposes." But in our experience, more often than not it is the competing demands (and the sometimes mixed messages sent from above) concerning the investment of scarce police personnel and other resources that account for what appears to be middle managers' resistance to "getting with the (latest) program."

In contrast to police "manager-leader" or "leader-manager" models, the "pure" police manager is a "controlling manager whose time is spent almost exclusively in his or her office, which serves as the 'command center' for the organization. The lion's share of the agency's paper originates from and returns to this office. [The pure manager] personally balances spread sheets, maintains statistics on most organizational/managerial processes. Coordination and control are accomplished principally by telephone, computer, and memoranda. [The manager] sees himself or herself, and is seen by others, as very analytical and dispassionate. [He or she] does a great deal of reading, most of it directly related to indices of organizational effectiveness and efficiency. *** New ideas are of interest if they are perceived as valuable in controlling the managerial process; intuitive and creative suggestions are often rejected with disdain. [The traditional manager is] seen by those 'in the know' as the one who controls resources and who has answers to most questions about the organization's past. Nonetheless, [this manager's] orientation is in the present, getting the job done today" (Stamper 1992: 169).

In any event, it seems clear to us that, in the most general terms, middle managers should continue to be responsible for protecting the organization and the community against a raid on resources that will be needed for public safety emergencies. What is critical is the *balance* struck between holding resources back and expending resources in a way that might solve current problems and leverage additional preventive resources for the future.

A litany of other functions traditionally performed by middle managers can be derived from observation and the literature on police management (see, e.g., Kelling and Bratton 1993: 4, 6-7, 9; Moore and Stephens 1991a, 1991b; Fyfe 1985; Leonard and More 1971; Wilson and McLaren 1972). These functions would include:

- ☐ setting operational priorities for their own units
- ☐ supervising operations
- ☐ public relations with neighborhood groups
- ☐ coordination with other patrol and detective units
- ☐ determining assignments
- ☐ scheduling work days and shifts
- ☐ providing operational notices to each shift (special attention to vulnerable locations/people, wanted persons, etc.)

□ transmitting departmental/division orders to personnel within their commands
□ communicating with senior officials and serving as a messenger between subordinates and senior officials
□ compiling periodic crime, arrest and other productivity statistics
□ keeping attendance, sick leave, and other logs for personnel units
□ preparing district/precinct budget requests
□ preliminarily handling citizen complaints against officers
□ running the service/administrative desk in district/precinct stations
□ procurement
□ authorizing use of equipment and keeping track of its location and condition
□ taking charge of complex crime scene investigations
□ taking charge of complex operations within the middle manager's area of specialty (e.g., hostage/barricade, SWAT, containing collective violence)

> *"[T]he role of mid-management...in policing during the past 50 years...has been [primarily] to extend the reach of management into the day-to-day operations of police departments by standardizing and controlling both organizational procedures and officer performance. As such, captains and lieutenants have been the leading edge of the control functions of police departments"* *(Kelling and Bratton 1993: 9).*

□ managing special projects (dignitary protection, crowd control at public events, holiday season robbery and pickpocket prevention efforts in shopping centers, order maintenance support when a mayor temporarily moves into her city's high-rise public housing to dramatize its deplorable conditions, etc.)
□ reviewing and approving shift reports on—and thus exercising some quality control over—field activity (arrests, follow-up investigations, use of force, etc.)
□ conducting roll call inspections (of weapons, the wearing of soft body armor and other uniform elements, etc.)
□ reviewing "early warning" system alerts concerning officers at risk of poor performance due to job-related or personal problems
□ supervising the supervisors below them

The list could continue. Couper and Lobitz (1991: 2) summarized what Hickman and Silva (1977) earlier called "old age" managerial skills. These include "setting goals, establishing procedures, organizing, and controlling." The architects of the strategic transformation from traditional to community policing will need to weigh carefully such long-standing roles for middle managers to assess which of these functions must be retained and adapted to provide leadership of and an infrastructure for community problem solving. While we shall not attempt in this book to react to each of the preceding items individually, generally we believe that almost any important organizational mission needs leaders who make the promises (articulate the vision and chart the overall direction), entrepreneurial followers who find imaginative ways to attain the goals, and managers who secure needed support services and attend to quality control, efficiency, and other crucial matters (see Stamper 1992: 150-58).

To be sure, some of the things middle managers currently do conflict with the core tactics of problem solving. Examples include inflexibility concerning work schedules, micromanaging officers' choices of preventive tactics, or punishing cops for infractions of silly rules that impede officers from building legitimate, trusting relationships with members of the public. Nevertheless, it would be unwise to jettison as *completely* superfluous the "old age" managerial skills of "setting goals, establishing procedures, organizing, and controlling." Whether a manager should "control" or "coach" or engage in other advisory, nurturing approaches depends on the tasks at hand and the people being managed. For many aspects of officers' collaborative efforts to tackle complex public safety problems, a controlling managerial approach would be counterproductive. But it still will be necessary for middle managers to maintain their skills in being highly directive when dealing with some types of problem employees (e.g., habitual abusers of force or authority and persistent sick roll abusers—Punch 1983) and with some kinds of

> *"Police officers have long been accustomed to doing their jobs 'by the book.' Detailed instruction manuals, sometimes running into hundreds, even thousands, of pages have been designed to prescribe action in every eventuality. Police officers feel that they are not required to exercise judgment so much as to know what they are supposed to do in a particular situation. There is little incentive and little time to think, or to have ideas. There is little creativity and very little problem solving. Most of the day is taken up just trying not to make mistakes"* (Sparrow 1992: 54).

operational challenges requiring highly coordinated team tactics. Examples of tactics necessitating precise team coordination include the service of high-risk warrants; hostage-barricade or terrorist incidents; neighborhood evacuations due to hazardous material threats or storm warnings; and risks to vehicles and pedestrians posed by unusually heavy traffic such as when major public events conclude.

Naturally, one would wish for middle managers in traditional or innovative organizations to treat their subordinates with the basic decency and respect due any coworker. But showing subordinates respect does not mean middle managers should be allowed to abdicate their responsibility when circumstances necessitate for telling some others precisely what to do and how and when to do it. Again, the challenge for the middle manager is knowing what the right balance is, in a wide variety of circumstances, between issuing nonnegotiable demands, making suggestions, and simply butting out so that dedicated and competent officers and supervisors can exercise—and learn from exercising—the discretion they have been paid to develop.

Similarly, the traditional middle management role of setting goals and procedures will have some continuing application in community problem-solving regimens, in our view. Frontline officers should be granted far more latitude than they have had historically to jointly set goals with the service population and tailor work methods to the idiosyncrasies of the problems being addressed. But even (or, as some might argue, *especially*) under a collaborative community policing strategy, there remains a risk that a team in one precinct or beat might monopolize the agency's training or printing or postage budgets to the detriment of colleagues and other neighborhoods. To prevent such problems and ensure the equitable distribution of resources and power among units or squads, the middle manager may need to coordinate and make decisions about goals, procedures, and priorities.

III. Why Middle Managers Oppose, or Have Been Considered Obstacles to, Strategic Innovation

Striking the delicate balance between delegating decisionmaking to frontline personnel and micromanaging, as well as trying to please all those above the middle manager in the organization (and external constituents), can be very difficult. That difficulty alone helps explain why middle managers might not welcome the chief's enthusiastic announcement that his or her department has embarked on a new and exciting journey into the land of community problem solving. In this chapter, we explore the litany of reasons why many believe the police organizational reformers' worst headaches will be mid-level employees.

"Reinventing" public, monopolistic agencies is not, of course, precisely the same as the strategic makeover of a private business, but expert advice aimed at private enterprise clearly has great resonance for an increasing number of public administrators—police executives included—who are well-schooled in and respectful of business management techniques (see, e.g., Bratton 1994). Thus, it may help to begin this chapter with a classic statement of popular private-sector thinking about the middle manager and his or her potential acceptance of organizational change. The views are those of James Champy, co-author of the best-selling book, *Reengineering the Corporation*:

> *"Listening with an objective ear to those who resist community policing would provide planners and would-be implementers with key information for a more effective plan of action"* (Mastrofski 1993: 10).

"[Middle managers] have gotten to a place in their careers under a set of rules that have been well understood. Now we come in and say: 'All the rules are going to change. There may not even be the place you thought you were moving towards when this reengineering job is done.' It's these people who are the most intransigent to change. The truth is maybe 75% of them aren't going to be there; at least not in their current capacity. This group also has the most difficult time 'transitioning' into a new model of work. What you're saying to those people is: 'Managerial work as you know it is over. Nothing personal in this, but in your work you have not added value to what we do. So what we want you to do is get back out there on the street, on the route, back out there with the customer, where we really need the value added.' Now, that's a new game for some of these people, who, frankly, thought that what a career was about was getting away from the real work" (quoted in Vogl 1993/1994: 54).

Experienced and insightful students and practitioners of policing generally subscribe to the view that *police* middle managers are no less likely than their *private sector* counterparts to throw a wrench into the reform works. While observing that in some police agencies "some middle managers are supportive" of strategic shifts, Goldstein (1990: 173, 174) notes that an effort to introduce problem-oriented policing *organization-wide* rather than in an "incubator" special unit will probably meet with mid-level resistance. Such a wholesale implementation effort, he suggests, "is bound to be diluted by those who are either passive or—as is *likely to be true especially of middle management*—actively resist and perhaps even attempt to sabotage the efforts" (emphasis added).

So the belief in mid-rank entrenchment is strong, deep, and widespread. Here, then, is an overview of many of the *reasons* why police middle managers have been, or at least are expected to be, obstacles to the implementation of police strategic reform.

☐ *They have mastered the current systems.* The middle managers, it is said, are the enforcers of the current enterprise and the current organizational culture. They play this role partly because of expectations set by superiors and partly because—in organizations where the middle managers rose through the ranks—they achieved their career successes by developing expertise in how to work the current organizational systems. As a St. Louis sergeant said in response to a department survey, "The traditional police manager...is committed to an orthodoxy which includes 'not making waves' and which excludes innovation. This commitment has served him or her well because they have advanced through the ranks by following the orthodoxy." Changing the orthodox systems, *even if they are deficient*, thus poses a threat to the middle managers' know-how (see Moore and Stephens 1991a: 108).

> *"A chief executive who inherits a smoothly running bureaucracy, complacent in the status quo, has a tougher job"* than one *"fortunate enough to inherit an organization that is already susceptible to change."* The task for the leader of a mediocre and content organization *"is to expose the defects that exist within the present system. *** The difficulty...is that [doing so]...may look and feel destructive rather than constructive. Managers within the department will feel uneasy and insecure, as they see principles and assertions for which they have stood for many years being subjected to unaccustomed scrutiny"* (Sparrow 1992: 52).

A middle manager feeling threatened may not, of course, express himself or herself candidly. Fear of the future may hide behind a mask of bravado about the benefits of traditional ways of doing business. Reacting scornfully to the enthusiasm his first-line officers were showing for problem-solving techniques and their rejection of "just-the-facts-ma'am-lock-'em-up" policing, one middle manager told us: "If it [traditional policing] was good enough for me, it's good enough for them." Not only does this middle manager ignore the possibility that problem solving is a more powerful crime-fighting approach than conventional, less flexible and less varied methods, he also confuses what Chris Braiden would call "the object of the exercise" of policing. It's purpose is *not* to be good enough for *the police*, but to be good enough for *the public*.

The notion that some human beings might prefer known bad systems to unknown improvements merits emphasis. This phenomenon has been observed in other kinds of organizations, such as prisons. Even prisoners who object to their conditions of confinement often do not welcome prison reforms because they have figured out how to manipulate the current system. They don't want anyone to upset the apple cart because they have figured out how to get the apples they want.

The kind of police middle management *know-how* that radical systemic changes may jeopardize typically includes mastery of the incident-oriented, crime-fighting strategy and of the department's punitively oriented rule manual. Sparrow (1992: 55) observes that British police forces moving away from voluminous rule manuals in favor of short, clear statements of "principles for action" have reaped appreciation from first-line officers but resistance from some mid-level managers. They "found the implied management style harder to accept and were reluctant to discard their old manuals."

In most types of bureaucracies, Wilson (1989: 131) argues,

"managers have a strong incentive to worry more about constraints than tasks, which means to worry more about processes than outcomes. Outcomes often are uncertain, delayed, and controversial; procedures are known, immediate, and defined by law or rule. It is hard to hold managers accountable for attaining a goal, easy to hold them accountable for conforming to the rules."

Neither as police officers in their earlier careers nor as sergeants and now lieutenants or captains have the middle managers normally had to move beyond taking reports, making arrests or providing other basic services in order to process incidents, victims and suspects. They have not had to tackle the challenges confronted every day by problem-solving officers—the challenges of getting results that the service population finds genuinely responsive to their concerns. People may understandably oppose moving from their comfort zones—familiar turf where they exhibit confidence and competence—to areas of greater challenge.

☐ *Power as a zero-sum game.* One of the principal ways in which the new policing strategies upset prior systems is by pushing power further down in the organization. Middle managers may perceive this power reallocation (correctly or not) as a zero-sum game in which they must lose authority for sergeants and officers to gain it. Under

> *"Power and money are like manure. If you pile them up in one place, they can really start to stink. But if you spread them around, they can make roses grow"* (Rev. Edward Harris).

traditional arrangements in police organizations, the most powerful people in the occupational lives of officers are peers, first-line supervisors and middle managers. (Ask a street cop almost anywhere for an opinion about his or her departments' chiefs over the years and the answer is likely to be a variant of, "All I really care about is who my sergeant is"—see Goldstein 1990: 157 and Byham and Cox 1988: 165.) Middle managers fearing that they will have less power if they give some away may subvert the attempt to spread power around (Skogan 1994: 177; Sensenbrenner 1991: 69; Greene, et al. 1994: 93). Some analysts believe that concerns about becoming effete accounted for mid-managers' resistance during the 1970s to team policing, a strategy bearing a strong resemblance to today's community problem solving (Sherman, et al. 1973: 107; Sherman 1975, 1986: 365; Skogan 1990: 123; Roberg 1994: 252; Stephens 1993: 3-4; Moore 1992: 133; Riechers and Roberg 1990; Walker 1993; Zhao, et al. 1995: 15). As Sherman (1986: 365) put it, "The demonstration projects often gave sergeants more power than lieutenants and captains, whose jealousy led them to countermand and sabotage the orders of the team leader."

The phrase "community policing" also includes a word that is scary to many police—"community." They infer, quite correctly, that not only will power be pushed down through the police organization but out of the organization and into the neighborhoods. Police who do not respect the governance role of the public in a democracy—or the limited role of government in a system of ordered liberty—will have substantial difficulty with the reallocations of power entailed in community problem solving (see Friedman 1994 for a community organizer's perspective on these issues).

In Chicago, where experimental implementation of community problem solving began in April 1993, police-community partnering occurred in different manners and to different extents across five "prototype" police districts. As Skogan, et al. (1995: 28) report:

> "Police and residents tended to act as partners in Englewood, Austin, and especially Rogers Park, working together as members of one team to coordinate their efforts and influence the neighborhood in a positive way. In Morgan Park, however, the typical [beat] meeting [between officers and residents] saw police and residents behaving as though they had similar goals but separate agendas, with police stressing certain aspects of neighborhood problems, citizens emphasizing others, and both acting as though their efforts were independent of one another. A different pattern emerged in Marquette, where police representatives normally took charge of organizing citizens and developing plans for them to implement" (see also Skogan, et al. 1995: 29-30).

Thus, Skogan and colleagues concluded that in four of the five pilot districts in Chicago, police in meeting with residents "downplayed the adoption of nontraditional roles by beat residents, and it seems unlikely that citizens dependent on police leadership will successfully adopt these new responsibilities on their own" (Skogan, et al. 1995: 30; see also Buerger 1994).

To the zero-sum thinker, sharing power *with* their subordinates is bad enough. Having also to share power *over* their subordinates *with others* can be extremely disconcerting. Indeed, depending on how radical a restructuring occurs in a police department to accommodate community problem solving, it may not only be *citizens* who have renewed "power" over police officers (arguably citizens already have more power, because of their ability to dial 9-1-1 on any telephone, than anyone *should* have over professional police officers). If a police department's restructuring supplants a unity-of-command system with a matrix management arrangement, then officers "may be responsible to other bosses as well" as to their direct superior (Kanter 1982: 98). If you think it angers a *citizen* to call a cop and have nobody come,

How many, if any, of the following insights about a manufacturer of computer products are applicable—or could be usefully adapted—to help a police department become more effective and efficient? "[M]anagers have broad job charters to 'do the right thing' in a manner of their own choosing. Lateral relationships are more important than vertical ones. Most functions are in a matrix, and some managers have up to four 'bosses.' Top management expects ideas to bubble up from lower levels. Senior executives then select solutions rather than issue confining directives. In fact, people generally rely on informal face-to-face communication across units to build a consensus. Managers spend a lot of time in meetings; information flows freely, and reputation among peers—instead of formal authority or title—conveys credibility and garners support. Career mobility...is rapid, and people have pride in their company's success" (Kanter 1982: 103).

you haven't seen exasperation until you envision a traditional police manager, thrust uncomprehendingly into a matrix management system, who calls one of *his* cops, only to find that the officer is unavailable because she is busy helping another of her "co-bosses." Travis, et al. (1993: 76-79) prompt the provocative thought that perhaps police supervisors should report not only to their middle manager but to a police-community problem-solving coordinating council. Moreover, maybe police officers should report not to a lone sergeant who tries to help them with all manner of problems but instead to an array of sergeants who have diverse substantive skills and can help officers with specialized challenges depending on the nature of the problem-solving project. Provocative and perhaps very useful, but to a rugged traditionalist, blood curdling heresy!

❑ *Zero tolerance for experimentation and failure.* Demands (by chiefs and/or the middle managers themselves) that middle managers play the role of rigid, punitive rule-enforcer cannot easily be reconciled with a policing strategy (or wider *government* strategy) that entails a great deal of unpredictable experimentation with new techniques by public servants (Osborne and Gaebler 1993: 108-37).

Zero tolerance for failure by a boss is detrimental to employee creativity. As Goldstein (1993: 5) put it, "Officers will not be creative and will not take initiatives if a high value continues to be placed on conformity. They will not be thoughtful if they are required to adhere to regulations that are thoughtless." We do *not* refer here to wilful, malign disrespect by officers for department policies, rules and regulations, which may very well call for intolerance and recriminations by supervisors. As Lee Brown said when he served as New York City Police Commissioner,

> "There are two kinds of mistakes—mistakes of the mind and mistakes of the heart. If you're doing something out of malice, then you've got a problem with me. But if you're trying to do your job and you make an innocent mistake that may violate a rule, the entire circumstances should be taken into account. If we want people to take risks, we have to tolerate mistakes" (quoted in Webber 1992: 32).

Middle managers who cannot tolerate good faith errors by officers attempting to meet ambitious community protection objectives will not easily embrace community problem solving (Chicago Police Department 1993: 22).

Zero tolerance for employee experimentation will quickly cause atrophy of the experimentation inclination. That malady not only deprives the police department of innovative ideas, it may make for cranky employees. There is a considerable body of medical science that shows what happens to the victims of sleep deprivation. Their ability to dream is impaired, which causes fatigue, resistance to cooperation, cynicism and other anti-social conduct. Wouldn't cops deprived of the ability to daydream—for example, about how they might leave the world a bit better than they found it—suffer similar symptoms? And what does each officer's withered dreams cost the rest of us? In his poem "Harlem," Langston Hughes asked: "What happens to a dream deferred? Does it dry up like a raisin in the sun? Or fester like a sore—and then run? Does it stink like rotten meat? Or crust and sugar over—like a syrupy sweet? Maybe it just sags like a heavy load. Or does it explode?" (Hughes 1959: 268; Hansberry 1958: vii).

Avoiding embarrassing the department is a higher goal than reducing community problems in some police organizations. As Braiden (1995) put it, "the allegiance is to the culture, not the cause." An easy way to avoid embarrassing the agency is to take no chances, to stay on the well-trod path. Never mind that the path is not going anywhere particularly useful. Where this thinking prevails, middle managers will find that the path of least resistance is to resist community policing. Wilson (1989: 132-33) illustrates part of why managers in various kinds of public agencies tend to be "risk averse":

> "Police administrators rarely lose their jobs because the crime rate has gone up or win promotions because it has gone down. They can easily lose their jobs if somebody persuasively argues that the police department has abused a citizen, beaten a prisoner, or failed to answer a call for service. School administrators rarely lose their jobs when their pupils' reading scores go down or win promotions when scores go up. But they can lose their jobs or suffer other career-impeding consequences if students are punished, controversial textbooks assigned, or parents treated impolitely. Under these circumstances it is hardly surprising that police captains spend a lot of their time trying to make certain that their officers follow the rules and that school principals spend a lot of their time cultivating the goodwill of parents" (see also Wilson 1968: 70-71).

If Kelling and Bratton (1993: 9) are correct in their history of police bureaucracy, then asking middle mangers to be risk takers and to welcome creativity and innovation is asking for a dramatic role reversal. "[O]ne of the basic functions of captains and lieutenants—their *raison d'être*," Kelling and Bratton report, "has been to forestall creativity and innovation."

What is at stake if middle managers demand that police responses to citizen crime and disorder problems be uniform and if the managers insist on controlling centrally all departures from standard operating procedures? The risk, in Leslie Wilkins' attractive metaphor (reported by Toch 1995: 5) is that the first-line officers fail to adjust their "flight path" to follow a moving target:

> "Wilkins...points to the difference between a predetermined flight-path missile and a self-homing missile which uses features of the terrain over which it is sent. Such a missile...needs to have an information gathering and processing device in itself, not one in headquarters. It needs also to have the power to adjust its path as it senses the 'better' course to follow."

❑ *Loss of promotional slots if organizations are flattened or downsized.* Implementation plans for the new strategies sometimes include reducing the management ranks (e.g., eliminating some or even *all* slots for deputy chiefs, majors, captains or lieutenants). The impulse to flatten the hierarchy often arises from the desire both to save money and to manage from values and communicate those values clearly. "In the larger American forces," observes Sparrow (1992: 55), "the number of ranks can vary from 9 to 13."[3] The layering of management insulates those on

---

[3] This, he quips, "is in contrast to the worldwide Roman Catholic Church (with over 600 million members), which does a fairly good job of disseminating values with only five layers." Maybe the Pope knows something public administrators need to learn. In their much-heralded *Reinventing Government*, Osborne and Gaebler (1993: 262) contrast the administrator-customer ratio in Chicago's parallel school systems: "Before its recent decentralization, Chicago had 500,000 public school students and 3,000 administrators; Chicago's Catholic school system, with 250,000 students, had *36* administrators."

both ends of the hierarchy against clear communication, much as "[w]e know from physics that many thin layers is the best formula for effective [thermal] insulation" (Sparrow 1992: 55).

So with recommendations abounding for shaking organizational trees and squeezing more out of tightening budgets (McNally 1991), it is little wonder that middle managers feel like deer frozen in the headlights. Vogl (1993/1994: 53) put the question bluntly to management consultant Michael Hammer: "If I'm going to lose my job, why should I participate in my own execution?" Hammer had no sugar-coated reassurances, except that those middle managers whose jobs survive the organizational review will probably be better off after the managerial weed-and-seed exercise than they are now: "[R]eengineering usually results in a smaller number of better, higher-paying jobs."

With corporate "downsizing," "right-sizing," "flattening" and other euphemisms for taking peoples' jobs away sweeping the corporate landscape, traditional expectations about joining private-sector organizations and keeping one's job with them for an entire career are changing radically. As one corporate consultant put it, "employees are no longer seen as long-term assets to be developed but as short-term costs to be cut." The focus for organizations feeling not only the squeeze of the competition but compassion for their employees thus has shifted from promising employees whole-career job security to giving them career skills they can transfer to other good jobs if they are no longer needed in their current positions.

Goldstein (1993: 5) candidly admits that middle and senior management resistance to strategic innovation in some police agencies is so strong that progress may come only through management attrition. "Perhaps early retirement should be made more attractive for police executives who resist change," he opines. He notes as well that consideration should be given, as it has been in England recently, to "the elimination of unnecessary ranks." For an excellent description of the strategic thinking that guided efforts to flatten and otherwise reorganize the San Diego Police Department during the 1980s, see Stamper (1992). Not surprisingly, those facing loss of prestige, loss of jobs, and diminished opportunities for promotion usually will resist the reform movement unless attractive alternatives are provided.

□ *It's not police work.* Egon Bittner has long and eloquently complained that a spirit of adventure rather than a spirit of service characterizes police cultures (see also Moore 1992: 151). Problem solving that is responsive to what really irks a neighborhood may mix with that culture like oil and water. For instance, one of the classic quality-of-life problems police are often asked to help alleviate by residents and business people on their beats is disorderly conditions. While sometimes these disorderly conditions contribute to drug marketing, burglaries, muggings and the like, they "are often important problems in their own right, and difficult to solve. They are not often the subject of police melodramas—and you'll probably never hear a television announcer say, 'Hero cop cracks disorderly conditions case! Details at eleven!'" (Farrell, et al. 1993a: 6).

Thus, middle managers (and others in a department) may believe the expanded information-sharing and problem-solving functions of the police under the new strategies should be carried out by other public and private entities, leaving the police with traditional roles. The battle cry of the police reform resister—"We're not social workers!"—often means that police are considered unable to help reduce the community, personal, or family problems that give rise to crime and related social disruptions.

"Family preservation workers know that something as easily fixable as a filthy kitchen can lead to a cycle of depression that can lead to [child] neglect. So they're trained to start with the readily fixable" (Barthel 1992: 40).

It is worth noting that resistance to tasks on the grounds that "I'm not a social worker" is hardly a lament limited to the *police*. Many other professionals—teachers, doctors and lawyers to name a few—have been heard to say that certain tasks are beneath them because they are not social workers. Moreover, even *social workers* sometimes disagree over what tasks are beneath *them*. For instance, it is debated whether case workers confronted with dysfunctional, poor families should help their clients accomplish some of the basic "housekeeping" necessities of normal living, like "scrubbing floors, cleaning out garbage, fixing sinks...." Those who advocate that social workers help with such chores suggest that, while the case workers are providing this help, they can be "'modeling' behavior and talking at the same time" (Barthel 1992: 40). An analogy for police might be helping a community clean up a vacant lot that has proven to be a hot-spot for crime while discussing how the community might protect itself in the future.

The "not-my-job" response arises both from the perception that police don't know how to make a difference in social problems and from the perception that nobody else in the community's human service system has—or is prepared to use—the power to *compel* people to behave civilly toward one another (Bittner 1970, 1975, 1980). Since compelling such civil conduct is a full-time job for the police, the argument goes, leave it to social workers and others to provide other societal services. Besides, the police don't want to use techniques that may give would-be lawbreakers the misimpression that the police are "soft on crime" (Greene, et al. 1994: 102; Skogan 1994: 177-78; Roberg 1994: 253). And it's hard to reconcile "touchy-feely psychobabble" (Yates 1994) with get-tough law enforcement. For those who hold such views, the words of a cops' cop, St. Louis Major Roy Joachimstaler, may fall on deaf ears. Joachimstaler, currently serving as his department's implementation manager for community problem solving, asks his colleagues: "What's police work? In my opinion, neighborhood association and community meetings are just as important as a radio call" (1995: 4).

Why would Joachimstaler say such a thing? Perhaps because he knows that at neighborhood association and community meetings police could investigate (or research) the problems confronting the community. Moreover, the police could also explore in such settings how well prior police efforts to alleviate neighborhood problems are playing among the public. But "research" hardly seems like police work, in the sense in which Bittner calls the police adventurers. Toch (1995: 2) captures the image problem nicely:

"[T]here are some persons for whom research has an effete and impractical connotation. Research smacks of halls of academe and of ivy-covered people who have a great deal of time to waste. It means that meetings are scheduled where work is called for, and that debating societies substitute for timely responses to problems.

One picks up warm testimonials to strongly felt resistances: Experience—one hears—teaches us experienced people what to do. One knows what one does when one does it, but can't be expected to spell it out. If we dissect life we destroy it. Real skills—such as those involved in doing police work or being an indigenous community organizer—are intuitive, and choices and decisions are ineffable. There is no point in Monday-morning quarterbacking one's actions when one has done the best one knows how. Everyone knows that research only undergirds the obvious [compare Cordner 1985]. Where it does not, it is wrong. Some people are built to act, and others are meant to talk about acting or to study those who act, and there is no mystery about which group are Real Men and Women."

Such attitudes, still entrenched pretty deeply in the culture of most police organizations, help create an atmosphere in which it is possible for middle managers to ridicule as "not police work" the analytic exercises which are a core part of the police problem-solving process. Toch's critique of the man of action's impatience with things cerebral recalls the aphorism that there is nothing so practical as a good theory.

One of the difficulties with police resistance to wearing "too many hats" is that, over the decades, most neighborhoods have suffered a steady attrition of social services (other than the police) which are available around the clock and which make house calls.

"If we think back to those days when the old-fashioned beat cop patrolled city streets, we should remember that those were the days when an official team of public service providers spent much of their time 'making house calls.' In that era, social workers routinely made home visits to see firsthand if children were neglected or abused. At the same time, the public health nurses might be out in the community visiting the homes of the young, the elderly, and the infirm. Probation and parole officers made scheduled and unscheduled home visits to ensure that their clients were living up to the terms of their release. Those were also the days when so-called truant officers were on the streets making sure that kids were not 'playing hooky'" (Trojanowicz 1994: 259).[4]

Over time, as Joseph Heller said, "something happened." Judge (1995) offers the interesting perspective that, among all the other things that happened over the past half century, something happened to erode democratizing social and recreational habits in America (ballroom dancing, etc.), in which people of different classes and cultures would mix and develop a nonthreatening sense of commonality. On the economic front, some observers, including *New York Times* columnist Russell Baker (1995), suggest that *something happened* long ago. In his view, a substantial amount of unemployment and poverty is simply part of the equation of a capitalist system. "Those vital paupers," he laments, are as functional to our economic system as the stock exchanges and entrepreneurship (see also Barlett and Steele 1992; Broder 1995).

So what's the answer to the current vacuum in community social support systems? For some police leaders, like former Baltimore County Chief Neil Behan and current Chicago street cop (and rap-group star) Eric Davis, the answer is simple: As compassionate and honorable members of their communities and professions, they can't afford the luxury of grumbling that

---

[4] Compare Barthel (1992: 21): Family social service "caseworkers in Newark find they're on the genuine front lines, sometimes meeting with families in housing projects so dangerous, so controlled by drug dealers, that even the law stays out. 'We go where the police won't go,' says Wil Taylor, administrative director of The Bridge, an Essex County, New Jersey, agency that provides family preservation [services]. 'Not that we're braver—but if you're going to have family preservation in an area like this, that's where you'll find the families.'"

somebody ought to do something; they just *do something* and let others sort out the role questions (on Behan's behavior, see, e.g., Delattre and Behan 1991; Behan 1986).

For Braiden (1995), the answer is to be found in response to the question, "What *was* police work intended for?" His reply:

> "It should be working on society's problems—that is, it should be *social* work in the broadest sense of the word. Instead of conforming the shape of policing to the object of the exercise, we've got it backwards. We take our form as a given and tell the world what functions that form will permit us to carry out. Those who subscribe to the form fight the change of function."

Despite the heroic aspirations of such dedicated exemplars as Behan, Davis and Braiden, as a general proposition, the police *cannot* and perhaps *should not* bear the burden of cleansing society's Augean stables. The police cannot *themselves* compensate for the dearth of public services for primary, secondary and tertiary crime prevention; remediate a broad range of interpersonal conflict; and foster healthy community and individual development. What the police can and should do, however, is use their expert awareness of society's problems to speak out compellingly for the enhancement of formal and informal systems that can help improve things. They should also broker access to existing support systems for members of the public in need. Too many police still waste too much of their time (and too many of our tax dollars) telling everyone they can't fix criminogenic problems. If only they devoted equal energy to looking for people who *can*. We bet they would come up with some good leads. After all, the Rand Corporation detective evaluations to the contrary notwithstanding (Greenwood and Petersilia 1975), police *are* pretty good at finding people.

If the world confronting police in big cities today is not scary enough, consider this 10-year projection by police, demographers, economists and others attending a recent "Futures Symposium" in Chicago: "Chicago was characterized as the most segregated major city in the United States, with the most segregated school system. High school drop-out rates were expected to continue climbing while the shift from [a] manufacturing to a service industry would produce an undereducated underclass of unemployed inner-city youth. In Chicago, the greatest proportion of those losing jobs would be blacks living in some of the poorest neighborhoods in the country. Poor inner city residents would get poorer, while better-off, middle-class minorities would continue to move out, leaving behind those with the fewest resources to go elsewhere. Tensions between police and citizens could be expected to escalate as the job of many police officers would be to keep the poor away from the rich. And, finally, unless the poor could be dispersed, Chicago was projected to be a place that would be inundated with unsophisticated, unschooled, unskilled people" (Skogan, et al. 1995: 12).

Different components of police departments may mount the not-my-job defense in differing degrees. For instance, Sparrow (1992: 57) suggests that detective units will be among the most likely sources of resistance and sabotage for community policing implementation plans. "Certainly," he opines, "the detective branch typically views the introduction of community policing as a matter for the patrol officers—'our job is still to solve crime'" (compare Greenwood and Petersilia 1975; Eck 1983).

Resistance to community policing based on the view that it's not real police work may mask the basest of human motives (racism, sexism, callous disregard for the plight of crime victims, etc.) and may call attention to people who made a basic mistake when they pinned on the police badge and took their oath of office. Many such people are not going to change to meet the needs of a community policing agency, and we might as well resign ourselves to that fact. As Yogi Berra said, "If the people don't want to come out to the park, nobody's gonna stop them" (quoted in Pritchett and Pound 1995: 16). The real misanthropes on our police forces have seen the light at the end of the police reform tunnel, and it's an on-coming train. It's a train that will test their compassion fatigue mightily.

Such managers are likely to view colleagues who are enthusiastic about the new vision of police-community partnerships not as brave pioneers but as opportunistic "management finks" (Sensenbrenner 1991: 69). The more threatened conventionalists feel by the new wave of police strategy and structure, the more likely they are to behave in organizationally and personally destructive ways. Two such behavior patterns are cynically packaging "their pet projects as [reform] initiatives" and trying to "entice some reporter into probing the [chief's] 'boondoggle'" (Sensenbrenner 1991: 69).

But some of the opposition by middle managers to a shift in policing strategy may stem from sincere doubts that the new strategies will serve well in protecting the community from crime and from unprofessional police officers. While we do not subscribe to an undifferentiated "lock-'em-up-and-throw-away-the-key" approach to crime control, we are not prepared to say that everyone who does is simply unconcerned about making neighborhoods safer, more livable places for all Americans.

    □ *Problem solving and community engagement don't make sense under current conditions.* We have encountered some middle managers who express genuine interest in a world in which police could be community problem solvers. They just don't believe they are living in such a world.

A frequent excuse is that the budget is tight, thus barring a labor-intensive "program" like community policing. More money, spent more wisely, may indeed be useful. But there is little or no evidence that *thinking critically about how to do one's job in a more publicly valuable fashion* requires more resources. So much time is

> *"Almost everything that we believe is true today was once seen as heresy—ask Copernicus and Galileo if you don't believe me" (Braiden 1995).*

squandered now by so many police departments that if a dollar were put in a basket for every wasted minute every year, before long there would be enough to pay cops what they deserve for doing one of society's hardest jobs.

Another common reason for saying the time is wrong for strategic reform is that politicians will not tolerate any meaningful police excursions into brokering community services for needy communities. The perception is that such brokerage is the mayor's or the ward boss' job—or perhaps even the community organizer's job (compare Friedman 1994)—and the police would be ill-advised to take it on themselves.

As another illustration, a police middle manager facing organized drug corruption, gang or mob infiltration of the sworn ranks, and egregiously excessive force within her precinct could be excused for looking askance at a reform that extols permanent beat assignments (Skogan 1990: 123; Cosgrove and McElroy 1986) and the empowerment of officers to use broader discretion, take unconventional initiatives, and the like (Roberg 1994: 252; Skogan, et al. 1995: 17; Oclander 1995a, 1995b; but compare Bracey 1992; Kelling, et al. 1988; Weisburd 1994: 275; Bratton 1994: 4).

One might not be surprised, given the drug and abuse-of-force corruption scandals that have commanded headlines during 1995, to find middle managers in New Orleans, Philadelphia, Los Angeles, New York, Atlanta, Chicago and other locales greet as lunacy the suggestion that the path to professionalism is along permanently assigned beats (Goldberg 1995). Yet, there is at least one problem with resisting employee empowerment in the face of a corruption scandal: Except in the most extraordinary circumstances, this still throws the baby out with the bath water by penalizing the mass of good workers for the visible misdeeds of a few. Indeed, as Atlanta Chief Beverly Harvard noted when six of her officers were charged September 6, 1995 with federal corruption offenses, it was the *good* officers in the Department—proud of their badges and taking their oaths to the people seriously—who first made the Department aware of the renegades in their midst (*Crime Control Digest* 1995: 7). Osborne and Gaebler (1993: 137) touch on the risk of throwing the baby out with the bath water:

> "Peter Drucker long ago pointed out that 'control of the last 10 percent of phenomena always costs more than control of the first 90 percent.' If it costs far more to eliminate corruption than we save by doing so, is it worth the expense? If by making corruption virtually impossible we also make quality performance virtually impossible, have we done a good thing? If by tying everyone up in rules we so demoralize public employees that they give up, is it worth the enormous cost we bear in dead-weight?"

While we are skeptical that it makes sense to oppose strategic reform for fear of exacerbating integrity problems, we are sympathetic to lieutenants and captains who might counsel selective delays in implementing some procedural and structural aspects of community policing. For instance, middle managers who are aware of pervasive deficiencies in the skills of their department's criminal investigators may be respected for opposing rapid *decentralization* of detective functions. Until skills are enhanced, the community may be better served by a centralized detective operation in which competent investigators and supervisors can closely guide the work of less capable employees.

Another reason why middle managers may object to a strategic reformer's decentralization of such functions as criminal investigation may be that the crime problems being targeted are "centralized." For instance, problem solvers may target city-wide and multi-jurisdictional illicit drug markets or criminal syndicate dominance of a region's cartage industry. Under such conditions, decentralization could impede the effectiveness and efficiency of the investigations.

Such strategic and tactical objections to decentralization of particular segments of police operations should not, of course, necessitate wholesale rejection of community problem solving, because there is nothing about this approach that counsels mindless decentralization (Bennett 1994). Yet if middle managers are not making such distinctions—or if they are confronted with ill-informed community policing advocates from within or outside the organization who assert that universal decentralization is a mandatory component of the new policing, one might better understand the middle managers' generalized resistance to change. Kelling and Bratton (1993: 7) discuss resistance by Madison, Wisconsin, police detectives to decentralization of investigative functions. The detectives in that highly admired police agency, presumably for reasons other than investigative incompetence, argued that decentralization lowered the quality of investigations (compare Couper and Lobitz 1991; also see Skogan 1990: 123).

Some police departments, Roberg (1994: 255) argues, may not be ready to try responsibly to implement community problem solving. These, he suggests, are departments that need to "become more organic in nature before attempting any movement at all." He worries about the prospects for denigrating community policing if agencies doing traditional, reactive, relatively ineffectual police work masquerade as using the principles and tactics of what should be a far more tenacious strategy (*ibid.*). The prospect of *sheep* in *wolves'* clothing is, indeed, troubling. Goldstein (1993: 1) voices alarm over the widespread lip-service being paid to community policing: "Carefully developed initiatives bearing the community policing label, fragile by their very nature, are endangered because superficial programs are so vulnerable to attack." The latest survey of a representative national sample of local criminal justice agencies revealed that "80 percent of the police chiefs and almost two thirds of the sheriffs...[said] they have adopted" community policing (McEwen 1995: 4). "This is a finding," McEwen warned, "that needs to be interpreted cautiously,...given the amorphousness of the concept" of community policing (*ibid.*: 11). Mastrofski (1993: 4) concurs with Sparrow, et al. (1990) that "only a few departments have moved much distance 'beyond 911'" (that is, beyond incident-driven policing) and into a problem-solving mode as their standard operating procedure.

Thus, we have little quarrel with the *motives* of some police middle managers who resist community policing. Their opposition, whether well-founded or ill-conceived, at least is animated by their desire to serve and protect the community. And in some circumstances, they may even be right to resist change on the grounds that they know their local governance culture or police

> *"Lieutenants, in the past, were on the leading edge of a prime mid-management responsibility: maintaining control and ensuring that operations functioned according to the book. Now lieutenants, attempting to maintain the standards that have been their reason for being, find themselves cast as the lagging edge: a major source of resistance to innovation. Such a characterization of mid-managers in policing is not surprising, given their basic function"* (Kelling and Bratton 1993: 9).

culture will not tolerate the methods and benefits of community problem solving.[5] "Chicago ain't ready for reform," proclaimed a cigar-chomping local pol several decades ago. He may have been right at the time. Today, Chicago's political and police leadership are among the most vocal and entrepreneurial exponents of community problem solving, although hardly immune to the rebellions of the middle ranks against this cultural revolution (Chicago Police Department 1994; Skogan, et al. 1994: 37; Skogan, et al. 1995: 23).

---

[5] Roberg (1994: 255, 256) would take issue with the notion that these are rarities. He asserts that "most departments throughout the country are not yet ready to assume the responsibilities required from" community policing and that "this approach can be effectively implemented by only a small number of 'elite' departments throughout the country."

□ *We didn't try it, and it didn't work.* A closely related reason why many middle managers express deep skepticism toward community policing is that, even if the concept sounds sensible on the drawing board, they believe the lessons of history prove the concept to have been a failure. It would be arrogant in the extreme for us to reject out of hand any and all examples of community policing's *conceptual* failures—where the strategy was given a fair test and flunked. But our belief generally is that most case studies and folklore about failed community problem-solving reforms are in fact stories about *implementation* failures (Bennett 1994: 233 reports, for example, on some implementation failures in Britain). Moore (1994: 295) expresses the view that

> "An important part of the reason for the difficulties in producing consistent operational successes may have less to do with the correctness of the theory of community and problem-solving policing and much more to do with the difficulty of implementing those theories correctly."

It is just as important to be clear about the distinction between conceptual and implementation problems in the police world as it is in a for-profit manufacturing context—where the distinction could be between a "design flaw" and a "manufacturing shortcoming," and where confusing the two could bankrupt a business (Kanter 1982: 98). Lavrakas (1995: 112) suggests another analogy: "In public health, a promising new medicine would not be abandoned prematurely because it was not properly or adequately tested." Having reviewed a considerable body of evaluation research on community-based crime-prevention initiatives, Lavrakas concluded: "The loosely formulated 'theory' of community-based crime prevention has never been adequately tested" (*ibid.*).

The pervasive problem of falsely interpreting *implementation* failures as *conceptual* failures was captured succinctly some years ago by Wayne Kerstetter. This seasoned police administrator-turned-academic wisecracked: "With little exaggeration, one could sum up the history of American police experimentation with innovative ideas in one sentence: We didn't try it and it didn't work."

Implementation failures, especially following an early successful pilot project, are hardly limited to the policing arena. The human services world knows too many of these misfortunes, as a foundation executive points out: "The landscape is littered with good ideas that were limited to a brief moment in the sun. Some could not be replicated. With others it proved impossible to teach new leaders to do what the founders had managed with such promise and enthusiasm. Some programs proved impossible to sustain and over a period of years were watered down, changed, or lost their way. Some were limited by the geography, culture, climate or peculiar circumstances in which they were introduced. Some could not be evaluated; their goals were too murky or shifting, their procedures varied too widely from case to case, and there were no baselines against which success could be measured" (Edna McConnell Clark Foundation president Peter Forsythe, quoted in Barthel 1992: 42).

The experience with team policing during the 1970s is a classic case in the police field of professional mythology that has misconstrued an implementation failure as a conceptual failure. Sherman (1986: 363) concluded: "The program failure meant that the theory was not properly tested." The belief that *team policing* was shown to be a bad idea (a bad strategy) taints the appraisals that some veteran police middle managers make of *community policing's* prospects for succeeding. As many commentators have discussed, the implementation failures surrounding the team policing experiments had much to do with the departments trying to graft team policing as a work approach onto unaltered, traditional police organizations and priorities (see, e.g., Sherman, et al. 1973; Sherman 1975; Sherman 1986: 364-65; Schwartz and Clarren 1977; Koenig, et al. 1979; Moore 1992: 132-34; Kelling and Bratton 1993: 5; and Walker 1993). Those organizations' incentive structures (assignments, performance appraisals, promotions criteria, award programs, disciplinary criteria, etc.) and support systems (training, supervision, R&D, etc.) were in varying degrees irrelevant or antithetical to the strategies and tactics team policing officers were asked to employ. Hence, successful work methods under team policing were largely *ad hoc* and not incorporated institutionally as the organization's basic way of doing business (see also Bennett 1994: 233-34; Walker 1993). Moore (1992: 134) adds that "[a]s long as the organization's most important task was getting to calls on time, and as long as the organization remained a steep hierarchy of commanders, it would be hard to fit team policing into existing police organizations" (see also Sherman 1986: 365).

☐ *I'm on the B-Team*. There is still another reason why a middle manager might resist community policing, even if he or she recognizes its conceptual soundness and believes that police and local government leaders are sincere in their support for this strategy. The veteran police employee has seen a lot of well-intentioned police programs and strategic changes come and go with short-term chiefs and mayors or city managers. Thus, there may be a "wait-and-see" mentality among middle managers, which can thwart the incumbent leaders' reform efforts. With police chiefs lasting in office only a few years in most sizable departments in the United States, waiting any substantial time to see what the chief's staying power is with community policing reforms is likely to lead to perpetual waiting.

It is, indeed, always possible that the next chief will announce that community policing was a bad idea and call for a return to the days of traditional crime-fighting. A number ·of observers believe the Houston transition in recent years exemplifies civic leaders rejecting—or at least neglecting—the advancement of the community problem-solving strategy (see Skogan 1994: 177; Roberg 1994: 253; Kelling and Bratton 1993: 8). This has alarmed more than a few national advocates of police strategic innovation, who look to Houston's rich legacy of candidly questioning conventional strategies and experimenting with alternatives under former police chiefs Lee Brown and Elizabeth Watson. Nowadays, it sometimes seems that Houston's local government leaders look at community policing like a Texas rancher might look at long-horn cattle: There's a point here, a point there, and a lot of bull in between.

> *"I find that, deep in the organization, people recognize the actual need for change, but they're increasingly cynical about their leaders, who haven't been able to produce change" (James Champy, interviewed by Vogl 1993/1994: 54).*

New York City is a somewhat more complicated case than Houston. New York's current experience is being powerfully shaped by two men: Mayor Rudolph Giuliani, whom *Time* magazine (Moody 1995) characterized as "a hard-nosed former federal prosecutor who has long made a subspecialty of studying local law enforcement," and the police commissioner he hired, William Bratton. Bratton, during the seminal, six-year-long Harvard Executive Session on Community Policing, was one of the early, articulate exponents of community problem solving. The resulting collaboration and give and take between these two New York City municipal leaders may provide an intriguing amalgam of the two styles and value systems (see Bratton 1994).

Under circumstances of genuine or wished-for ambiguity, middle managers may take the position, like a number of senior managers did a few years ago when Vincent Lane was named to head the Chicago Housing Authority (CHA), that "We're on the B-Team: We'll *be* here when you arrive, and we'll *be* here when you leave." (As the spring 1995 newspapers attest, the CHA staffers were *right*.) Thus, the short tenure of most police chiefs and many local government administrations—as well as the vacillations of federal leadership and funding priorities from one administration to another—create an environment in which it is feasible, if not wise, for a goodly number of police middle managers to simply go slow and wait for a possible change in the winds of reform. Middle managers who ardently do not want the proposed organizational changes sometimes *covertly* resist them. "Other times," reports management advisor James Champy, they "[ignore] the effort entirely. Just pay no attention and believe this, too, will pass" (Vogl 1993/1994: 54).

To be sure, *middle managers* are not the only police ranks who might be expected to sit on the sidelines waiting to see if the chief's reforms need to be taken seriously. First-line officers and sergeants also may resist rapid enlistment in the chief's reform programs, thinking those initiatives are "faddish" (Sensenbrenner 1991: 69)—just another "flavor of the week" (see Vogl 1993/1994: 54). Roberg (1994: 252) observes that a here-we-go-again attitude among agency personnel, while not insurmountable, will be

> *"Though [an] atmosphere of uncertainty creates opportunities for a few, it generally limits risk taking. *** It is difficult for managers to get commitment from their subordinates because they question the manager's tenure"* (Kanter 1982: 104).

more difficult to overcome if the attitude has risen to "a general level of cynicism with respect to organizational change." Of course, it will be more tempting for personnel to conclude that the demand for organizational changes to support community policing is just a passing phase—and it will be more difficult to overcome such views—if the chief exhibits inconsistent commitment to his or her own announced reform agenda.

☐ *Pluralistic ignorance*. Still another explanation for reluctance to embark on ambitious change even though the straggler has no conceptual difficulty with the proposed change is associated with the problem of pluralistic ignorance. "The phenomenon...consists of a liberal majority laboring under the misapprehension that most people's views are hard-bitten and cynical (Toch and Klofas 1994)" (Geller and Toch 1995: 329). Middle managers who think *they* are the only enlightened ones in the command staff can impede the organizational development process in at least two ways. First, such managers inhibit discovery that a critical mass of support for reform *already exists*. This ignorance, in turn, deters action by those who like company if they are going to leap off cliffs. Second, managers who believe they have a monopoly on progressivism will likely engender divisive resentment from the other commanders, who view the middle managers at issue as self-righteous.

Many police chiefs privately express the view that most of their senior command staff are dinosaurs. Sometimes the chiefs are correct. But if and when they are wrong, their pluralistic ignorance can become a self-fulfilling prophecy, allowing the "dinosaurs" to play out the chief's low expectations for them. Sometimes the problem is compounded by withholding specialized training from the dinosaurs that might alert them to the coming of a new era and how to cope with it. While Greene, et al. (1994: 106) do *not* suggest that the Philadelphia commissioner, embarking on community policing in the late 1980s, miscalculated in sending only select members of his top command staff for specialized management training, still they note the unintended consequence of such disparate treatment. The department sent 44 police managers

> "to [an] independent executive-level managerial training [program]...conducted by Harvard University, in conjunction with the Police Executive Research Forum. *** Upon returning from the Harvard experience, these police managers, Harvard coffee cups and T-shirts in hand, had begun to develop a change ideology and a change vocabulary. They became a core element of police managers to spearhead change efforts within the Philadelphia police. They were formed into policy committees producing recommendations for changing the service delivery, organizational, and managerial systems within the Philadelphia Police Department. Although it ultimately took a few years for these 'policy reports' to take hold, the 'seeds' of changing the internal administrative culture had been placed. The 'Harvard 44' nevertheless labored under a continuous bombardment of senior-level commander control, in part because these senior managers had been consciously excluded from participation in the Harvard program."

The middle manager suffering the syndrome of pluralistic ignorance may find it helpful to inventory, through some credible process, what his or her colleagues candidly believe about key issues confronting the organization. Perhaps the feeling of being vastly outnumbered will be allayed. Robert Orban, quoted by Pritchett and Pound (1995: 34), struck a cautiously optimistic note, confiding: "Sometimes I get the feeling that the whole world is against me, but deep down I know that's not true. Some of the smaller countries are neutral."

The inventory of others' true beliefs might be helpfully supplemented by a little introspection if an individual is feeling cynical himself. As Toch (1995: 9) suggests, one of the many things he has learned from a considerable number of police over several decades is that "the veneer of cynicism displayed by officers was often thin and transparent. There was latent idealism to be found under such veneer, a desire to be of service and to contribute to improving the world."

☐ *Accountability beyond authority.* In traditional police organizations, middle managers' accountability for failures often exceeds their responsibility, authority, and methods (technology) to avert them. Thus, middle managers may be highly skeptical that any additional, ambitious department innovations could possibly work out to their benefit. Greater goals mean greater scapegoats.

> *"Fix the problem, not the blame." — a Japanese business management credo*

Why is it that middle managers often get blamed for conditions they are powerless to prevent or correct? One reason may be the specialization of inspections, internal affairs, and other quality-control functions (Reiss 1992: 79). The police employees who are in the best position to observe slips in quality may not be the ones charged with identifying and addressing such losses. The ones who witnessed a problem may lack the power to correct it, and the ones responsible for correcting it may not know it has occurred.

As it embarked in 1995 on reengineering, the New York City Police Department expressed a determination to "increase the authority, resources, and responsibility of the commanders in the department's 76 precincts" (Bratton 1994: 3) (emphasis added).

Senior managers may also put middle managers in untenable positions by holding them to account for defects in police performance but declining to delegate available power to correct those defects. Among such prerogatives hoarded by senior managers might be the power to assemble effective work teams by changing an officer's assigned partner or shift; the ability to reallocate responsibility for conducting full investigations of simple crimes from detective squads to patrol units; the authority to mandate in-service refresher training on conflict management or problem solving; the opportunity to reduce the stresses in an employee's work setting through various procedural changes; the power to safeguard subordinates' careers by removing obvious temptations to corrupt practices; and the opportunity to resolve a wide variety of conflicting demands placed on officers' time and talents by running interference for the affected officers with the chief and other sources of those conflicting demands.

In fairness to senior managers, sometimes there will be formal departmental restrictions on such delegations of power. These restrictions might stem from labor-management contracts that allow officers to select their own precincts and shifts of assignment on a seniority basis (Chicago Police Department 1994: 137, 141) or that constrain management flexibility in allocating investigative functions between detective and patrol squads (Sparrow 1992: 57). Barriers may also come from "civil service laws [and] arcane government procurement practices" (Bratton 1994: 5). In a meeting between St. Louis Chief Clarence Harmon and a number of his lieutenants about progress in implementing community problem solving, one participant raised a concern that "the Fair Labor Standards Act inhibits flexibility in shift scheduling for both officers and commanders. This inhibits some creative problem solving" (St. Louis Metropolitan Police Department 1993b: 2). Even when there are no *formal* administrative or statutory inhibitions on organizational rearrangements, however, unionized police officers can mount mighty resistance to any modifications they think may impair their working environment (Greene, et al. 1994: 99 discuss the Fraternal Order of Police's power to resist change in Philadelphia).

Another way in which middle managers could be held answerable for problems beyond their control would be if community policing departments failed to develop the techniques, procedures and resources needed for accomplishing traditional and still important control functions. For instance, departments may insist generally on the empowerment of first-line officers by their superiors but may be excessively vague about how, while granting officers wide discretion, supervisors are supposed to avert officer dishonesty (payroll abuse or worse) and abuses of force and other authority. If and when the inevitable lapses occur, the lieutenants and captains in the errant officers' chain of command may be blamed for events they had little guidance in how to avert. To be sure, there are few proven techniques under *traditional* policing for preventing *all* officer integrity problems and abuses of authority. Accordingly indicting community policing for failing to develop *fail-safe* systems for quality control would be unfair.

□ *You want it WHEN?* A perfectly good reason why some middle managers oppose a chief's shift to community policing is that the proposed pace of change is so unrealistic that the competent middle manager concludes the chief really can't be serious—or that the results of precipitous change may make the department even less productive than it has been under traditional strategies. More than one police department has announced with great fanfare its kick-off date for community policing and promised that within six weeks (or whatever the actual time is before the mayoral election campaign will be at full tilt) community policing will be running smoothly. Most of the architects of community policing suggest that the change process will take a decade or more (e.g., Moore 1994: 288; Sparrow, et al. 1993: 21; see also Sensenbrenner 1991: 74)—hardly consistent with the usual tenure of police chiefs or their elected overseers.

Malcolm Sparrow, a gifted former British police executive, cautioned that expecting too much too soon from middle managers and others expected to drive community-policing implementation is ill-advised:

"A simple lesson, well understood by truck drivers, helps to frame the problem...: greater momentum means less maneuverability. The professional truck driver does not drive his 50-ton trailer-truck the same way that he drives his sports car. He avoids braking sharply. He treats corners with far greater respect. And he generally does not expect the same instant response from the trailer, with its load, that he enjoys in his car. The driver's failure to understand the implications and responsibilities of driving such a massive vehicle inevitably produces tragedy: if the driver tries to turn too sharply, the cab loses traction as the trailer's momentum overturns or jackknifes the vehicle.

Police organizations also have considerable momentum. Having a strong personal commitment to the values with which they have 'grown up,' police officers will find any hint of proposed change in the police culture extremely threatening. Moreover, those values are reflected in many apparently technical aspects of their jobs—systems for dispatching patrols, patrol officers constantly striving to be available for the next call, incident-logging criteria, etc. The chief executive who simply announces that community policing is now the order of the day, without a carefully designed plan for bringing about that change, stands in danger both of 'losing traction' and of throwing his entire force into confusion" (Sparrow 1992: 49; see also Goldstein 1990: 154).

Still, as Stephens (1995a: 3) cautions, "It is very difficult to determine the correct pace of change." A chief who wishes to protect his or her employees against precipitous innovation must also protect the department against mid-managers and others who disingenuously decry the pace of innovation when in fact they simply object to innovation. Middle managers who are sincerely willing to change sometimes don't appreciate their capacity to adapt to accelerating progress, Stephens suggests:

"Organizations and people have limits to what they can absorb, but I believe they both develop a greater capacity for the pace of change—just as people are often more productive when expectations increase. I hear middle managers complaining a lot about the pace of change being too great [even though] I feel it is too slow. It is also not unusual to hear [managers'] complaints about the things that need to be fixed at the same time they are complaining about too much change."

Pritchett and Pound (1995: 13, 17) counsel that high-velocity change may be easier than slower movement in the long run (like pulling a bandaid off quickly) and, in any event, may be unavoidable:

"Let's say we push for a slower pace of change...less pressure to perform...a more relaxed, low-keyed atmosphere in general. And let's say we prevail. Top management cuts us some slack.

Chances are we enjoy some temporary relief. Our stress level drops, and maybe we point to that as proof that the organization made the right move. We'd probably be drawing the wrong conclusion.

There's a lot more evidence these days to suggest that slow-changing organizations are headed for the most trouble. Sure, we can do things to minimize stress for today—we can buy a little time—but we have to mortgage the future. We actually end up living closer to the edge.

It's pretty obvious to people that the stress of a rapidly changing organization can be difficult and unpleasant. What's not so clear to us sometimes is how much *more* trouble we're in for if the organization fails to change. It just means denying the problems and delaying the pain. All we're actually doing is postponing tough times for tougher times.

Given the choice, which is really in your best interests: being part of an outfit that's struggling with all the stress and problems of progress, or feeling good (for the moment) and failing?

You can pick your poison. But the hard truth is that the stress of high-velocity change is here to stay. ***

Some people *** really don't *mean* to resist change, but they do want to stay in their comfort zone. Their plan is to minimize stress by 'pacing themselves.' This behavior is based on several faulty assumptions.

First of all, let's examine the mistake that comes in assuming we'll feel less stress if we move slowly to change. Sure, we *might*—but not if we're falling further behind with every day that passes. Not if our employer starts putting more heat on us because we're bogging down the rest of the organization.

Still another wrong assumption is in thinking we have the privilege of choosing almost any rate of change that 'feels right' personally. Frankly, the organization can't give its blessing to that kind of behavior. Some people, given their preference, would take forever to adapt.

We can *call* ourselves cooperative. We can even give ourselves credit for not *deliberately* resisting change. But our thinking is badly off key, and we're headed for trouble, if we're not changing as fast as the world around us.

The simple fact is that failure to keep up with the organization's rate of change *is* resistance. Intent is not the issue here. Impact is. We might be innocent so far as our motives are concerned, but we're guilty of resisting change whenever we slow things down. We also create tension between ourselves and the rest of the organization."

A middle manager may object to the pace of change because he or she believes there has been insufficient analysis of pertinent facts to support the change. In this regard, one is challenged to find the right balance between thinking things through and acting before it's too late to make a difference. In some respects the police are terribly conservative and slow to make decisions. In others the relationship of analytic processes to action decisions can best be characterized as "ready, fire, aim." Colin Powell's rule of thumb for how much information he needed to support a decision when he served as Chairman of the Joint Chiefs of Staff intrigued us:

"I have a timing formula, P=40 to 70, in which P stands for probability of success and the numbers indicate the percentage of information acquired. I don't act if I have only enough information to give me a less than 40 percent chance of being right. And I don't wait until I have enough facts to be 100 percent sure of being right, because by then it is almost always too late" (quoted in Gates 1995: 67).

Gates (1995: 73) reflects on people who cling tenaciously to moderation and compromise in all things—apparently unwilling or unable to make a bold leap for the brass ring of dramatic, speedy (and perhaps invidious) improvements. He worries that ideals can be shattered on the rocks of moderation and accommodation, declaring: "Extremism in pursuit of moderation may be no virtue."

☐ *The middle managers' bosses encourage traditional policing*. Just as we earlier noted that in some agencies avoiding embarrassment to the department is a higher goal than reducing community problems, in some organizational cultures *singular* importance is placed on pleasing higher-ups (Stamper 1995a). A chief who takes the approach that he or she can make community policing happen just by announcing it probably has a pretty superficial commitment to making the strategic transformation. Most savvy cops will detect the shallowness of such a chief's resolve. The brown-nosers will mimic the boss' lip service.

Suppose for the moment that a police force's chief and senior command staff were all sincerely and skillfully pushing a clear and sensible strategic change agenda. Even under these relatively "ideal" circumstances, many lower-ranking managers and first-line workers would cling to old ways. As Pritchett and Pound (1995: 19) observed about private-sector companies:

"You don't have to look very far to find employees who are focused on doing things right, but who are failing to do the right things. These are the people who act as if they'll be held accountable for their old jobs, when—in large part—those assignments don't even exist anymore. Often they just can't understand why they're no longer getting accolades, even though they're doing their old jobs as well as ever. Their key mistake comes in ignoring how priorities and management expectations have changed."

If Pritchett and Pound are correct that such lag time is to be expected in the filtering of new ways of doing business from top bosses to the rest of the employees, then consider the plight of the well-intentioned middle manager who gets unmistakable signals that his or her superiors are *ambivalent* about fundamental change. That ambivalence usually is revealed in mixed messages from the top bosses about what they want (Stamper 1992: 100-09; Greene, et al. 1994: 105). One of the clearest ways to send mixed messages is to call for changed behavior but use the same old infrastructure, such as conventional performance evaluation criteria and reward/punishment systems.

When he served as NYPD Commissioner, Lee Brown frowned on the performance evaluation systems traditionally used by his own agency and others. Under such approaches, he suggested,

"we evaluate officers on how many arrests they make, how many summonses they issue. But the ultimate evaluation should not be the arrests but the absence of arrests, when there's no crime. If you have no crime on your beat, then you are doing the job you should be doing. There's peace of mind in the community" (quoted in Webber 1992: 32; see also Moore 1992: 151).

After Commissioner Brown left New York City to serve as the nation's Drug Czar, New York Mayor Rudolph Giuliani echoed Brown's point to an interviewer:

"One of the most commonsense measures [of police effectiveness] links cops' promotions and future assignments not to the number of arrests they make but to their ability to keep crime out of their territory. 'An arrest is almost a failure,' Giuliani explains. 'The better way to manage a police department is to prevent crime in the first place and find ways of measuring that'" (Moody 1995).

And a police officer in a large city whose chief is an ardent advocate of community problem solving confided in an agency survey:

"Officers with total justification know that if they answer their radios, don't call in sick too often and turn in a couple of summonses and tags each week, they are going to be rated high enough for any reward, increase in pay, transfer, promotion or choice assignment they desire. 'So why do more, why risk screwing up with problem solving?' is a common attitude all over the department."

Similarly, Chris Braiden pulled no punches in chastising his beloved profession for its pattern of honoring employees who don't deserve to be honored:

"In most departments the wrong people get rewarded. Sycophants get rewarded. We should be rewarding the rebels, those who dare to challenge conventional thinking and find better ways to accomplish the police mission" (Braiden 1995).

It's easy to tout patrol as the "backbone" of the police department, Burgreen and McPherson (1992: 77) argue, but the cops will take the true message of the administration to be just the opposite if the system persists in which "any officer who errs or fails elsewhere in the organization goes 'back to patrol.'" Benjamin Ward, when he served as New York City Police Commissioner, ridiculed the prevailing culture, saying, "Sometimes I daydream about the day when I can take a bad *patrolman* and bust him to *detective*!"

Some departments believe that the best way to deal with vigorous opponents of community policing within their ranks is to take a permissive attitude toward employee participation in the new strategies. Such agencies reason that this approach will allow skeptics eventually to see their less reticent colleagues put community policing into practice and may motivate the skeptics to get involved themselves. The Kansas City, Missouri, Police Department is one such agency. As Nunn (1995: 131) told a regional police conference,

"[W]e've got some supervisors, we've got some managers, we've even got some officers that don't really like the concept [of community policing]. So in order to get around that, at least...at this point since we still have a very high level of calls for service, we don't make it mandatory that everybody participate. 'If you want to be involved in community policing objectives, fine, we want you to be involved, but we're not going to put you out there into a neighborhood by force to...do nice things for the community, because if your heart and soul and your mind isn't in it, it isn't going to take very long for those citizens to find out that it's more song and dance—they're not serious about [it]—and it just leads to more apathy.'"

The opinions of professionals will differ concerning the Kansas City approach—whether this is simply hard-nosed, candid realism or setting sights too low at the early stage of reform when sending a clear vision and expectation to the entire workforce can be crucial to long-term success. To be sure, Kansas City can be proud of various community problem-solving attempts by a number of its officers who did decide to board the train toward strategic innovation (Seib 1995: A16).

> *"The principal task facing police leaders in changing the orientation of their organization has been identified as the task of communicating new values. In order to stand a chance of communicating values effectively, you need to believe in them yourself, and to be part of a community that believes in them, too" (Sparrow 1992: 58).*

In any event, in an environment where *significant mixed messages* are sent about whether community policing really matters, the status quo is likely to be king, and the middle managers will be his loyal subjects. No point in getting anyone miffed by telling the emperor his new clothes are a bit skimpy. Under a lip-service reform regime, the middle managers, as gatekeepers of organizational resources, often win more praise for conserving these assets than for treating them as "venture capital" to be invested wisely by officers in the development of community problem-solving technologies. It would take brave lieutenants, captains, and civilian managers indeed to resist the explicit or implicit cautions of their immediate superiors and higher-ups against "squandering" the departments' personnel and other assets in pursuit of "speculative problem-solving ventures" when there are "tried and true" technologies such as random preventive patrolling to underwrite.

Faced with conflicting role demands (e.g., maintain the status quo vs. become an agent of change), middle managers often choose the familiar. For instance, unit managers frequently are pressured by senior police officials, prosecutors, mayors, media, and others both to maintain *all* the existing system's outputs (arrests, response times, number of calls for service handled, tight control of officers, standardization of approaches, etc.) *and* to shift to a strategy (problem solving) that makes those outputs important only insofar as they help the community (Kelling and Bratton 1993: 10). Indeed, the ardent pursuit of quantity may undermine the quality results sought by community policing, both because attaining the numbers is time-consuming and because some of the numbers (e.g., unforgiving ticket quotas) may work at cross-purposes to the development of respectful partnerships with the public (Brann and Whalley 1992: 74; Delattre and Behan 1991: 539-40).

It is said that the speed of the boss is the speed of the crew. It should be little wonder if middle managers resist community policing when they interpret their bosses' *true* attitudes (lip service to the contrary notwithstanding) as hostility to the strategy. "It is disheartening," Goldstein (1993: 5) admits, "to witness a meeting of the senior staff of a police agency in which those in attendance are disconnected and often openly hostile to changes initiated by the chief executive and supported by a substantial proportion of the rank and file."

    ❑ *A desire to stay in the loop.* Information is a police department's best tool, and savvy

> *A "kill-the-messenger" environment causes middle managers to hide bad news from superiors, thus minimizing the open discussion of problems and their resolution before they blow up (Kelling and Bratton 1993: 10).*

middle managers know that. If it's not *what* you know but *who* you know that usually gets you ahead, maintaining a good relationship with *who* you know may nevertheless depend on continuing to know *what* you know. As processors of information flowing between the ranks above and below them, middle managers become gatekeepers of police departments' internal communications systems. As any child who has played the game of "telephone" realizes, repeatedly relaying a message often transforms it beyond recognition. The transfer of instructions, advice, inquiries, complaints and complements along a chain of command thus predictably results in "a substantial amount of 'incremental whitewashing,' as well as legitimate filtering of information" (Stamper 1992: 157). A St. Louis police officer put the matter bluntly in a staff meeting with his chief: "Many good ideas die on the way up the chain of command" (St. Louis Metropolitan Police Department 1993a: 1). Some middle managers are threatened by the prospect of being uninformed about key communications between those above and below them. Since most efforts to bring community problem solving to full potential entail a substantial opening of avenues for officers and sergeants to communicate with others inside and outside the police organization, some middle managers will resist the strategic reform.

☐ *Paramilitarism*. Weisburd, et al. (1988: 32), citing Murphy and Muir (1985) and Reiss (1985), argue that "the fundamental principles of the paramilitary model, which are a closed system, compliance with rigid formal rules, centralized decision-making and specialization, are incompatible with the goals and strategies of community-oriented policing." The paramilitary organization of police departments (including the military titles of supervisors and managers) feeds the myth that good ideas can only flow *down* the chain of command (Goldstein 1990: 157). Paramilitarism also typically pushes decisions *upward* in the chain of command. "Constantly gazing upward," as Chris Braiden (1995) put it, "causes you to trod on those below you" and is inconsistent with community problem-solving approaches. The middle manager enamored of looking only upwards for decisions and innovations will very likely resist the current changes in the way of doing police business.

Woe be to the peon in the militaristic setting who is misled by disingenuous rhetoric from bosses about participative management and really letting one's hair down and saying what we think about one another in this organization. Charles McCrary, an assistant chief in the St. Louis Metropolitan Police Department, recalled a gullible middle manager some years ago who thought his chief (not the incumbent, community policing advocate Clarence Harmon) really *meant* the invitation to be frank at a command staff retreat on community policing:

> *In Chicago, many lieutenants resented being grouped with people of lower ranks in community policing training. Said one: "You can't be buddy buddy and then lead the patrolmen on the street" (Skogan, et al. 1994: 4/33).*

> "The board members were there, the top commanders..., and the president of the board got up and gave his pep talk [on team building], then he sat down. Our former Chief got up to give his pep talk.... [O]ne thing about our former Chief,

he was from the old school. Nothing more needs to be said. He was...a no-nonsense type guy. He had given a speech and about half way through the speech one of our senior commanders raised his hand and [the chief] says, 'Yeah, what do you have to say?' This commander stood up and he proceeded to talk, and he was really saying things that were against some of the things that the Chief was saying, but I guess he felt this was in the spirit of the team-work and he could say it. This commander had his say and he sat down and for about ten seconds there was dead silence. You could hear a pin drop. I knew and I think that everybody else in that room knew that the hammer was about to fall, and believe me it did fall. The Chief was on that commander like a sturdy shirt, and I said right there, and everybody else in the room felt it, this seminar is going downhill quick. It's going to hell in a hand basket, and it did. So needless to say, a lot of us were sort of gun shy from that episode, and we were a little suspicious whenever anybody started talking about commitment, especially commitment from the top" (McCrary 1995: 134).

Nice clothes, Emperor.

Bosses such as McCrary's former chief may proclaim that they have an open door policy, but all except the densest employees or the most cockeyed optimists soon learn what that really means: "If anyone doesn't like the way things are done, management shows them to the open door" (Spitzer 1995).

Similarly, a militaristic culture may foster an organization (and middle managers) closed to outside influences. Since the engagement of community members and institutions in genuine power-sharing partnerships is a central tenet of community policing, police employees jealous of their customers gaining influence over decisions can be expected to resist change.

Community problem solving calls for a plethora of new partnerships involving police as one party. Most of these relationships imply power sharing among police and community people who may not consider themselves equally powerful. The early "courtship" stages of these partnerships may produce trepidations for either or both parties. Woody Allen captured the point when he observed, "The lion and the lamb shall lie down together, but the lamb won't get much sleep." Mastrofski (1993: 8) distrusts the modern reformers' professed belief in police-community partnerships among equals. Their "ideal [community] partner," he opines, "appears to be the domesticated one."

Some such middle managers will simply misunderstand what community policing advocates intend when they speak of police sharing power and decisionmaking with stakeholders outside the department. "Too many people," Braiden (1995) suggests,

"think community policing means the police abdicate their mandate and just do whatever the public wants them to do. Police can't simply ask the public what they prefer because they will ask you to do some illegal things, like old people wanting young people who are doing nothing wrong taken off the street. Another reason is that police are responsible for the outcome of their service. If I go to a barber and ask him to shave half my head and color the rest of my hair bright green, he can go ahead and do it without expecting anyone to hold him accountable for doing what I asked. The police don't have that luxury; in our business, the customer is *not* always right. We should ask the public what bothers them, but we shouldn't simply defer to them to set the police agenda and determine our tactics."

Ray Davis (1985), former chief in Santa Ana and a pioneer of community empowerment, similarly acknowledged that power sharing does *not* mean that police should relinquish responsibility for decisions or authority that properly are theirs. He cautioned against "a blind pilgrimage to the temples of community control" of the police.

Still another reason that police should not simply cede responsibility for various decisions and planning to the public is that doing so might unduly constrain the imaginativeness of problem-solving approaches. Although it is true that the fresh perspectives of people unschooled in police science are also valuable in creative problem-solving, Robert (1995), commenting on the private sector, argues that expert knowledge must be deployed to invent new options that will benefit customers:

> "Don't ask customers about future products. Customers can identify performance gaps in the products they are using currently. They can't, however, identify future trends and turn those into future needs. No customer asked Thomas Edison to invent the light bulb, for example, or Spencer Fry to invent the Post-it, or Akio Morita to develop a Walkman, or Steve Jobs and Steve Wozniak to develop a personal computer. To create the products of the future, you have to monitor the trends and develop products that the customer won't be able to do without—in the future."

The militaristic structure also allows middle managers to rely on authority rather than competence (creativity, people-managing skills, intellect, etc.) and respect among peers as the basis for influencing subordinates (Kanter 1982: 103; 1983; Goldstein 1990: 157). We acknowledged earlier that not every decision a police department needs to make can or should be made democratically (for an account of officers' democratically electing their district-level bosses, see Wycoff and Skogan 1993: 22; Osborne and Gaebler 1993: 261). But there is far more democracy and rugged individualism in a creative problem-solving unit than there is in a spit-and-polish, by-the-book approach to police work. The "because-I-said-so" middle manager may well interpret community policing as an invitation for subordinates to be insubordinate.

There remains, for even the ardent advocate of community policing, the daunting challenge of how to maintain a preparedness for unquestioning obedience to authority—when operational needs require this—among officers who spend most of their time in a contrasting system that values their independence, creativity, and similar traits. "There are strong arguments in support of quasi-military organization," argues Goodbody (1995: 12). He continued:

> "The police do need the ability to mobilize quickly and act decisively. *** The key...is not to deny what is inherent to policing, but to determine how the bureaucracy can be reformed to accommodate the day-to-day functioning of a problem solving approach to the work."

The perception of widespread insubordination under community policing may be fed by general grants of officer discretion that reduce expectations of full and rigid compliance with formal rules. Department manuals, Sparrow (1992: 54) suggests, "have been used as much to allocate blame retrospectively after some error has come to light, as to facilitate the difficult work of patrol officers." As such, the rule manual has been a useful crutch for supervisors who could not or would not be able to extrapolate specific guidelines from more general ones. The trend among community policing organizations is away from rigid reliance on cookbook approaches: "Many departments, in implementing community policing (which normally involves a less militaristic and more participatory management style), have de-emphasized their instruction manuals" (Sparrow 1992: 54). The Commission on Accreditation for Law Enforcement Agencies, according to Commissioner (and Skokie, Illinois, police chief) Bill Miller, is also making substantial progress in reducing the number of formal standards that some had criticized as encroaching on the flexibility required by community problem-solving teams (Miller 1995; the criticism is illustrated by Watson and Williams 1991). Nevertheless, a manager who manages for rule compliance rather than for results (attained by honorable means) will rebel at the latitude granted officers under the new policing styles (Chicago Police Department 1993: 22-23).

Organizations mimicking military structures are also likely to embrace a great deal of specialization and standardization of function within areas of specialization. Community policing, by contrast, champions generalist problem-solving employees wherever possible and recognition that neighborhood problems come in myriad sizes and shapes and change over time in ways that require great adaptability by problem solvers with some continuing stake in the resolution of the problem. Middle managers in departments featuring standardization of function within areas of specialization can develop large amounts of expertise on a small number of topics. Their conventional claims to competence can thus be eroded by a department's strategic reformation.

> *"Managers in companies know all about organizational pyramids and rigid lines of reporting. As paramilitary organizations, police departments follow that same model but to an even greater extent. The command-and-control culture of the police department doesn't treat officers as intelligent, creative, and trustworthy people. It allows them very little discretion. It's designed to make sure that they don't get into trouble, don't embarrass the department, and don't get their supervisors into trouble" (Lee P. Brown, quoted in Webber 1992: 27).*

People who embrace military discipline, national pride and *esprit de corps* as essential cultural elements for a well-managed police department may overlook the possibilities for engendering the same sort of loyalties, self-discipline and enthusiasm through other management styles and organizational value systems. While morale is undoubtedly very high in a number of military units, one wonders whether that derives as much from contextual factors (e.g., having a particular battle mission or, nowadays, *peacekeeping* mission in which the soldiers can believe) as it does from strong command-and-control structures (Peters, date unknown).

It is important to note, before one becomes too entrenched in critiquing police departments for their adherence to militaristic mores and manners, that at least some management experts believe the military model is getting a bum rap. Properly understood, asserts management guru Tom Peters (date unknown, included in Chicago Police Department 1994 and Ramsey, et al. 1994: 43), the military model embraces many of the tenets of high-performing organizations. Peters argues:

"[M]ost business executives are confused about what makes for success in military units. The idea of toughness for toughness' sake, strict adherence to the chain of command and mindless obedience to orders could not be further from the nub of military effectiveness. Instead, victory on the battlefield depends on nine traits.

1. **An inspiring vision.** ***
2. **Leadership by emotion.** ***
3. **Managing by wandering around.** ***
4. **Improvisation, autonomy and creativity.** The do-as-I-say military image is the saga of losers. The most successful leaders, from the pinnacle of command to the squad-leading corporal, have been difficult-to-manage innovators in time of battle. Boot camp teaches soldiers to duck without thinking. But, it also teaches them to improvise, a requisite on the always ambiguous battlefield. Charles de Gaulle once asserted, '...Those who have done great deeds have often had to take the risk of ignoring the merely routine aspects of discipline.... Pelissier at Sebastopol stuffing the emperor's threatening dispatches into his pocket unopened and reading them after the action was over. After the Battle of Jutland and the English failure to take the opportunity offered them of destroying the German fleet, Adm. Fischer, then first sea lord, exclaimed in a fury after reading Adm. Jellicoe's dispatch: He has all of Nelson's qualities but one—he doesn't know how to disobey!'
5. **Small group dynamics.** ***
6. **Partnership.** ***
7. **Execution and the 'little things.'** ***
8. **People, not technology.** ***
9. **Removing boot lickers and bureaucrats.** De Gaulle, Patton and Montgomery, among others, had been sidetracked as too flamboyant in peacetime, where cocktail-party technique counts. When times got tough, the boot lickers shriveled and the irritating innovators scored success after success.

These factors also are decisive in business, church choirs, Brownie troops, local United Way campaigns, baseball and semiconductor-making. The purpose of every human organization is at once to harness and release the human spirit, creativity and talent to pursue a chosen end. Business people need not avoid military analogs. They should, however, endeavor to use them correctly" (Peters, date unknown).

Among the well-respected centers of high-performance managerial training in which senior military managers have been enrolled over the years is the Center for Creative Leadership. This 25-year-old institute, headquartered in Greensboro, North Carolina, caters mostly to Fortune 500 executives. If Peters is correct about the modern American military, then the "defects" of *paramilitary* infrastructures for community problem solving may involve at least as many *implementation* defects as *conceptual* defects.

But former Attorney General Ed Meese observes that, despite numerous ways in which the military model may have inched American policing forward through the decades, that model

"inadvertently downgrades the position of the primary figure in police service: the individual officer. Too often the basic police officer is viewed as comparable to a private in the army, the lowest ranking military person, who has virtually no individual authority. Such a perception is understandable when several police officers report to a sergeant who, in turn, reports to a lieutenant, and so on up the chain of command. *** [If the military model is to be retained,] rather than being considered as the equivalent of an army private, the police officer should be given the distinction of an aviator in the military services. Aircraft pilots initially are appointed as lieutenants in the Air Force or ensigns in the Navy, not because of the number of personnel reporting to them (which is usually small or nonexistent), but because of the great responsibility entrusted to them when they are given charge of an expensive and potentially dangerous aircraft. Just as military pilots must exercise considerable judgment on their own and accept that their individual actions may have grave consequences, so police officers on the street should be considered the equivalent of commissioned officers, with concomitant respect, authority, and discretion" (Meese 1993: 3).

□ *The management of community problem solving is hard work.* One of the reasons we noted above that conventional wisdom pits the militaristic structure *against* community policing is that militarism grounds influence in authority rather than competence. Put bluntly, another reason why some middle managers may oppose the shift to community policing is that they find their traditional authority-wielding responsibilities simpler than managing problem-solving officers (Trojanowicz and Bucqueroux 1990: 347; 1994). They may applaud and feel a momentary adrenalin rush after pep talks which insist that "any victory that came easily doesn't mean anything" (Braiden 1995), but they'll

"Lieutenants and sergeants should be aware of their officers' problem-solving projects and offer guidance and direction as they progress through their efforts. This method of supervision asks supervisors to be responsible not only for handling the radio call load...but also requires them to take an active role in management of their personnel and the problem-solving process" (Joachimstaler 1995: 3).

recover pretty quickly and remember that managing problem solving is not easy.

Why is managing community policing harder than managing conventional policing? For one thing, it is easier to manage (check up on) officers doing routine, repetitive tasks (e.g., preventive patrol, rapid response to calls, minimal engagement with victims) than to manage varied, innovative, unpredictable problem-solving efforts (Goldstein 1990: 157; Kelling and Bratton 1993: 3; Weisburd, et al. 1988: 47 n. 11). Moreover, it is easier to find defects in officers' work (especially with many prohibitory rules) than to help subordinates succeed in meeting the community's needs.

It is also simpler to *count* arrests, summonses, preventive patrol tours, response times and other traditional indices of productivity than to assess the *quality* of problem solving and problem-prevention *efforts* and *outcomes* (Chicago Police Department 1994: 120). And the challenges are fewer when applying rules and directing operations with a mechanistic consistency than when middle managers attempt to be judiciously flexible yet fair.

Even in a quality-driven organization such as the Madison, Wisconsin, Police Department, analysts discovered a pattern in which some lieutenants "were bothered by what they perceived as inconsistency in handling calls for service, complaints, disciplinary procedures, and other procedural matters" (Kelling and Bratton 1993: 7). To be sure, these dissatisfactions with such inconsistencies may reflect more the intolerance of the responding *lieutenants* for ambiguity and variegated approaches than any inappropriateness from the point of view of problem-solving officers or the community customers. Or, the dissatisfaction may simply have been envy by lieutenants whose officers were not yet participating in the less punitive disciplinary processes employed in Madison's much heralded "experimental police district" (EPD) (see also Greene, et al. 1994: 106). As Wycoff and Skogan (1993: 27) report,

> "supervision and discipline are deliberately more informal at the EPD than in the rest of the Department. Managers consciously attempt to accept honest mistakes. *** Accordingly, disciplinary actions are more likely to begin with an attempt at reconciliation between citizen and officer. When looking at incidents between officers and citizens or officers and other officers, EPD managers are not quick to label incidents as complaints and to institute formal processes."

Insightfully observing and facilitating community problem solving is hard work not only for middle managers, but for first-line supervisors. Lieutenants, captains and their civilian counterparts need to appreciate how, especially for sergeants, traditional supervision is easier than community problem-solving supervision. Thus, an added burden for middle managers is inventing ways to help their sergeants succeed (Weisburd, et al. 1988: 47 n. 11; Chicago Police Department 1994: 120).

Herman Goldstein has emphasized in many of his publications and presentations the importance of the police and the public coming to grips with the fact that policing is a highly complex undertaking. Still, he acknowledges that concentrating on complexity can be a mixed blessing: "Dwelling on complexity...can be overwhelming and intimidating. It is difficult. It turns many people off. But for those who get involved, the results can be very rewarding" (Goldstein 1993: 6).

While we respect the difficulties entailed in managing results-driven policing, we should note that, done *well*, middle management even in a traditional police organization is not—or should not be—a straightforward matter. Middle managers' (and sergeants') *traditional* responsibilities should be wide ranging, including helping officers conform their work (and attitudes) to department goals; conducting substantive performance appraisals; developing training and other incentives to improve performance; and monitoring to avert misconduct (Weisburd, et al. 1988: 32). Thus, those middle managers who resist the new policing because their work will become difficult probably haven't been pulling their fair share of the load up to that time.

❑ *The line don't like rate-breakers.* Those who have not been pulling their weight are one type of problem. Perhaps a more pervasive problem is one of those who do just enough to get by (Spitzer 1995). Like assembly-line workers, they keep up with the flow of work, and they have developed routines that accommodate the pace comfortably. Perhaps they are only marking time—only eight-and-a-half more years until retirement. Such employees often deeply resent the rate-breaker—the assembly line worker who

> *Those who "announce that...significant changes in the direction and operations of the organization are required, and that they are determined to bring them about *** [may be accused of being] arrogant, self-seeking grandstanders vying for public attention" (Moore and Stephens 1991a: 107).*

picks up the pace of production and thereby forces everyone else down the line to do likewise. Peer pressure to go along if you want to get along can be a powerful feature of organizational life, especially in a *police* organization, which is characterized by high levels of employee solidarity, insulation from outside values, and interdependence for protection of career and physical safety. The middle manager who enthusiastically joins the "chief's" team on a reform initiative and gives 150 percent will very likely be ostracized by many colleagues for "making life more difficult for the rest of us."

There are at least three possible answers to the resentment of rate-breakers. First, and perhaps most obvious, is that those lagging behind need to find ways to emulate the high-performers and "speed up." The second is that it makes no more sense to have one "fast" speed for all employees than it does to have one moderate speed. In the final chapter, we address the need for middle managers to get help creating an organizational environment that respects employees' individuality, including their different packages of strengths and weaknesses. The third response is that, fundamentally, the new strategies ask officers to work *smarter*, not *harder* (Stewart 1985).

☐ *We're too busy to change.* Although we believe that most of the time people are able to make time for what they want to do, it will be true in some organizations that people are too busy to change. This will be the case if the senior leadership insists that middle managers continue doing all the old things they shouldn't be doing plus all the new things they should. The classic problem here is being too busy bailing out the boat to fix the hole in the hull. If you don't take time to mend the hole, eventually exhaustion will win, the bailing will cease, and so will the bailer.

Preoccupation with the task at hand prevents people from pausing to reflect critically on whether what they are doing has any value. Pritchett and Pound (1995: 12) remind us of a *Saturday Night Live* "deep thought" from staff soothsayer Jack Handey: "The other day I got out my can-opener and was opening a can of worms when I thought 'What am I doing?!'" When reflection on "what you're doing" reveals it isn't contributing value to the organization's service to the public, what to do? Conceding that their advice may be easier said than done, Pritchett and Pound (1995: 20) are clear and crisp in their prescription: "[D]itch those duties that don't count much, even if you can do them magnificently well."

Beliefs that police are too busy to change can be compounded with fears that community policing will only intensify the workload. When supervisory and management personnel of the Chicago Police Department were surveyed during in-service community policing training in 1994, 76 percent of the respondents said they expected the Department's commitment to community problem solving to lead to a "greater demand on police resources" and 66 percent predicted "more unreasonable demands on police by community groups" (Skogan, et al. 1995: 17). Unhappily,

> *The National Assessment Program, a survey of criminal justice practitioners by the National Institute of Justice, found that, in 1994, most police chiefs and sheriffs believe two things: (1) their workloads are higher than ever; and (2) it is important that they implement community policing in order to accomplish more under these trying circumstances (McEwen 1995).*

these opinions were *evenly distributed* across supervisors who were familiar with community policing in five pilot districts and their colleagues who had not actually lived through the

Department's efforts to launch a new way of doing business (*ibid.*). Community organizer Warren Friedman, who has helped design and deliver training for Chicago police personnel, takes a different view: "[W]hen the community is an organized, informed, and active partner, the problem-solving process is not so labor intensive for the police as some have asserted" (1994: 268). Still, as Major Roy Joachimstaler of the St. Louis Metropolitan Police Department observes, in many agencies, "the main reason usually given as an impediment to...expansion efforts [for problem-oriented policing] is the amount of radio calls—[they say], 'We're too busy running from job to job to solve problems'" (Joachimstaler 1995: 6).

Vogl (1993/1994: 52-53) asked management consultant Michael Hammer about his proposal that corporations commit substantial resources to self-reengineering. "Putting myself in readers' shoes, [a] reaction you'd likely get is: 'Reengineering looks as if it'd be terribly disruptive to my company. Do I need that on top of all my other problems?'" To which Hammer replied: "[Y]ou don't need it on top of all your other problems; you need it *instead* of all your other problems."

"Too busy to change" and other such objections may not, of course, be ingenuous. Sometimes they veil overt opposition to reform. Hammer opines that middle management resistance to change

> "usually manifests itself as covert. Resistance includes 'Gee, that idea will never work,' 'We tried that idea and it didn't work,' 'I really think that's a great idea, but this is our busy time, and then we have the holidays and the vacations, so come back a year from Wednesday' and 'That's a good idea, but we should really do it slowly and carefully to get it right.' Like, let's take about 10 years" (Vogl 1993/1994: 54).

Kanter (1982: 101), too, suggests that often middle managers who are themselves quite entrepreneurial and innovative, when they encounter resistance from colleagues and subordinates, will find the resistance manifested in *covert* ways:

> "Entrepreneurial managers encounter strikingly little overt opposition—perhaps because their success at coalition building determines whether a project gets started in the first place. Resistance takes a more passive form: criticism of the plan's details, foot-dragging, late responses to requests, or arguments over allocation of time and resources among projects."

❑ *Distance from customers.* As Sparrow, et al. (1990: 170-71) observe, compared with police chiefs, rank-and-file officers, sergeants, first-line civilian police employees and their immediate supervisors, middle managers have less contact with the service population (are more internally focused) and may feel less public pressure for modifying police operations:

> "The community contact experienced by the top and bottom ranks differs considerably. The contact at the top is largely political consultation and such hobnobbing as is commensurate with high office. The contact at the bottom is the business of serving the department's clients and hoping to satisfy them. The rest of the work tends to be internal to the department, and most middle managers spend much of their time in their offices. The picture that begins to emerge from

this division of labor matches very nicely the perception of operational police officers, patrol officers, and their immediate supervisors. *** They regard themselves as the only officers who know 'what goes on out there.' They see the whole of the police management structure, even with its politicking, as a comparatively cozy internal world. In their eyes one of the attractions of promotion is its offer of protection from a harsh and demanding external world. Patrol officers can therefore be forgiven for thinking that they insulate the rest of the organization from the public. It would be unfortunate, though, if this pattern of community contact and concern continued. Middle managers should wherever possible interact as fully with the community as the most senior and most junior officers."

In departments where middle managers are insulated from "community contact and concern," these police employees may have a harder time than people working at ground level perceiving that hard-won gains in police *efficiency* are irrelevant to a neighborhood being treated with *ineffective* tactics. Doing more of a useless thing and doing it more efficiently is not of much value to the intended beneficiaries. For instance, "random patrol," Burgreen and McPherson suggest, "is little better than sleeping on duty" (1992: 77).

Increased random preventive patrolling and speedier responses to 9-1-1 calls about cold crimes, in the face of neglected crime hot spots, may well seem to the afflicted neighborhood like the cartoon of the bus driver who fails to stop the bus at a crowded bus stop. When asked why he did that, he declared, "If I stop to pick the people up, I'll fall behind schedule." This is what Chris Braiden refers to as police *function following form*. When that happens, he suggests, officers may acquire backwards views about service to the public. For instance, "we put 'We Serve and Protect' and the department's phone number on the side of our patrol cars and then we get annoyed when people call the police asking for service."

Arguably, even worse than withholding minor services from the public or providing them grudgingly is unwittingly providing police services that are affirmatively harmful to a community (we have also noted this problem elsewhere in this volume). Often there are not perfect choices in policing between tactics that produce "known harms" and tactics that produce "known benefits." But greater proximity to customers helps service providers such as police keep in touch with the basic question of whether their labors are seen *by customers* as relevant to the customers' needs. It is easier for middle managers and others kept at a distance from the public to oppose community problem solving on the grounds that, since current police strategies don't seem broken, there's no need to fix them.

It's also easy for people removed from contact with the intended beneficiaries of programs to harbor resentments when the gargantuan efforts they've expended designing, launching, and maintaining irrelevant programs go unappreciated. Why so many police confuse the *tactics* that a police strategy might pull out of a tool kit with the *object of the exercise* is a bit baffling to many who are not accustomed to police culture. But too often the police are living examples of the proposition: "When you're up to your ass in alligators, it's hard to remember that your original purpose was to drain the swamp." The Edmonton Police Service helpfully reminds us that

"[r]eal community policing is how police work with the community and not how they organize themselves to police the community. In other words, a police officer could ride a bike, walk a beat, or patrol a zone, but never do community policing [see also Cordner 1994; Bennett 1994: 228]. Foot patrol, bike patrol, zone policing, and team policing are often held up as examples of community policing, but they are really examples of how police organize to provide services *to* the community. Community policing is about how police provide policing *with* the community" (Hornick, et al. 1993: 46).

Former Edmonton Chief D.D. McNally cautioned his own middle managers, as they strove to find better ways to serve the public, not to let "the process...overwhelm the task" (McNally 1991: 1). Commenting on lessons learned in Joliet and Aurora, Illinois, Wilkinson and Rosenbaum (1994: 124) warned that, while "some amount of record keeping is critical to the problem solving process," still "problem solving can become means-oriented policing if officers get lost in the bureaucracy of paperwork and forget the larger objective." St. Louis police sergeants were asked in an internal survey what middle managers do both to *encourage* and to *discourage* officers and supervisors from engaging in problem solving. One sergeant differentiated the effects on subordinates of two types of middle managers. On the one hand, there are those who supported problem-solving projects *pertinent* to community needs. On the other hand, some middle managers, in their anxiety about "getting with the program," demanded that officers engage in large quantities of problem solving, oblivious of the particular priorities of specific neighborhoods. The sergeant declared:

> "Neither lieutenant...desired to have the officers initiate projects of little or no significance to appease the Captain or Major. Furthermore, whenever a project was initiated, the lieutenants merely monitored the progress without interfering. The Captain, on the other hand, seemed to want to make a project out of every radio assignment dispatched. [He was] constantly demanding memos and printouts of the activity related to the project. Basically, the Captain did nothing to encourage problem solving."

Goldstein (1990: 35), too, noted how police alienation from, or simple lack of information about, customers can cripple police capacity to set appropriate priorities. He called on police to "go beyond taking satisfaction in the smooth operation of their organization" and to "extend their concern to dealing effectively with the problems that justify creating a police agency in the first instance."

❑ *Boosting expectations: If you think our crime clearance rates look bad, wait 'til you see our problem closure rates!* While the *benefits* of solving problems are fairly easy to describe, the *likelihood* that any given group of officers and community members in any given jurisdiction will be able to successfully solve very many of a community's myriad problems is much harder to predict.

Skogan, et al. (1995: 35) report (using a source that probably *understated* the success rate) that in Chicago what they call a "closure" rate on specific problems was "less than five percent during the first year" of strategic reform in that department. "Closure," in their definition, is reached when "a problem was identified, a solution suggested, and some action taken." The total number of problems that had been presented in officer-resident "beat meetings" was 1,079 problems (of which 49 reached "closure"). While we can readily assume that problem solving was occurring at a higher rate throughout the city than is captured by their data source, we are somewhat perplexed at their definition of "closure." In a results-oriented strategy such as community policing, we would have thought that a problem file wouldn't be closed until a temporary or enduring solution was found, rather than when "some action" was taken (compare Skogan, et al. 1995: 38).

Be that as it may, still the point remains that nobody can reliably predict that problems will be solved at a higher rate than the clearance-by-arrest rates that police currently tally each year. When politicians and others scoff at what they falsely interpret as a department's "drop in productivity" because, compared to its current *clearance* rates, its *problem closure* rates are smaller numbers, what is the buffeted chief—or the middle manager behind whom the chief is standing—to say?

Perhaps the critics could be told that doing more of a marginally useless thing, and even doing it with greater finesse, is still marginally useful. Better to have *some* success at eroding problems than lots of success at activity that, under the circumstances, simply doesn't reduce the factors that are producing crime, disorder or fear. In the words of a Native American proverb, "It is better to limp in the right direction than run in the wrong direction." Maybe the critics could be told, too, that some of the things police do, such as randomly patrolling by driving through neighborhoods scowling at everybody (Braiden 1995), not only do little good, they do affirmative harm. The 50-cent word for this concept is the medical term "iatrogenic," which means helping to spread the disease the doctor or medicine seeks to cure. "It would require substantial improvements in the American criminal justice system," Norval Morris told a community crime prevention conference in Illinois some years ago, "for the system simply to live up to the physician's oath to 'do no harm.'" Nevertheless, middle managers who are accustomed to the unkindness of the news media, politicians, and interest groups who prefer not to be confused with the facts may well look with trepidation on the new era in American policing. They may see it as one in which reformers create unattainably high expectations for what the police and the community can do to reverse social decay.

> *Trying to fundamentally retool police operating systems at a time when fear of crime is rampant, budgets are growing leaner, and public opinion of government generally is plummeting may sound highly impractical. Even if we don't know quite enough yet about how to deploy better strategies—even if our "problem closure" rates may look unimpressive, is it better to fight the noble fight and risk going down in a blaze of glory than to not even try different approaches? Is it better to do something novel, even if it's not great, than to stick assiduously to tried and untrue methods? Clearly many middle managers have answered these questions "yes" with their words and their deeds.*
>
> *As Harris (1995a: 83) said, "Anything worth doing is worth doing badly. *** We all have to start somewhere. *** We can't be 'perfect' and we miss out on much that is good in life if we try to be. *** Do [whatever is important to you] badly to begin with and go as far as you can with it." Under the circumstances, where current methods are demonstrably unimpressive, we simply cannot afford to delay trying other approaches until someone gives us an ironclad guarantee that they will prove superior. The compassion that police express by tirelessly trying to find better ways to serve the public counts for something important, even if they fail to get the results everyone wants.*

☐ *People hate change.* Resistance to change is not new and hardly limited to police middle managers (Coch and French 1948). An ancient Chinese curse is: "May you live in times of transition." A more contemporary social commentator observed that the only people who *like* change are babies with wet diapers. We have already suggested above many of the reasons why people resist change. Another possibility is that resistance tends to increase with age. Harris (1995b) suggests: "As you get older, most change looks like change for the worse." Doesn't it seem that every generation of adults laments that the current generation of youth is going to hell in a hand basket? "When *we* were kids, life was simpler.... You kids today have it easy—you don't know what rough is...when I was a kid I had to get up at 6:00 everyday and do chores before I walked two miles to school.... When I was young, 'right' and 'wrong' meant something..." and so forth. Such longing for the "good old days" may sometimes be more nostalgia for one's fading youth than an objective appraisal of changing conditions. As someone once suggested, all this affection for the good old days is largely "an apocrypha of Norman Rockwell's imagination."

Organizational change experts Pritchett and Pound (1995: iii) predict that, as rough as *today* seems to employees in changing companies, tomorrow will be more complex and more stressful. These days, they opine, "will be remembered as 'the good old days'." Remember when the American dream felt feasible—at least to middle- and upper-class people—and we generally expected life ahead to be better in almost every way? The future, as they say, ain't what it used to be. So even if change in an era of American dreamers was less scary, today most change may be presumed to be for the worse (Barlett and Steele 1992).

Whatever the prospect of change means for one's memories of bygone days and expectations for the future, it is also possible that change threatens one's sense of *identity*. Bryson (1995) touched on this point in writing about the evolution of language in America. He focused on the loss of local colloquialisms because of our transitory population and the homogenizing, standardizing effect of television and other mass communications on subculture. For instance, Vermonters used to say "so don't I" when they meant "so do I." The conversations of North Carolinians living on the remote Outer Banks island of Ocracoke, first settled in 1715 but now a popular tourist retreat, used to be peppered with such wonderful, curious words as "*fladget* (meaning a piece of something), *begombed* (to be soiled or smeared), *airish* (for a stiff breeze) or *quamish* (for queasy)." Bryson reports that the erosion of local linguistic idiosyncracies "is quietly robbing us of turns of phrases, pronunciations and other dialect features that once gave many localities a stamp of distinction." This "may alarm traditionalists" he writes, but

> *"[P]eople are scared to death...because, even if they keep their jobs, it ain't gonna be the same job. The jobs are different, and they have great anxiety. 'Gee,' they ask, 'will I be able to do the job? What will my future be? The career path doesn't look the same. The pay system is different'" (Vogl 1993/1994: 53).*

> "many authorities take a more philosophical view. 'People nearly always see linguistic change as a deterioration when in fact it is just change,' says Dr. Julie Roberts of the University of Vermont Department of Communication Sciences.... 'Dialects don't die, they evolve.... I have no doubt that 50 years from now people will be decrying the loss of expression they heard in their childhoods in the 1990's. It has always been so.'
> Indeed, there may be what Roberts calls 'a prestige factor' at play in perpetuating local speechways. A classic study on Martha's Vineyard in 1963

found that certain traditional pronunciations...were in danger of extinction, but then staged an unexpected rally. A main force for preservation, it turned out, was natives who returned to the island after living away and embraced the old speech forms as a way of distinguishing themselves from the mass of non-natives.

Similarly, a survey of Ocracoke [Island] speech...found that middle-aged people—those who grew up in the 1950's and 1960's, when tourism first became a dominant motif of island life—...'exaggerate their island dialect features, whether consciously or not, because they want there to be no mistake that they are *real* Ocracokers and not tourists or new residents recently relocated from the mainland'" (*ibid.*).

Analogous points have been raised about young African Americans' adherence to "Black English" as an emblem of cultural pride (see Major 1994, Smitherman 1977, and Poet X 1995). Might it also be that seasoned *cops*, trying to cling to their identity as the *real* cops, may resist "new fangled" policing methods, which during their careers have not been among the central defining activities of good police work?

Among the various possible reasons for unhappiness over change, one should not discount the likelihood that some employees are just unhappy people—with or without pronounced changes afoot. Their burden in life is a heavy one, captured wryly by Pritchett and Pound (1995: 10): "I feel so bad since you've gone. It's almost like having you here." An organization without a few such malcontents on its payroll is either very lucky or very much worth studying for its motivational and employee support systems.

Another likely wellspring of opposition to change is simply fear of the unknown. As bad as things might be, they can always get worse. And, if leaders are mistrusted, things will be *expected* to get worse. Worst of all, they can get worse without *me* being around to experience the disaster, if my job is jettisoned in a downsizing exercise. A condition of unpredictability and risk, as Trojanowicz (1994: 261) put it in one of the last publications he authored before he passed away so early, becomes a test of individual and collective character. He asked: "Will uncertainty about the future draw us together so that we work collectively to solve our problems or will it pull us apart so that we selfishly attempt to protect only ourselves?" Pritchett and Pound's (1995: iii) prediction is not a happy one:

> "Most of us just wish that change would go away. Or at least slow down. When it doesn't, we look around for someone to blame it on or for someone we think should be responsible for relieving our stress."

For those with reasonable expectations of retaining a job in a reconstituted organization, distaste of change also stems from a thoroughly understandable desire for predictability, which police more than many in society may covet (Moore and Stephens 1991a: 108). Sparrow (1992: 52) observes that "the process of generating a questioning, curious, and ultimately innovative spirit within the department" creates uncertainty. "Police do not like uncertainty within their own organization," he argues. "[T]hey already face enough of that on the streets." Like many of the rest of us, police feel a strong desire to know exactly how they fit into the picture. As a St. Louis police officer put it,

> "[T]he real problem seems to be attitudes of most officers. We are too busy. We

don't have time. How can we work with the public to problem solve? The sum total of course of all the excuses could be summed up as I just don't want to change, because I know how I fit into the way we do it now."

Seriously probing the psychological bases for human resistance to change is beyond our competence. Our armchair psychological judgment, however, is that people do not really resist change on a wholesale basis. Rather, we believe people resist the change if is forced on them or they conclude it is not in their self-interest. And, as Brann (1995b) observes, even those who resist change directed at *themselves* often voice little or no objection to changes affecting only their coworkers. Such employees may even grouse about the need for organizational reforms—but reforms involving *others'* sacrifices.

A St. Louis police officer underscored the tendency of many people to recoil at change forced on them by others. During a staff meeting about implementing community problem solving, he told Chief Clarence Harmon: "Veterans often say this is what they did 15 years ago, but they don't want this style of police work 'forced down their throats'" (St. Louis Metropolitan Police Department 1993a: 1). Sparrow (1992: 57) echoes the point about self-interest influencing one's attitude toward change: "The most robust resistance to any change in values within an organization will come from those parts that stand to benefit most by the perpetuation of the old set of values."

Another commentator suggested that people don't resist change so much as they resist *being* changed. In any event, so simple is the proposition that people only resist change which they believe runs against their interests that it may not help advance our thinking very much. Or maybe it does lie at the core of why we cling to some optimism that middle managers, despite all their potential reasons for opposing community policing, might instead be supported and motivated in ways that convert them from opponents to proponents of strategic innovations.

IV. Reasons to Believe that Middle Managers Can Be Willing Partners in the Reform Movement

"We senior executives in policing have to be willing to look at ourselves and our behavior to see whether it's consistent with the values we espouse. I'm concerned that we're creating a false perception and a false barrier to implementing community policing by saying middle managers are the great obstacle to change. I think we're using them as scapegoats. If we chiefs and other senior managers really walk our own talk, our middle managers will take their lead from us" (Brann 1995a).

"Example is not the main thing in influencing others. It is the only thing."—Albert Schweitzer

Both experience and some theoretical considerations encourage us that middle managers can efficiently and effectively help design and implement community problem solving. We do not claim that *all* middle managers can become valued agents of change, but that is hardly the issue. The question at hand is whether a critical mass of police middle managers can contribute productively to strategic reform so that the reforms come quicker, deeper, and more enduringly. Precisely what that critical mass needs to be very likely will vary from department to department.

Writing in the *Harvard Business Review*, Rosabeth Moss Kanter (1979: 96) argued theoretically and empirically that middle managers can and do serve as organizational innovators (see also Kanter 1983; Kelling and Bratton 1993: 2). Although she was not addressing public organizations such as police departments, her insights may prove applicable beyond the context of private businesses in service industries and manufacturing.

One of the reasons Kanter considers middle managers suitably positioned as innovators derives from the maxim that the job of the leader is to make promises and the job of the manager is to keep them (Stamper 1992). "[T]op leaders' general directives...mean nothing," Kanter observed (1982: 96), "without efficient middle managers...able to design the systems, carry them out, and redirect their staffs' activities accordingly." Such a perspective on the relative roles of police CEOs and middle managers led Braiden (1995) to opine: "It's not the chief's job to run the department well. It's the chief's job to be sure the department is run well by others." St. Louis' Major Roy Joachimstaler made a similar point: "Our main job in the administration should not be to dictate to the...District Commanders how to manage their areas of responsibility, but instead to hold them accountable for expanding the problem-solving philosophy throughout their commands" (1995: 2).

The power and responsibility to convert leaders' words to organizational deeds places great innovation challenges in the bailiwick of the middle manager. Middle managers may have to step up and proactively exercise the power they have implicitly or explicitly been delegated by the organization's CEO to effectuate the department's mission and goals. But the opportunity to step up is there for those with initiative and competence. It is also crucial, of course, for senior management to help show the way for mid-level officials who may not already know (although some know *better* than higher-ups) where things need to head. As Sparrow notes,

> "The likelihood of a change in policy and style surviving, in the long term, probably depends as much on its acceptance by middle management as on anything else. The middle managers, therefore, have to be coached and reeducated; they have to be given the opportunity and incentive for critical self-examination and the chance to participate in the reappraisal of the organization. Some chiefs have invested heavily in management retraining, seminars, and retreats, taking great care to show their personal commitment to those enterprises" (1992: 56).

Kanter also argues that middle managers' proximity to operations can help them "conceive, suggest, and set in motion new ideas that top managers may not have thought of" (1982: 96). Admittedly, proximity to the field does not favorably distinguish middle managers from their *subordinates* in terms of capacity for conceiving innovations. As noted earlier, the subordinates typically have a much closer view of the customers than do the middle managers. But the middle managers' *combination* of proximity (as compared with more senior bosses) and *breadth* of vision within the organization (e.g., they are not narrowly focused on just one police beat) may equip middle managers to imagine strategic improvements that use but do not hoard departmental resources. As Center for Creative Leadership researcher Leonard Sayles (1993) argued, "It is the much maligned middle managers who are...often the only ones with the technical knowledge and perspective that allows for sensible trade-offs."

Since the middle managers have to worry about meeting the needs of *all* subordinates under their domain, they may avoid the false starts of innovations that unfairly rob from Officer Peter to support Officer Paul. One of the best ways to kill an innovation in policing is to make it available only to a select few favored employees, then watch the resentment of the deprived cops undermine the credibility and effectiveness of the innovation in myriad subtle and overt ways. Federal "COPS Office" Director Joe Brann (1995b), who enjoyed the benefits of *agency-wide* introduction of community policing when he served in the Santa Ana, California, Police Department, concurs: Officer resentment "is one of the primary drawbacks of implementing community policing or problem-oriented policing through elite units or incrementally."

"It is fairly easy to see how the chief..., district commanders, and individual beat officers can have a clear territorial responsibility. What about the remainder in middle management? There is a danger that community contact and concern will be the preserve of the highest and lowest ranks..., with the middle ranks living a cozy internal life of administration. Middle-ranking officers can continue to be a barrier to the dissemination of the new values unless they too are made to live by them. This is perhaps best accomplished by making each rank correspond to some level of aggregation of beats or of community concerns. Thus middle managers should interact as fully with the community as the most senior and most junior officers. They thereby become a meaningful resource for the patrol officers rather than just one more level of supervision. They then can provide contextual frameworks, at successively higher levels, to assist subordinates in the understanding and resolution of particular community problems" (Sparrow 1992: 57; Sparrow, et al. 1990: 171).

Middle managers also may welcome the opportunity, which they can be given during a campaign for organizational transformation, to display one of their strengths: expert knowledge about the department's current and previous culture. Middle managers are unlikely to have risen successfully through the ranks without a fairly intimate knowledge of the organizational culture with all its splendor and warts. The good middle managers have, among other things, spent "time learning the location of vested interests and where other patches of organizational quicksand lurk..." (Kanter 1982: 98). Moreover, a good middle manager in the private setting, in order to sell an innovation to superiors, frequently has had to "prove to people that [she knows] more about the company than they did" (*ibid.*).

To fundamentally change an organization's strategy, one must know its culture so that obstacles to reform and pressure points can be identified and either neutralized or used properly. Particularly if a reform police chief has been hired from outside the organization, middle managers who can keep the CEO well briefed on the landmines and escape hatches afforded by the organization's heritage of mores and informal practices can spell the difference between the new chief's success or failure (Braiden 1995).

Knowing the existing culture is also necessary for figuring out when unobtrusive but important things are changing. For instance, *Reinventing Government* authors Osborne and Gaebler (1993: 173) highlight PERF staffer Mary Ann Wycoff's insight into the shifting culture of the Madison, Wisconsin, Police Department:

> "Fairly early after they began getting the customer reports, one officer got one back that was quite critical. He read it out loud to his colleagues, quite sarcastically, expecting them to agree that it was ridiculous. And there was dead silence. It was clear that the group did not necessarily agree with him. That kind of change in peer relations can have a big impact on people. That officer was very surprised."

While middle managers, unless they entered laterally, will usually have been in an organization long enough to have mastered its culture, Greene, et al. (1994: 97-98) argue that, compared with *senior* management, mid-level managers may not have been around long enough to have been *mastered by* the culture. They may, therefore, be more amenable to organizational change than their superiors. Assessing efforts to introduce community policing into the Philadelphia Police Department, they argue:

> "[M]iddle-level police commanders...had a more long-term stake in the reform of the Philadelphia Police. Unlike their chief inspector counterparts—often referred to as the department's dinosaurs—these lesser ranked commanders were most likely to want change: They had only moderate investment in maintaining the historical past, they had been exposed to more ideas about police reform, they had more time to remain within the department, and they were more likely to feel the long-term consequences of the tainted image of the Philadelphia Police [Goldberg 1995]. While there were certainly several individuals within these upper and middle management ranks who had allegiances to senior commanders and to chief inspectors, a significant number of others did not. As a result, this stratum of management within the department appeared more willing to adopt the change agenda of the police commissioner. Some of this acceptance was due to an

acknowledged need for change, some was political—trying to be on the right side—while others joined the change effort without a clear alternative."

Eck (1993) makes a point related to the observation by Greene, et al. (1994) that today's police middle managers have more exposure to reform ideas than their longer-in-the-tooth superiors. As Roberg (1994: 252) summarizes Eck, "current managers have the advantage of the popular management literature that is more supportive of flattening police hierarchy and decentralizing authority, and other types of constructive changes associated with contemporary corporate management practice" (see also Bratton 1994).

The Eck-Roberg point presents a double-edged sword. Much good can and has come from modern middle managers becoming conversant with the current, best-selling management reform literature. A possible downside, however, is that some managers may accept uncritically the advice given—including the now-conventional prediction that middle managers are almost certain to be obstacles to organizational reform. The problem that concerns us is that of *labeling*: whether dealing with youth who are prematurely labeled "juvenile delinquents" or with lieutenants and captains who are prematurely labeled recalcitrants, people often tend to live down to our expectations. When the drivers of the bandwagon make serious errors of judgment or simply don't get their facts right, those of us hopping on the bandwagon may get a ride we end up regretting. The management gurus are fallible human beings, subject to the same occasional murky thinking and poor research as the rest of us. One of the most popular management consultants, for example, has characterized two public sector criminal justice organizations in ways that don't square remotely with the facts as we or our colleagues know them to be. In one instance, the error was in characterizing a police department, along with several private companies, as one of the nation's highest-performing organizations. While this particular organization *does* have determined and gifted senior leadership who, in time, may be able to elevate the department to the point where it could reasonably be described as high-performing, that simply is not the *current* reality as we know it. It appears the management expert read the brochures and bought the car without kicking the tires.

Another reason for optimism that middle managers can be part of the solution rather than part of the problem in the transformation of police agencies from low- to high-performing organizations concerns the capacity of many middle managers to pay attention to details. The *post mortem* on many failed, ambitious projects includes the truism that "the devil is in the details." Where talented *traditional* middle managers have acumen in—and take pride in—attending to details, they might be enticed to help the community policing implementation effort. A winning approach for such individuals might involve appealing to their *technical* management expertise more than to their concurrence with a grand vision of customer-oriented public administration. If everybody in the department is a *visionary* and nobody worries the details, the agency may have some great retreats but it's less likely to make much progress in changing organizational *behavior* in an enduring way.

> *"One can imagine a department in which lieutenants become mid-level managers not simply by dutifully writing out the shift schedule and staffing the station house but by proposing tactical solutions to problems, devising innovative police operations, or working with community groups to identify their priorities" (Moore and Stephens 1991b: 44).*

An eminently practical reason for optimism that police middle managers *could* contribute mightily to organizational innovation is that, in prior waves of police strategic reform, and in the current "quiet revolution" (Kelling 1988) within policing, middle managers *have* made significant contributions. Just as police are too quick at times to dismiss a poorly tested idea on grounds that it was tried and found wanting, they are also generally quick to impress on the basis of real-world examples of counterparts' organizational successes. In the early successes with team policing efforts in Cincinnati, St. Paul and Los Angeles—and in a series of experiments in Kansas City, Missouri (assessing preventive patrol, rapid response, special operations, peer review of uses of force, and other initiatives)—middle managers were given key responsibilities as change agents and performed well (Kelling and Bratton 1993: 4-6; Moore 1992: 133; Koenig, et al. 1979). Kanter (1982, 1983) adds evidence that mid-level employees have also excelled as agents of change in private-sector organizations; see also Naisbitt and Aburdene (1985); and Byham and Cox (1988), whose fictional world of high-performing middle managers is grounded in years of real world success stories.

If one believes that the desire to move upward within an organization is a powerful motivator for at least some middle managers, then their career aspirations are still another basis for believing they can be motivated to actively facilitate community policing—even if they don't personally believe it is a valuable strategy. Police employees are conditioned to follow orders, so those who aren't inspired to contribute may be directed at least not to impede others.

> *"Nay-sayers [within police departments] scare easily when they see you're going to take them on. But take them on for the right reasons" (Braiden 1995).*

For example, Captain Al Sweeney, who heads the Boston Police Academy, recounts an experience with a sworn member of his staff whose conduct was not helping shape the organizational culture needed for community policing:

"Sometimes a handshake works and other times you need the hammer. An officer whom I selected to join my Academy staff brought with him eight years of street experience and 12 years of military background—in the Marines. Shortly after he arrived at the Academy I passed by his office and noticed a meticulous work area with every certificate imaginable from his service days. Centered prominently on the wall behind his chair—so you couldn't possibly miss it when talking with him—was a large Corps flag in all its glory.

I told him I appreciated his pride in the Corps but that I was concerned that the flag displayed in this manner conveyed a message to people who had not served in the Marines that they didn't quite measure up. In any event, the mission of the Marines was not identical to the mission and philosophy of community policing in Boston. I also asked him whether he had read a report about management problems in the Boston PD authored a few years earlier by William St. Clair. The 'St. Clair Commission Report,' among other things, specifically criticized Marine Corps posters in the Academy. He replied, with some defiant pride, that he had not read that report.

I thought I'd gotten my message across. I even suggested that he could place the flag on a staff pole and move it to the corner near his citations. How smooth and subtle I felt was the message. Too subtle, I guess, for a week later I passed his office again and noticed nothing had changed. It wasn't insubordination because I never gave him a direct order about the flag. I summoned the officer to my office and asked whether he had read the St. Clair Commission report yet. He told me he had sent for it. So I took a copy from my desk, opened it to the page containing the criticism of military flags in the Academy and asked him to read it on the spot. I told him my style was to encourage discussion and debate on such issues as the wisdom of displaying military flags in the Academy. I'd be happy to talk about this issue as long as he liked, because it was important to me that he understand *why* I was concerned about the flag.

I asked what his reaction was to the page from the report, and he said he disagreed with the report. He disagreed with it when it was issued and still did. He made it clear that no amount of discussion with me would change his mind. His closing remark was, 'But you are the commanding officer!' So much for my persuasive abilities, my logic, reasoning and belief in consensus. I thanked him for his candor. I told him how important it was to me to be able to discuss issues with my staff. Then I looked him in the eye and ordered him to move the flag immediately to a staff pole and off the wall. I also told him to have a great day" (Sweeney 1995).

Trojanowicz and Bucqueroux (1990: 351) relate the view of Robert Lunney, Chief of the Peel Regional Police in Ontario, Canada, about the necessity for being directive with some who resist the shift to community policing.

> "[T]raditionalists who will never embrace community policing offer both good news and bad. The bad news is that you will never change their minds, no matter how long and hard you talk and how logical you think your arguments are. The good news, however, is that traditionalists subscribe to the importance of following orders. The goal therefore is not to change attitudes, but to change behavior" (see also Block, undated: 2).

That's the good news and the bad news. But there's *worse* news yet. The tactic of seeking cooperation through edicts may not work with some of the more savvy obstructionist middle managers, for despite their conditioning they may only follow those orders they can't imaginatively evade (and those who know police are frequently awed at their talents for evasion).

Chris Braiden (1995) suggests that, to avoid the inefficiencies of trying to outfox resistant middle managers, police agencies should make far greater use of lateral entry of middle managers. "This is a good way to control what middle managers do. Hire them with a contract to carry out certain tasks. If they don't perform as desired, don't keep them on the payroll."

"Sergeants learn early on that using the power to formally discipline an officer for minor infractions, or enforcing strict conformity, usually comes with a price tag. Officers on the street are solitary workers who have many means available to them to get even with a 'wayward' supervisor. The first, and easiest, is taking the full amount of time allotted by the rules to handle each and every assignment. In a busy precinct this could spell disaster for the supervisor. Punishment-centered supervision only teaches cops the finer points of how to avoid the punishment. Little if anything else is accomplished" (Goodbody 1995: 12).

Whether aimed at lateral entrants or long-time agency veterans, for nonnegotiable directives to have a chance of overcoming a mid-manager's personal doubts and impulses to skate by with minimal compliance, the messages sent from those with the power to help or hurt the middle manager's career need to be consistent, clear, convincing, and fraught with consequences for the willful straggler. One way to maximize compliance among the serious resisters, argues Michael Hammer (Vogl 1993/1994: 54), is to create "a sense of inevitability" about the coming changes (see also Wilkinson and Rosenbaum 1994: 124). Hammer—with a more draconian bent than we find palatable—illustrates:

> "At one company I know, the union was about to go on strike over reengineering. On the eve of the strike, management went to the union and said: 'Listen, we understand your concerns, but you must understand, this company is customer driven, not union driven. We must do this. We're going to do it. We'll do it with you, we'll do it without you, but we are doing it.' The union called off the strike.
> ***
> Bluntly, the way to deal with this resistance is with a combination of relentless communication, support, incentives and a bloody axe. Al Capone said: 'You get a lot further with a gun and a kind word than with a kind word alone.'[6] ... [The] Hallmark [Company]...has been very successful in reengineering. Bob Stark, president of the card business, had a famous line when he started reengineering at Hallmark: 'We're going on a journey. On this journey, we will carry the wounded and shoot the stragglers.' That says it perfectly" (Vogl 1993/1994: 54).

Pritchett and Pound (1995: 11) give this advice to workers who consider trying to play the immovable object against the irresistible force of corporate change: "[I]f you think *adapting* is tough duty, just see how difficult life becomes if you *don't*." Braiden (1995) concurs that some employees need tangible ways of understanding the inevitability of their involvement in the new stratagem: "There's a job to be done. I remind coppers that community-oriented policing is the same as paycheck-oriented policing."

But Braiden (1995) also suggests that some of the middle managers whom more senior officials can motivate are not actively opposed to community policing. "They don't see themselves as part of the problem or the solution. They see themselves just as functionaries." Explaining how they can be a part of something that really makes a difference in the overall police mission may be an effective prod to such middle managers.

One need not leap, however, to the cynical view that the essential challenge for chiefs is driving middle managers out of reluctance, ambivalence, or apathy into embraces with community policing. For in our experience, a substantial number of police middle managers, just like their frontline co-workers, heartily believe that traditional, incident-driven policing is a flawed strategy and that community problem solving makes far more sense (see also Strandberg 1992). Many middle managers also hold the view that the paramilitarism of police organizations

---

[6] Trojanowicz (1994: 260), extolling the array of capacities that police officers bring to community-oriented government teams, put Capone's point a bit differently: "[T]he community officer has the broadest range of options, ranging from a pat on the back for a job well done to the use of deadly force in dealing with the problems that the community may face."

is inappropriate for the missions assigned to the police. They point out, as Chris Braiden (1995) has, that "the civil police were created in the first place in order to *replace* the military in performing domestic policing." Indeed, Reiss (1992: 80, n. 10) reports that police departments in the United States, which were organized as full-time, paid forces in the mid-19th century, did not adopt the military rank structure until late in the 19th century.

Displaying the emerging quantitative and anecdotal evidence that community problem solving is a more powerful, more aggressive way than previous approaches to engage and defeat crime, disorder and fear is beyond the scope of this little volume. The reader is referred to the footnote in Chapter 1 containing a lengthy citation to the fast-growing descriptive and evaluative literature on community policing. That body of work explores many of the operational and reputational benefits police departments have reaped from their commitment to community policing. The National Institute of Justice in

Middle manager Michael R. Longfellow, of the Ormond Beach, Florida, Police Department reflected on conclusions he reached about the competing policing strategies. His views were based on his own experience and conversations with his chief, Robert L. Stewart:
"Studies conducted more than thirty years ago proved that the methods in traditional policing were not effective. Routine patrol does not effectively reduce crime. Rapid response does not affect our ability to apprehend the perpetrators who have already fled. Locking ourselves in the metal cocoon of a patrol vehicle and dealing with the public only when required created a fear of the police and an unwillingness to cooperate. *** [Think about] the methods, management styles, and results of traditional policing versus community oriented policing. Anyone who truly studies these differences and the results obtainable from each method cannot help but see how COP is better for all involved" (Longfellow 1995: 4).

1995 developed an impressive research and evaluation agenda on community policing (Travis 1995), and the results of those studies should make further important contributions to the literature.

Our point here is that there are a fair number of middle managers who, for their own reasons, believe in the superiority of community problem solving as the way to do *tough* and *real* police work. Many of them concur with the position Lee Brown took as Commissioner of the NYPD:

> "Community policing is not soft on crime. Community policing is tougher on crime than traditional policing because it's smarter. A good community police officer will make more arrests than the regular beat officer because he or she will get more information" (quoted in Webber 1992: 29).

For many mid-manager community policing enthusiasts, confidence in this strategy is born of looking into the faces of "officers who enjoy their work and find satisfaction in solving recurring problems, and in [seeing] community members who are pleased with the effectiveness of police services..." (Burgreen and McPherson 1992: 78). In city after city, middle managers are aware that "officers feel as if they are making an impact on long-standing problems rather than only 'shoveling sand against the tide'" (Weisel 1992: 137; also see the description, in *Reinventing Government*, of the Tulsa Police Department's successes under the leadership of former Chief Drew Diamond—Osborne and Gaebler 1993: 50).

Many middle managers also cannot abide using the same old mops to clean up predictable floods of social distress—they would rather see if they can help someone figure out how to fortify the village against the troubled waters. The commonsense appeal of preventing problems—shutting them off at their source if possible rather than having to do triage emergency care to the victims—tugs powerfully at most police who have direct and unrelenting exposure to the victims. One social services practitioner suggests the metaphor of

> "a village on a cliff. Everything's fine, except the kids keep falling off. The community elders get together and decide that the solution is to build a clinic at the bottom of the cliff. That's the classic government answer: build clinics. What the village needs is a fence at the top, to keep kids from falling" (Barthel 1992: 14).

One of the fence builders we admire is St. Louis Police Major Roy Joachimstaler, who as a district captain afforded his first-line officers an inspiring blend of autonomy with accountability. He noted that a

> "misconception [about problem-oriented policing]...is the belief that it is public affairs, a public relations endeavor. Some of the skeptics should witness the energy and enthusiasm of uniform patrol officers executing their own search warrant on a drug house in their beat as part of a problem-solving project. Or they should personally witness the satisfaction of the residents when problem properties are condemned and boarded up, before they throw a 'public affairs' label on this type of policing" (Joachimstaler 1995: 2).

Such testimonial data would not suffice for formal social science process and impact evaluations of community problem solving (see, e.g., Greene and Taylor 1988; Lurigio and Rosenbaum 1994: 160-61; Bennett 1994: 244; Buerger 1994; Shadish, et al. 1991; Mastrofski 1993; Cresap Associates 1991; and Skolnick and Bayley 1988: 17-19; compare Roberg 1994: 254). But this kind of testimony is a rich source of encouragement and guidance for those charged with leading strategic change efforts in police departments around the nation (Weisburd 1994). These

> *"The evaluator...can be rewarded as much for negative as positive evidence [of a program's accomplishments]. His or her commitment 'is to knowledge, not the success of some program'.... Moreover, the evaluator does not want to be seen as 'going native'—as becoming too much a part of the enthusiasm of the program process. From the perspective of practitioners this skepticism is often irritating"* (Weisburd 1994: 275).

reformers should not, of course, denigrate or ignore whatever convincing evaluative studies are available. Nor should they, however, overlook the fact that, "by the very nature of community policing, it is difficult to prove that a philosophy works" (Leighton 1994: 220). Bayley (1994: 278) is blunter:

> "The success of community policing will never be evaluated. The reason is simple. Community policing means too many things to different people. Its practices are so varied that any evaluation will be partial or challengeable as not being authentic 'community policing.'"

Even if reasonable consensus could be reached on the elements to be evaluated, however, Roberg (1994: 253) and Moore (1994: 288) remind us that this strategic reformation is expected to take ten years or more to reach fruition in any given locale. As a result, it should come as no surprise that community problem-solving efforts generally show unimpressive results in *impact* evaluations conducted during their earliest years (Lavrakas 1995: 110). Moreover, Weisburd (1994: 275) offers the observation that police practitioners' "enthusiasm," however impractical seeming, "often contributes to the successful operation of the program." Enthusiasm produces an impact in part by "motivating others to become involved" (see Skogan, et al. 1995: 20 for a description of contagious enthusiasm in the Chicago Police Department). Ralph Waldo Emerson declared: "Nothing great is ever achieved without enthusiasm" (quoted in Braiden, "Policing—From the Belly of the Whale": 9). And the philosopher, Goethe, urged: "Whatever you can do, or dream you can do, begin it! Boldness has genius, power, and magic in it. Begin it now." So faith can shape fortune. In any event, the cops, as Weisburd (1994: 275) reminds us, "cannot afford to be skeptics on the sidelines."

Middle managers and other police may perhaps be understood, if not forgiven, if their view of ivy-tower evaluators who subject fledgling programs to penetrating scrutiny resembles actress Tyne Daly's opinion of drama critics. "They are the people," she said, "who never arrive at the battlefield until after the battle is over and then walk around shooting the wounded." If there seems to be an anti-intellectual tone here, it is not intended. What we favor, with others (e.g., Moore 1994: 287) is greater scholarly sensitivity to the problem that, in the fragile, early stages of a new movement, prematurely

> *During the creative process, things can look pretty messy, ugly, unproductive or unpromising. That is when intolerance and impatience must be checked. Remember, the caterpillar retreats to a seemingly useless state of dormancy only to emerge as a butterfly.*

exposing it to the "third degree" may become a destructive, self-fulfilling prophecy of failure. This risk is heightened if the interrogator commences an evaluation with the cynical presumption that, probed deeply enough, *everything* will turn out "not to work" (Toch 1995: 2). The history of humankind is full of people who have attained miraculous results, partly because nobody informed them that what they were attempting wouldn't work. The history of daring social programs is full of caregivers who got to attend their own funerals. It may strike the collaborators in a goodly number of successful community policing partnerships that the reports of their demise (e.g., Buerger 1994) or stillborn beginnings (Mastrofski 1993) also have been greatly exaggerated.

At the same time, practitioner-change agents may be wary of academics who "try to 'rationalize' the untidy developments now occurring in the field, and bring them under some form of central control designed to ensure that the one best form of community policing is tested and implemented" (Moore 1994: 287). There are perils in both extremes to which some researchers are inclined—precipitous scrutiny and intolerance for "creative chaos." ("Creative chaos," the saying goes, "is better than tidy idleness.") The consequence that practitioners rightly fear from either form of academic excess is that

> "the search for better ways to police America's communities might be aborted or crippled. *** The danger associated with too heavy-handed a research intervention is that by trying to learn too quickly and too systematically, society could actually shrink its capacity to learn what works. In trying to answer the question of whether community policing works before society and the field have had ample

opportunity to explore the possibilities of the complex idea, we might unwittingly stop the prospecting just before we found gold" (Moore 1994: 287).

The risk might otherwise be expressed in the metaphor of the eager novice botanist who wants to see how a young plant is doing so he keeps pulling it up by the roots to check its growth. The exposure is revealing but lethal.

Middle managers whom we have observed leading the charge toward strategic innovation and conducting the "bureaucratic garage sales" that Chris Braiden urges upon the policing industry do not see their own interests as conflicting with those of their department's customers. Community satisfaction is a defining feature of good job performance for such managers. (One can find a number of middle managers of this type in Reno, Nevada, for instance, which achieved notable improvements in public attitudes toward the police after commencing community policing—Glensor 1990; Peak, et al. 1992: 38; and Bigham 1993; for an early indication of similar results in Chicago, see Skogan, et al. 1995: 89). The way in which excellent middle managers think about their business is that good policing is about getting good public safety results by honorable means. Accordingly, they explore intently to discover whether progress is being made toward that goal. If it is, then such middle managers believe that police at all ranks should take job satisfaction, even if the content of their work has changed in ways that may not be as adventurous.

> *The process of organizational innovation will necessarily be "very fluid" and "context-dependent," argues NYPD Sergeant William Goodbody (1995: 14). "Thus, we will learn much from what we do, and this will in turn become the basis of our practice. ... [A] core of proven strategies and practices is already emerging. Every new situation need not be a new adventure. Information must be shared so that officers do not waste valuable time reinventing the wheel when confronted with new problems and circumstances" (ibid.).*

Moreover, many middle managers simply take pride in showing their ingenuity in solving organizational problems that would otherwise impede police effectiveness and efficiency. Braiden's theory (1995) is that some people simply enjoy the creative problem-solving process and some people prefer a highly structured work and private life. "The best problem solvers in policing," he opines, "are handymen (and women) in real life. People who are handy with their hands are handy with their heads. Successful human beings are problem solvers."

Maclean's best-selling historical novel, *Young Men and Fire* (1992), underscores Braiden's point about the creative spectrum spanning cerebral and tactile processes. Maclean recounts how a few "smoke jumpers" (firefighters who parachute into forest fires) several decades ago invented a firefighting technique—with their hands rather than their heads—that is used to this day. For these young men, necessity was definitely the mother of invention. They conceived and produced the first-known *backfire* while a horrific conflagration swiftly closed in on them from all sides. Most of their fellow firefighters on the scene thought the proposal—to set fire to the safe ground on which they were standing and then lie down in the ashes—was the demented product of the fear of impending death. The few among them who followed this unprecedented and seemingly illogical advice were the only young firefighters to survive the infamous Mann Gulch fire.

To bolster our assertions that police middle managers not only *could* contribute greatly as leaders or facilitators of community policing, but are actually doing so, we offer a few illustrations. (If time and space permitted, literally *hundreds* of such examples could be presented.[7]) Following these anecdotes, we shall enumerate the kinds of steps and conditions that these and many similar experiences suggest will support and motivate middle managers as agents of police strategic change.

Some Examples of Middle Managers Facilitating Community Problem Solving

Two things should be kept in mind while reading the following illustrations of middle management leadership or facilitation of strategic change in police departments. First, the mid-managers featured are *admirable* people. Second, they are—in the fondest sense of the word—*ordinary* people. As management expert Rosabeth Moss Kanter observed after describing similar people whom she admired in *corporate* middle management, "the middle managers described here are *not extraordinary* individuals" (Kanter 1982: 96) (emphasis added). The second point is *not* bad news. It's *good* news. It means that, under the right organizational conditions and the right kind of senior leadership, there are many people in organizational mid-ranks who can make a significant contribution to change. The most successful among them very likely will share the kind of qualities that Kanter observed in her sample and that we observe in ours: "comfort with change, ...clarity of direction, ...thoroughness, ...participative management style, ...[and] persuasiveness, persistence, and discretion" (Kanter 1982: 96). The men and women featured below are the heroes of the story this book tells. They are, indeed, heroes to us personally. In the relatively cynical era in which we live, it seems both predictable and useful that many of our society's genuine and enduring heroes come from the ranks of "ordinary" people (see Milloy 1995).

1. Birds in the attic, a hose in the alley, and the meaning of empowerment

In Evanston, Illinois, a suburb of about 75,000 on Chicago's northern border, department comedians had chided Officer John Birkenheier for years over the histrionics he displayed after handling a 9-1-1 call about "birds in the attic." He got the birds out of the lady's attic, but for days afterward he was spitting and sputtering around the stationhouse: "Birds in the attic is not police work! I've got better things to do than go get the birds out of some lady's attic!" While his spirit of public service may have left a little to be desired, still nobody could deny that he had a point. Nobody denied it, but nobody did anything about it either.

Some years passed, and in the summer of 1994 Birkenheier and partner Don Pflaumer got another classic dispatch: "A hose running in the alley." The officers, especially Birkenheier, were fit to be tied, but they responded to the call and stopped the hose from running. When Birkenheier and Pflaumer returned to the station, they loudly voiced their displeasure to Sgt. Everett Erlandson. In publishable paraphrase, the pair of officers were less than enthused about

---

[7] An excellent example that is well documented elsewhere is the Baltimore County Police Department's C.O.P.E. (Citizen-Oriented Police Enforcement) unit. This was a fear-reduction project that hit pay dirt using the then quite new problem-solving techniques that were being described by Herman Goldstein, John Eck, Bill Spelman and a few other innovative strategists. The best succinct case study of the C.O.P.E. effort is by Taft (1986).

working in a community in which criminals remain at large while well-trained police officers run on hose-in-the-alley calls.

"Do you have a better solution?" Erlandson asked them. Birkenheier piped up, "Well maybe. The town I live in handles a lot of the B.S. garbage type calls over the phone. As a matter of fact, I had an occasion to make this type of report myself." Erlandson seized the

If the main role a particular middle manager is playing in the community policing implementation effort is that of quiet, behind-the-scenes bureaucratic problem solver, it may take a "Where's Waldo?" search to detect his or her contributions to overall success. The search is worth it, for it will illuminate the mundane but still essential infrastructural reform contributions without which continuing improvements in operational effectiveness—the headline stuff—may not be possible.

moment. He had listened with interest a year earlier when his new chief, Gerald Cooper, told a Department retreat that he wanted officers and others at the operating level of the department to take significant initiatives to make their work easier and more effective. Erlandson was one of the members of the Department who decided he might as well take the chief at his word. So the sergeant told Officers Birkenheier and Pflaumer:

"Both of you guys take the squad and go *right now* and take a look at how they handle these calls where John lives. And if you find other towns in the area that are doing something similar, go there. Then, when you come back, and if you think you have a better way for us to handle these calls, we will try it."

They did just that. Birkenheier and Pflaumer started the Evanston Department's differential response effort from the ground up. After they implemented it and set up the operating procedures, differential response was so well received by the day shift patrol officers that it was added to the afternoon shift. An officer from that shift, Mark Berndt, had only been on the differential response team a short time when he recommended moving the unit out from behind a desk in the station and into a marked squad car with a cellular phone. That way, he reasoned, the officers could field the differential response calls, provide visible patrol for Evanston, and be ready to roll if they were needed for any emergency calls. Berndt's suggestion was adopted. No elaborate chain-of-command was brought to bear on second-guessing the team's decision—a sharp departure from the agency's historical top-down, mother-may-I approaches to matters far less consequential than redeployment of personnel and assignment of vehicles and cellular phones. The lack of obstruction and facilitative role of several middle managers at this juncture was crucial to the launching and eventual institutionalization of differential response in the agency.

When Berndt began to get serious static about his involvement in differential response from a couple of his sergeants, the afternoon shift commander, Lt. Mike Gresham (a cop's cop who can lower the boom with the best of them) let the sergeants know in unmistakably clear terms that what Officer Berndt was doing was helpful to the department and that the sergeants should let him do his job. Were it not for this middle manager's timely and distinctly *unmixed* message to take down the roadblocks, Berndt's voyage into differential response might have been a short ride indeed.

The unit's four officers from the day and afternoon shifts dealt, usually by telephone, with birds and hoses and other such minor miscellany. As in any differential response call-back unit, the officers returned the call of the person who had requested police service and, where possible, connected the community resident to a more suitable public or private service provider.

What is striking about the development of the Evanston differential response unit is not, of course, the idea of differentially responding to calls for service depending on their nature and level of emergency. That is a tried and true program that many police organizations have had in place for well over a decade (Farmer 1981; McEwen, et al. 1984). The remarkable feature of the Evanston story is that this programmatic modification—which entailed taking four officers out of the regular patrol rotation, securing an extra squad car, equipping it as a roving "call-back office," and abandoning the long-standing Evanston tradition of sending a sworn officer in person to every call for service—was conceived, designed, implemented, and operated totally by first-line officers.

When developing a differential response system, the methods of response selected may have implications for exacerbating or solving particular kinds of problems, as the Edmonton Police Department discovered some years ago. They were taking nonemergency reports of theft and burglary by telephone. The Department discovered that there were a great many Ping golf clubs reported stolen. In fact, comparing crime stats to information gathered in a merchant survey, the Department learned that "[t]here were more Pings stolen than there were Pings purchased." The Department changed the policy to require the victim of a Ping club theft to stop at any police station, any time that was convenient, 24-hours a day, and to bring receipts for the purchase of the pricey gear. "They had a 30% reduction in thefts in the first year" (Briggs 1995: 139).

They did inform their sergeants and lieutenants what they had in mind at key junctures, but none of these supervisors ever tried to micromanage the project—other than the couple of afternoon shift sergeants who were openly hostile to the entire initiative. Nor did the middle managers (the lieutenants) feel obliged to run to the patrol commander or the chief for permission to let their officers try out a differential response capability. They knew their department's history was replete with examples of chiefs who would have called middle managers on the carpet for allowing such latitude to their officers. But, like Erlandson, lieutenants George Scharm and Mike Gresham had heard Chief Cooper's inaugural talk about empowerment and problem solving, and they too assumed he meant it.

Some in the department who were not directly in the enterprising officers' chains of command recoiled at this departure from conventional patrol methods and at the idea of bottoms-up innovation in the department. They decried the idea of first-line officers daring to invade middle managers' traditional turf by devising programmatic responses to operational problems. "What next?" they wondered. But to Sgt. Erlandson, shift commanders Gresham and Scharm, and Lt. Dennis Nilsson (an ardent devotee of Herman Goldstein's work on problem solving who some years earlier had addressed a Harvard Executive Session on community policing), the appeal of differential response was commonsensical: It could free officers for more problem solving. Those who bridled at the innovation illustrated the truth of management expert Kanter's observation that "most innovative achievements cut across organizational lines and threaten to disrupt existing arrangements" (1982: 97).

By the time Chief Cooper found out, a few weeks after the hose-in-the-alley call, that a few of his officers were experimenting with a new operational unit in the department, the program was already proving popular among the public and rank-and-file personnel. Members of the public appreciated not having to wait at home for a responding squad car on a minor problem. They could go about their business and take a phone call from an officer at a time of mutual convenience. The public also liked the fact that patrol officers were more available for the neighborhoods' serious problems because they were not tied up on low priority calls.

Fellow patrol officers appreciated that the four-member differential response team was relieving them of handling trivial calls and of listening to Birkenheier's ranting. The Chief was delighted. The officers who took the initiative to invent something felt powerful and effective—and, in more than one case, reversed their waning enthusiasm for police work. Their idea turned out to have staying power. Within a year, the Evanston Police Department formalized the experimental unit and ensconced it in the order book as a part of standard operating procedure. The officers on the team trained new members as they were rotated into the unit.

While the middle managers' roles could easily be missed in this success story, these unsung heros deserve a tuneful thanks. They had the good sense to leave the officers alone long enough for them to figure out what to invent, and the bravery to stand up against pockets of internal resistance to the officers' differential response experiment.

2. *You're only left out of the chain if you allow yourself to be the weak link*

When Cheektowaga, New York, a suburb of about 100,000 just east of Buffalo, was hit with a number of well-publicized crimes in its Harlem Police District, residents of the area became fearful and publicly quite vocal over the slippage in their quality of life. In this climate, one evening in June 1993, as Cheektowaga Chief Bruce Chamberlin tells the story, "ten black kids on bicycles beat up two white kids" in one of this neighborhood's parks. "Though this was not a serious assault," he reports,

"it infuriated the neighborhood, which is white; and rumors of the incident seemed to spread across the entire police district. By ten o'clock the next morning, we had received numerous calls from citizens saying that community leaders were calling for taking the streets back with shotguns and baseball bats. We realized we had to do something fairly fast, and we also realized that we were not fighting so much a crime problem as one of fear and racism that was being fueled by some community leaders and some political leadership."

"During a period of organizational reorientation the communication between the chief and the rank and file needs to be...more direct [than usual]. *** This is not proposed as a permanent state of affairs, as clearly the rank structure has its own value and is not to be lightly discarded. During the period of accelerated change, however,...it is necessary to ensure that the message is not filtered, doctored, or suppressed (either by accident or as an act of deliberate sabotage) by intermediate ranks..." (Sparrow 1992: 56).

Chief Chamberlin spent the entire day in a series of meetings with police employees of all ranks, community and political leaders. "By five o'clock that afternoon," the Chief says,

> "people in the Harlem District knew that something had changed. I gave some fairly simple instructions to the patrol officers, which mostly had to do with ways of being highly visible in the neighborhoods and making contact with key neighborhood residents.
>
> Patrol officers were told that their effort should be centered around reducing crime, reducing fear, and doing anything in their power to accomplish that, without forgetting about constitutional rights. They were told that they were in the best position to know how to do that; ...were to figure out the specific tactics we would use and report back to us; and not to look at arrest as the only way of solving a problem."

Even though middle managers had not been left out of the loop (they were in the planning meetings earlier in the day when the Chief gave the officers their problem-solving mission) the Chief had touched an unpleasant nerve for some of his mid-level staff: "The response from most of the command-supervisory staff was like I just stepped in from another planet." In their minds, "I had of course violated a number of the rules here, such as chain of command."

But fortunately for Chief Chamberlin and the residents of Cheektowaga, Lt. Fredrick Roll and his captain "were two of the few who seemed to understand the first time around the concept of what we were trying to do." Two things distinguished this pair from their fellow middle managers: "They grasped some new ideas and were not threatened by the concept of the patrol officers having a great deal of direct input as to how we were going to do policing in that neighborhood."

Fear-reduction efforts made by the problem-focused officers, working in concert with community residents, began to make a positive difference. What Lt. Roll and his captain made possible in Cheektowaga, by supporting first-line problem solving, was a *practical demonstration* that problem-oriented approaches to fear reduction could work, and not only in San Diego or Newport News or other meccas of strategic innovation, but in Cheektowaga.

But these middle managers had only *begun* to reinvent the *modus operandi* of their agency. Not long after the Harlem District problem solvers started tackling the fear and crime problems, officers in the adjacent William District asked for a meeting with Lt. Roll. They told him, as Chief Chamberlin indicates, "that they did not agree with the 'Chief's approach,' and they proposed a challenge project in the William District." They proposed to see whether they or their Harlem District counterparts could reduce more crime within comparable patrol areas.

Here was a critical juncture. An insecure police chief or middle managers with heavy sycophantic tendencies might well have squelched the challenge as unsupportive of the chief's agenda. But seeing an opportunity to harness the energy of potential "nay-sayers" for the betterment of the community, the middle managers went to the chief with the recommendation that he go along with the challenge project. "Of course," the Chief replied, "I can't lose either way." And "as it turned out," the Chief reported with evident pride, "the William District project was the most successful of the two."

A central question in the strategic reform of police organizations is "how should top management behave to ensure that those in the organization who have been the organization's champions for standardization and control—captains and lieutenants—become its leading edge for creativity and innovation?" (Kelling and Bratton 1993: 10).

"How in the world, I wondered, do we get bureaucrats to strive for 'continuous improvement'? They invented the status quo" (Sensenbrenner 1991: 64).

So here we have a police culture being reengineered. The message was clear: It's OK for the chief to talk directly to patrol officers and smart for the middle managers to listen carefully and then figure out how they can help facilitate the accomplishment of the assigned task. A savvy middle manager realizes, as Kanter (1982: 96) observed in a passage quoted earlier, that the "top leaders' general directives...mean nothing without efficient middle managers" doing their part to help the workers meet their ambitious goals. Moreover, it was not only *possible*, but *desirable* for employees to speak out when they thought the boss was wrong in his tactical choices—so long as the critics coupled their challenge with an offer to jump in and help meet the boss' goals in their own fashion.

Chief Chamberlin (1995a) gives the lion's share of the credit for the strategic shifts his department has made in the two years since June 1993 to these maverick middle managers:

"The role that this Captain and Lieutenant played was critical. They worked with the officers and encouraged them, kept me informed on what was working and what wasn't, and actually formed the basis for what we are doing today. At a recent training conference it was mentioned that two thousand departments are awaiting training in community policing. We had none prior to that, but what we did have was creative middle management. *** A lot has been written about middle management being the reason why nothing works or gets off the ground, and that certainly can be the case. We are fortunate in that I would say for the most part our middle management has been our strength. Lt. Roll, being one of the most senior and one of the most respected lieutenants, has had a great deal of influence on the rest of the management team in moving us further and further toward community policing. We are currently taking the next step in strengthening our management team using many of the principles of the Quality Movement."

3. A tale of two detective unit leaders

One of the things middle managers have done well is to strategically and wisely stay out of the way of proactive officers—and help ensure that other institutional players also give the first-line people appropriate running room. Another way in which middle managers have risen to the community policing challenge is by taking an active leadership role. In two widely respected North American police agencies—Edmonton, Alberta, Canada, and San Diego, California, detectives have been led through a cultural revolution in their thinking and work methods by lieutenant-level managers. The first story is excerpted from Ogle (undated).

In the Edmonton Police Service, Staff Sergeant Bill Mowbray (the equivalent of a lieutenant in an American police department) heads the downtown detective division. He explains the challenge for strategic leadership within a detective bureau:

"What we are asking now of detectives is infinitely more difficult than what we asked before. Before we asked them to go out and investigate this or that, but now we ask them to investigate, plus look at the overall picture, plus give us solutions to problems. That is very difficult for officers who have never worked that way in 20 or 25 years. They're running for cover now, the old fellows."

Mowbray helped the detectives understand and begin to make substantial problem-solving contributions through a four-step process of (1) "identifying your customers" (who were deemed in Edmonton to be crime victims as well as uniformed officers); (2) "building teams"; (3) "seeing the monkey on your back" (i.e., understanding that your responsibility in police service extends to cutting crime's harm to the community, not just making arrests regardless of their impact); and (4) "forming partnerships to get the monkey off."

The whirlwinds of change churning through policing must feel to many veteran police—detectives especially—like the tornado that transported Dorothy and her little mutt in The Wizard of Oz. "Toto," she said when they finally landed, "I don't think we're in Kansas anymore." So, too, as Moore (1994: 285) puts it with elegant simplicity: "Something is clearly afoot in the field of policing."

The downtown Vice Unit exemplifies problem solving by Edmonton detectives. To reduce public prostitution, which had persisted despite huge numbers of arrests over the years, Mowbray helped his personnel form partnerships with drug counseling and other social service agencies.

"Mowbray explains how this works: 'The detective goes out there and obtains a conversation, just as he would with any other communicating charge. But rather than charge that person, rather than write up a court file, he simply takes that individual before [any of several] predetermined...inner city agencies interested in getting prostitutes off the street and says, Here, now you do the job.'"

The cultural revolution—the paradigm shift—required for many of the detectives was enormous:

"[T]he officer must now realize that the prostitute is also a victim. Traditionally, the detective has seen these people as lawbreakers; therefore they go to court. Yes, they are lawbreakers, but there is a reason for them doing that. In fact, there are many reasons, and, if we can get to those reasons, we can solve the problem, and that person will no longer break the law."

The "huge shift in goals and objectives" that Staff Sgt. Mowbray helped his team embrace is that "[a]rrest is still there as an option, but it is now seen as a means to an end, whereas before it was seen as an end in itself. This changes the way in which the work is managed and measured."

The results—for Edmontonians and for Edmonton's police? "It's working: 30% of the prostitutes are no longer showing up on the street. Now the detectives can see tangible results" (Ogle, undated).

* *

In San Diego, Lieutenant Jim Caster managed the daily operations of the Police Department's street level drug enforcement unit. His six sergeants and 36 detectives, all plainclothes and veterans, used informants, surveillance, and information from uniformed officers to make arrests. An investigation began with a little bit of information and ended with an arrest. The focus was on the largest seizures, the most arrests.

And why not? Success was measured by numbers: the number of arrests, warrants, probation and parole searches, drugs confiscated, and, especially money seized. Statistics were kept on individual members and teams, by the month and year. And to ensure continuity of the unit's culture and methods, the supervisors were only selected from among those who had served as detectives in this same unit.

The unit's members—all good at their craft—had but one tool: enforcement. They suffered the two afflictions of the man whose only tool is a hammer: Too many things began to look to him like nails, and too many jobs seemed impossible because they couldn't be accomplished by banging. Indeed, if it looked like a complaint could not lead to an arrest, it was not considered a valid complaint by the unit. If arrests failed over and over to stop a problem, then it was considered the fault of the criminal justice system, not a mistaken choice of tactics by the unit. The unit's enforcement expertise was aimed strictly at drug marketing. Stolen property, health issues, and other problems directly associated with drug markets were not even on the drug unit's radar screen. "Successful" operations in this unit too often called to mind the critique: "The operation was a success; the patient died."

As community policing worked its way into the agency, the Chief supported it and demanded that everyone in the Department do likewise. But to most, supporting it meant not sabotaging it. Lieutenant Caster listened carefully and did what most police officers do with any new process or strategy. He asked, How does this apply to me and where I work now? He decided to accept the Chief's challenge.

Caster's starting points for changing the *m.o.* in the narcotics section, he determined, would be to emphasize (1) shared responsibilities; (2) dealing with more than simply law enforcement and crime; (3) supporting the experts (officers and citizens); and (4) being responsive to the changing needs of the neighborhoods.

The lieutenant began by looking at how his narcotics unit was working and searched for ways to slowly move it to practice community policing. Each decision he made was based on the criteria that it would have to be in the best interests of the detectives and community members. He realized that a key foundation was to ensure that the desired working relationships between detectives and community members could be established and maintained.

Caster assigned each team to a geographical area based on the amount of narcotics complaints received from citizens. This was similar to the deployment approach used by patrol. Citizen complaints came from a variety of sources and made their way to narcotics. Each one was logged, entered into a database, and assigned to a detective. Detectives were given five days to speak with the citizen, if the citizen wanted to be contacted. They had 90 days to work the complaint.

The geographical assignment and response deadlines moved the detectives from solely focusing on informants or their own expertise to determining what was best for the community. Even though the unit operated out of a centralized office, the responsibilities were decentralized. The only time a detective would need to venture out of his or her area would be when the investigation led the investigator elsewhere. And in those cases, the detective would notify his colleagues working in the area he was about to enter so they would know about his activity (for safety and other operational reasons) and could assist.

Detectives will persist in the view that their job is only to solve crimes, not help prevent them, "until they are removed from the group that reinforces that perception. Their goals will remain the same until their professional territory is redefined. Their professional territories, if the detectives are to adopt and understand the ideals of community policing, should be defined segments of the community" (Sparrow 1992: 57).

Previously, the detectives could only close a complaint after an arrest or search or after an enforcement activity was thwarted (e.g., because of insufficient probable cause). They were now encouraged to refer the complaint to the appropriate agency even before enforcement options were exhausted. Calls to the Housing Commission, Drug Abatement, Code Compliance, and Health Department became new devices on the detectives' tool belts. Lt. Caster even developed drug abatement procedures in which the owners of property where drug activity was taking place were notified of the problem. This dramatically reduced the repeat complaints to these locations.

"Not only can mid-managers...demonstrate considerable creativity and resourcefulness in project or tactical innovations, ...experiences in Madison, Houston, Baltimore County, Reno, and the New York City Transit Police Department suggest that mid-managers also are at the heart of strategic innovations" (Kelling and Bratton 1993: 9).

Weekly meetings between the lieutenant and the supervisors allowed free flowing discussions on systems or resource problems. It also kept the teams and unit focused on the goals of community policing. Examples of how the teams were working with patrol and community members were the centerpiece of these meetings. Another feature of these meetings were discussions of *internal* department issues, which were necessary to make corrections and to study successes. Detectives, not required to attend these meetings, thus did not need to take time to study charts or talk about equipment and other infrastructural issues. Their focus was external, in the community.

There was a marked expansion of the *information* that the unit considered essential for accomplishing its mission. Information that was released and studied by the unit centered on the geographic areas. The location and number of complaints and any enforcement or displacement, and drug market profiling replaced the bean-counting tallies of arrests and seizures. The beans were still used but not as the unit's driving force. Detectives could now look at information that related to an area. The investigators were provided details about the number of apartments, the design of key homes, the outside conditions that allowed street dealing, the agencies that worked in that area, and the patrol officers who policed that area. Detectives were encouraged to use new information-processing technology to help them work their areas. Mobile digital terminals could send electronic mail. Databases that tracked code and abatement cases were also used.

Once the basic relationships were developed, Lt. Caster formed a partnership between patrol officers, community members, and the narcotics section. He established a rotation system that allowed *patrol* officers to work one to two weeks in the unit. They would learn how to conduct surveillance, obtain search warrants, and handle complaints. More important, they could see what narcotics could do to support them in their problem-solving efforts.

Caster also created a citizen volunteer force for the narcotics section. Community members who wanted to volunteer their time for civic reasons could support the police agency in a time of decreasing resources. These community volunteers began by identifying the property owners of places raided by the Police Department, preparing information for community presentations and assisting detectives with their workload.

> *Many police agencies have made creative and effective use of residents willing to volunteer their time and talents. In Ormand Beach, Florida, "a community with a high number of retirees,....many of our residents had the types of skill and knowledge that [the police] needed.... A volunteer program was established that brings residents into the Department to help with a number of tasks, thus freeing our employees for more critical tasks. At the same time these volunteers provide us with the benefit of what they have learned in their professional lives and give us constant feedback on the job that we are doing" (Longfellow 1995: 5).*

What Lt. Caster did in developing community policing in his unit was to focus on the system. He did not worry about how the detectives were applying community policing or whether they understood it. That was the job of the supervisor. The lieutenant's job was to secure support for the detectives from other agencies and resources, remove those policies and procedures that prohibited integration, and evaluate the unit based on more sound criteria. Caster's change strategy was based on the insight that when the information base changes, the workload emphasis is altered, and the kinds of assistance needed to handle the caseload shift. When good things are accomplished using the new work methods and recognition follows, those employees who have been reluctant to adopt problem-solving approaches will begin to try a little harder to join the winning team.

Lt. Caster was managing the change at a pace that was acceptable to the unit, its members, and the community. He did not issue any mandates to the detectives. That was the job of their supervisors. He did not single out any individual but concentrated on the unit. His new quality control check was not a "recap sheet" of numbers but a "growth chart" of progress for community policing. This approach paralleled cutting-edge developments in the private sector. For instance, Spitzer (1995) describes the switch from performance appraisals linked to rewards or punishments to a "performance development process."

4. *A patrol watch commander challenges and facilitates his subordinates*

Lt. Hank Olais, also with the San Diego Police, asked his patrol officers what community policing meant to them. They responded, "getting to know the community better." When asked how they do that, the officers said confidently, "We tell them how we work and we listen to their complaints." When Lt. Olais pressed further by asking if this isn't what we have always done, the officers said defensively, "No! We used to just arrest and take reports. Now, we actually have to listen to them." (Such listening can be pretty boring for those who, as Ambrose Bierce quipped, define a bore as "a person who talks when you wish him to listen.")

Lt. Olais knew that what his officers were describing was not community policing but community relations. They simply added public relations to their enforcement nature and called it community policing. The emphasis was still on enforcement.

The challenge for this middle manager in trying to implement community policing in patrol was different than the challenge faced by a specialized unit commander but equally ominous. How do you manage the change to community policing with existing resources and 50 years of enforcement culture? Patrol personnel and the nature of that assignment dictated a different approach than that used by Lt. Caster in the San Diego narcotics squad. The knowledge and experience base of the uniformed personnel was different, the work environment was more restrictive, and the contact with the community was much closer. Patrol work is generally seen as extremely reactive, consisting mostly of "first-response" to calls for service. The largest obstacle, in Lt. Olais' opinion, would be changing the patrol members' mindset from being reactive to being goal-oriented.

The lieutenant met with his patrol sergeants and asked them what directions they provided to their officers. "Answer calls, take reports, make traffic stops, and know your area." When he asked what community policing meant to them, it was neighborhood meetings, route slips, and telling the officers to get out of their cars and talk to people. Their understanding of community policing was little better than the officers'. In order to integrate community policing into patrol, the concept first would have to be introduced correctly.

The lieutenant did not get the approval of his boss for what he was going to do. The captain had told Lt. Olais that community policing was the operating philosophy and to make it work. How it was developed, introduced, and evaluated would be left to him. Olais read everything he could touch on the subject of community policing and problem solving. He also researched the history of the Department to understand the transitions it went through to get to this point. He met with several local experts on the subject, and he spoke with other lieutenants in patrol to see what they had done to implement community policing.

How does a police department develop enthusiastic, hard work by employees who need to collect operationally-pertinent information about community problems? Toch's (1995: 7-8) reply could be expressed in one word: ownership. But how does one produce such ownership? Toch suggests four steps and two quality-control techniques: "FIRST, The question being asked ought to be your question; SECOND, You ought to get the answer yourself; THIRD, There should be closure or task completion; and FOURTH, The inquiry should carry what you see as meaningful consequences. Two requisites that relate to the context of such research are: FIRST, The project should be a team effort with both task sharing and specialization; and SECOND, There should be support, training and assistance available to ensure competent performance and quality of product."

Next, Lt. Olais asked for information on the communities for which his patrol unit was responsible. This included demographics, workload demands, crimes, calls for service, and a list of other agencies and private businesses that operate in the area. He spoke with the other police units (DARE, narcotics, domestic violence) that worked in those neighborhoods. Then, he met with his sergeants again. This time, he asked them if they had any suggestions for introducing community policing in their areas. He wanted them to offer plans and strategies, to develop more ownership—and he wanted to learn from them.

After doing this research, Lt. Olais formulated a plan. His focus would be to:

☐ eliminate the structural barriers to community policing
☐ provide information that would compel area ownership
☐ allow mistakes and experiments in order to develop a sense of risk taking and creativity
☐ supply resources, time, and constant feedback on integrating community policing
☐ do less managing of people and more managing of systems

Lt. Olais met with his supervisors once more to discuss what the officers were going to accomplish. Crime control, workload reduction, and order maintenance were selected as the goals of the patrol unit. He decided that all messages, reinforcement, and recognition had to support those three goals. The lieutenant would focus on adjusting the work system, while the supervisors would concentrate their efforts on the officers.

A list of resources for the area was quickly published to assist officers with their new responsibilities. Briefings now included agencies such as code enforcement, utilities, social and community groups, schools, and other organizations that traditionally had not participated in policing activities. Lists were published identifying the ten locations that drew the largest number of radio calls each month in each beat. Every two weeks lists were disseminated showing which businesses were most frequently victimized in the area. Newspaper articles listing particular community problems were posted in the briefing room.

The technique of sharing these lists with the patrol unit was intended to draw the officers' attention to the various types of problems and resources in their areas. The wide variety would allow officers to choose a problem that was comfortable for them. Lt. Olais saw this strategy as reinforcing ownership, since the officer chose the problem. Moreover, Olais tried to post problems that were not so large that they would overwhelm the officers. Exposure to problem solving, Olais believed, is the best learning tool.

> *"Often, a disproportionate number of calls for service come from a relatively small number of locations throughout a city. In the past, the police all too often simply responded to those repeat locations and moved on to the next call. Attempts to examine patterns in those calls to address the underlying problems were rare. As a result, the problems proliferated. Through problem-solving strategies, the underlying causes can be identified and solutions can be developed to abate the underlying issues"* (Brann, et al. 1992).

Lt. Olais began asking officers to attend supervisors' meetings to discuss their problem-solving efforts. This reinforced their work and helped focus the sergeants. These presentations opened the eyes of supervisors about the potential and creativity of patrol officers. The presentations reinforced Olais' belief that first-line officers will take risks and address problems if acknowledged by the supervisors and not micromanaged or interrogated about their efforts. The lieutenant also had his supervisors send summaries of the officers' efforts to the Chief's office to demonstrate the work being done by patrol. The Chief in turn would send personal notes to the officers thanking them and reinforcing their work. The old system of reading commendations at briefings ended because most officers found that embarrassing. More informal recognitions, such as in front of friends, were conducted.

In order to reduce workload to assist officers, Lt. Olais developed a cadre of volunteers and reserves to take reports that do not necessarily require a sworn officer. This included vandalism reports, reports about assorted cold crimes, and requests for crime prevention seminars and vacation house checks. The supplemental staff also made it possible to take reports of auto thefts and no-injury accidents over the telephone.

In addition, some of the sergeants developed a differential response program among their squads. Each day, some officers would volunteer to conduct investigations for the day. They would call the victims, set appointments, and manage their day. This allowed more freedom for the other patrol officers, gave realistic response times to the victims, and improved the quality of reports.

In Hayward, California, "[t]rue to the philosophy of valuing the employee, recommendations were solicited from managers, supervisors and line personnel [for changing the performance evaluation system]. Consistent with the new decentralized organizational focus, all work units are devising their own evaluation instruments and processes. Each is being designed around the specific services the work unit provides, emphasizing creative solutions and problem solving approaches" (Brann and Whalley 1992: 74).

The next step for Lt. Olais was to develop evaluation tools for the officers' reports. He did this because he considered it important for middle managers to know what impact their officers' efforts were having on the community and surrounding areas. The evaluation was designed to measure not officers' activity but the impact of the work effort. (On innovative performance evaluations of community policing officers generally, see Wycoff and Oettmeier 1993; Jordon 1992; Trojanowicz and Bucqueroux 1992.)

As Lt. Olais reflected on the role of a middle manager in implementing community policing, he concluded that key to his unit's accomplishments was his targeting three principal objectives: First, recognize that when the workload is reduced to allow for problem solving, the officers will have more idle time and may become bored or lazy. Accordingly, be ready to challenge the officers with problems that deserve their attention, such as problem locations, repeat offenders and high-rate victims (Bieck, et al. 1991). Second, approach the lack of resources needed for problem solving as a challenge and not an obstacle. Middle managers can tackle the question of how to develop assistance and resources for their officers in the same fashion that officers approach resolving community and crime problems—with creativity (Williams 1985; Shanahan 1985). Finally, ensure that community involvement with the police department expands substantially. The "eyes and ears" role for citizens, Lt. Olais came to understand, is outdated. Today, police know that citizens also have brains behind those eyes and ears. And, as Lt. Olais helped his department and community realize, so do police officers.

5. *A building block of partnerships for problem solving: Communicate before it's too late*

Some police departments struggling to implement community problem solving have the unusual good fortune to have *within* their ranks one or more of the most highly esteemed national experts on the design and operation of this strategy. The Seattle Police Department is such an agency, with Chief Norman Stamper at the helm and Nancy McPherson serving at the assistant chief level as the Director of the Bureau of Community Policing. We are grateful to Nancy McPherson (of whom both authors are particularly proud since she is a former staffer of the Police Executive Research Forum and the San Diego Police Department) and to Seattle Captain Clark Kimerer (whose story this is) for their assistance in providing this anecdote.

In the twilight of a cold March evening in 1993, Seattle Police Captain Clark Kimerer directed his personnel to begin removal of over 50 homeless advocates from an abandoned and decrepit downtown hotel, the Pacific Hotel. The occupation was commenced in order to protest the perceived lack of low-income, transitional housing in the downtown core. Yet that purpose was being lost in the sensationalist reductions of the media, which also occupied the streets and sidewalks encircling the Pacific Hotel. For five days, the police negotiated with a loosely knit coalition that called themselves Operation Homestead. On the sixth day the City was informed—through the media—that a core group of 13 trespassers would only leave the building under arrest. After escorting the demonstrators who did not wish to be arrested from the building, Captain Kimerer's officers began methodically arresting the remaining trespassers. While Kimerer reports that the officers displayed remarkable professionalism, competence and humanity, the streets that night still were filled with the rhetoric of anger and acrimony.

The Seattle Police Department's Nancy McPherson—like Sandy Kaminska in the Joliet, Illinois, Police Department, Mike Scott (when he was head of community problem-solving implementation for St. Louis Chief Clarence Harmon), and others around the nation—plays a critical organizational role in the transformation from conventional to more diversified policing strategies. As Chief Stamper described Nancy McPherson's role: "She is a 'process conscience' for the Seattle Police Department—an internal expert to keep the Department on track" (Stamper 1995b).

Negotiations with the 13 trespassers continued throughout the arrest and removal process. Captain Kimerer vividly recalls one of the arrestees indulging in a nonstop verbal assault on his character, values, politics, choice of profession, posture, and hairstyle. "I waited for the inevitable moment when he had to re-oxygenate," reports Kimerer,

> "and asked, 'How can you say such things about someone you don't even know?' His response resonates in my memory to this day: 'You're right. I'm sorry. But it's not like I get the opportunity to talk to you or other cops except when I am in handcuffs, sitting in the filth of some dark building, waiting to be arrested. I can't get to know you now. It's too late.'

> The challenge of defining and realizing community-police partnerships is summarized for me in reflection on this exchange. First, our relationships have been largely limited to stereotypic roles: You are an activist; I am a defender of the 'system.' You have a personal, emotional stake in your advocacies, while I am detached, neutral and aloof. You are the arrestee, and I am the arrestor. Second, if we lack forums for discussion that include even the most volatile issues as represented by the most strident advocates, then we will continue to have few options other than confrontation and arrest to address the inevitable dynamics of our society. And third, it is almost impossible to undertake a meaningful exploration of issues in the midst of confrontation, let alone get to know the

participants as possessing human frailties and excellences. At such a point it is just too late."

During the Department's after-action critique of the Pacific Hotel occupation, Captain Kimerer related his experience with the strident demonstrator who only talked to cops when it was too late. The discussion that followed was, for officers of the West Precinct, ground breaking. "We need an open line of communication to the people we think of as our enemies," began one sergeant. "Our community-police 'guest list' is usually made up of our friends and allies," echoed the precinct's Operations Lieutenant, "and we seldom invite the people we saw at the Pacific Hotel to precinct meetings and forums." One of the senior footbeat sergeants put it with eloquent simplicity: "When people are talking to one another, there is hope. Over and over again I have seen the connection between silence and violence."

At this point, Captain Kimerer floated the idea of establishing a regular forum composed of precinct command staff and various human service providers, including homeless advocates, mental health caseworkers, and activists and counselors who regularly work with street people. By the close of the meeting, the West Precinct Service Provider Forum had been conceptualized.

Even before the Forum met for the first time, the police interest in such a gathering had been reciprocated by a number of downtown human service providers. The director of the City's largest shelter called the police and pledged to do everything possible to make the Forum a success, including volunteering to broker invitations to veteran activists who had spent the past few years "in the shadows." The captain reports: "I even received a call from my interlocutor at the Pacific Hotel, who said that he wished 'to continue our conversation,' and who promised to forgo further commentary on my hairstyle." Numerous social workers, when they called to RSVP, commented that members of their human service provider community seldom explored relationships outside of their tight group of like-minded advocates. It sounded strikingly like the police to Clark Kimerer. Several of the human service workers expressed the opinion that the upcoming first meeting of the Forum represented

As in virtually all the police departments whose middle managers' leadership and facilitation is lauded on these pages, the Seattle Police Department has other middle managers who also provide excellent role models and put the lie to the experts' cynicism about the capacity of middle management to help promote fundamental organizational change. One such captain in the "Emerald City" of Seattle is clearly showing her officers and her community that "they are not in Kansas anymore." Captain Wanda Barkley, who heads the Youth Crimes section of the agency, exemplified an openness to collaboration and problem solving in a recent planning session in Seattle's International District—a small commercial/residential area in which 30 to 40 languages and cultures—all Asian and Pacific Islander—coexist. The objective of an ambitious new project there is for the police to forge a problem-solving partnership with a community economic development corporation, which necessitates unconventional thinking about police roles and responsibilities. Captain Barkley, along with several other sworn and civilian Department employees of other ranks, quietly persisted during the planning workshop in helping the working group imagine the what if's and the could be's instead of getting mired too soon in the can't's and won't's. As anyone knows who has attempted to forge untraditional partnerships, in which accepted roles need to be fundamentally reconsidered, the body language and comments of influential managers at the outset can make or break the prospects for a powerful and effective collaboration.

"an opportunity of unprecedented significance" for Seattle.

The first Forum was attended by more than 60 human service providers and activists. The meeting was held in the West Precinct roll call room, which had only hours earlier been used as the prisoner processing center for a large narcotics buy-bust operation. The meeting opened by reflecting on the words of Martin Luther King: "It is hard to hate a man when you know his name and have heard his story." Captain Kimerer reports that "this very human truth became the organizing principle of the first and subsequent Forum meetings." The participants agreed, he recalls "that our paramount goal would be problem-solving through access to one another's philosophies, concerns, fears, experiences, limitations, and—particularly as concerns the police—non-negotiable duties." The police and service providers agreed to "dignify all points of view but avoid reveries of self-righteousness." And most important, the group agreed to meet regularly, regardless of the politics, agendas and antipathies of the moment.

During the first several meetings of the Forum, the participants:

■ Attempted to identify and formalize common advocacy positions. For example, the Forum articulated positions on community diversion of mentally ill misdemeanants; funding for a comprehensive database networking shelter providers; street outreach protocols to deal with runaways and juveniles at risk; and reciprocal training programs jointly staffed by human service providers and Seattle Police personnel.

■ Agreed to continue meeting at the West Precinct and, where possible, to increase the Forum's visibility to line officers, business leaders and other downtown stakeholders. As part of this initiative, precinct officers and sergeants were regularly invited to attend and participate in each Forum meeting.

■ Established an emergency notification protocol designed to bring together key human service providers and the police with a view to constructively resolving confrontations like the one at the Pacific Hotel.

■ "[D]emystified and enhanced the credibility of the citizen complaint-internal investigation process," and addressed numerous concerns about specific police actions. In some cases, complaints were formalized and forwarded to Internal Investigations, while others were resolved by the thoughtful deliberation of the Forum as a whole.

■ Discussed the dangers and demands of police work and the legal standards—which sometimes conflict with the priorities of human service providers—that define the options available to the police.

A key event in the Forum's history occurred in July 1994, just a week before a regularly scheduled Forum meeting and several month after Norm Stamper had been named to head the Seattle Police Department by Mayor Norm Rice. A group of approximately 100 homeless men and women had constructed a virtual shantytown in a wooded area abutting the interstate. Numerous significant health, fire, and public safety concerns were identified about the encampment, which the media (and the occupants) dubbed "the Jungle." According to Captain Kimerer,

"The subsequent attention focused on the police and fire department activities in tearing down the shantytown became more symbolic than substantive, and some invested a great deal of energy to ensure that the day the 'Jungle' was scheduled to be razed would be marked by acrimony and confrontation. What ultimately distinguished this incident from the occupation of the Pacific Hotel, however, was the fact that we now 'knew each other's names and had heard each other's stories.' The protocol for emergency notification was invoked, and the confrontation prophesied never occurred."

Consistent with their pledge to meet without regard for momentary conflicts among Forum members, the Forum convened the following week as scheduled and presented a thoughtful, candid critique of the operational response by the police to the shanty-town. "Listening to this discussion," Captain Kimerer confides, "I had the momentary sensation that I had fallen through the looking glass and entered an antithetical universe. But on reflection I found that the fundamental truths identified by Martin Luther King and my veteran footbeat sergeant had been validated."

The common traits that Kanter (1982: 96) saw in corporate middle managers who were successful innovators—good but "not extraordinary individuals"—were:

"☐ Comfort with change. They are confident that uncertainties will be clarified. They also have foresight and see unmet needs as opportunities.

☐ Clarity of direction. They select projects carefully and, with their long time horizons, view set-backs as temporary blips in an otherwise straight path to a goal.

☐ Thoroughness. They prepare well for meetings and are professional in making their presentations. They have insight into organizational politics and a sense of whose support can help them at various junctures.

☐ Participative management style. They encourage subordinates to put in maximum effort and to be part of the team, promise them a share of the rewards, and deliver on their promises.

☐ Persuasiveness, persistence, and discretion. They understand that they cannot achieve their ends overnight, so they persevere—using tact—until they do."

The West Precinct Human Service Provider Forum meets in the headquarters roll call room on the third Friday of every month. "Those intolerant of different viewpoints," Clark Kimerer reports, "are not encouraged to attend."

6. Leading and sustaining long-term, multi-faceted problem-solving efforts

Prostitutes and "johns" are finding it increasingly difficult to do business in the city of St. Petersburg, located on Florida's west central Gulf coast. Working together with residents and business owners along a major thoroughfare where street-market prostitution was flourishing, Lt. Debbie Prine and a team of seven officers devised an unusually comprehensive effort to bankrupt the world's oldest profession. Lt. Prine reports that the team, which came to be called the Prostitution Core Group, was convened because

"I wanted our officers to work collaboratively with one another and they wanted to become involved in a major team effort that was a high priority to the community. People were frustrated with the police because prostitution was prevalent. So the entire team got together for a brainstorming session about how to address that problem."

This anti-prostitution program could not have evolved without the St. Petersburg Police Department's commitment to the community policing philosophy, which was introduced shortly before Darrel Stephens arrived as Chief in 1993. Under Chief Stephens, members of the Department at all ranks were encouraged to look for and undertake innovative problem-solving efforts. The St. Petersburg Department was the beneficiary of the pioneering work Darrel Stephens had done over the past two decades helping to invent community problem solving. His contributions to the cause have been made in his service as police chief in Newport News, Virginia, as executive director of the Police Executive Research Forum, as a member of the Harvard Executive Session on Community Policing, and in other venues.

Darrel's determination to improve American policing (Stephens 1995b) was put into practice where the rubber meets the road by middle manager Debbie Prine, who commenced her work with the Core Group as a sergeant and then had the interest and drive to continue providing leadership and facilitation to the team after being promoted to a mid-management rank. The unusual breadth and duration of the anti-prostitution program necessitated that Lt. Prine and her team be patient, imaginative, and doggedly committed to their mission. During her early work on this project as a community policing sergeant, she received excellent encouragement from her lieutenant, Don Quire, who has since been named a major in the Vice and Narcotics unit. "Don Quire, along with the chief, was extremely supportive when we needed the help," reports Debbie Prine. "Any resources we needed—vehicles, other equipment and so forth—we got."

The team commenced its work with several months of analysis, including defining the scope of the prostitution problem in their Sector 70 and identifying strategies used in other police agencies across the country. Officers examined relevant Florida state statutes that could be enforced. The team pieced together a plan that combined elements they thought had the best chance to impact the problem, then presented their ideas to neighborhood residents and business owners for their input and support. This was not a window-dressing consultation. Indeed, over the next three years the team would continue to consult with members of the community and every six months formally survey the neighborhood to see whether the public approved of the team's efforts and accomplishments.

After securing the advice and consent of the local residents and businesses, the team revised and fine-tuned the plan, and then presented it to Chief Stephens and his staff. Lt. Prine did not anticipate much resistance to her team's rather unconventional plans *within* the agency. Her confidence came both from a belief that the plan was sound and from her reputation within the organization. As she confides,

> "I'm known as a used car salesman around the Department. If I really want to get something done and they tell me no, I keep at it until I find a different angle that works. Not that there was really great opposition to what the Core Group wanted to do, but maybe part of that was because a lot of people knew it was a waste of time to tell me no."

Debbie Prine knew that she would have to make the sale to the chief if she stood a reasonable chance of convincing the mayor's office, the city council, and the county's chief judge. With Chief Stephens' help the mayor consented, and the Chief and Mayor in turn helped secure the approval of the chief judge and council. With the council's assent, the Prostitution Core Group took to the streets. "As I've told the many departments which have called us about this program," Lt. Prine reported, "the key for us in launching it was taking things a step at a time and winning the solid support of the Department first so they could help us persuade others."

> *"Some...have argued that community policing is social work and that cops are not social workers. But, with over-crowded prisons and a stagnated criminal justice system, simply arresting individuals does not necessarily solve crime problems. Cleaning up a neighborhood, freeing it from drug pushers and prostitutes, and restoring a safe, healthy environment does solve crime problems"* (Galvin 1992).

The Prostitution Core Group's first task was to raise public awareness and make it known that prostitution, or soliciting a prostitute, is a crime. The team turned to the Police Department's Public Information Manager, Bill Doniel, to spread the word via his monthly "Police Report" TV show. That show airs throughout the city on a local government access channel, reaching an audience of nearly 70,000 homes.[8] But using this TV program to reeducate the public about their legal responsibilities was just the tip of the team's tactical iceberg. A segment of each monthly program was devoted to scrolling the names of convicted johns and prostitutes, including their addresses, birth dates, fines and sentences. The city council's approval had to be won for this tactic because it was an unconventional use of the local government's cable TV system. Because the team had gotten its ducks in order—lining up the community's, Department's and mayor's support first—the council showed the courage of voting to support the plan despite the controversial tactic of listing the names of prostitution offenders on TV.

The public naming of lawbreakers reflects an ancient tradition, which anthropologists have noted in many cultures, of "shaming" aberrant members of the village. The operative crime-control theory is that naming and shaming will lead to the offender's being shunned by neighbors and to his or her changing unwanted behavior or departing from the unreceptive village.

Another component of the St. Petersburg team's prostitution control effort has been the "Dear John" letter. It is sent to each convicted john's home address, reminding the recipient that patronizing a prostitute is a criminal offense which risks not only penalties but major individual and public health hazards—HIV/AIDS and other sexually transmitted diseases. The hope is that these letters will catch the attention and alter the behavior of the johns by confronting them with the fact that they are known to authorities and are endangering their own and others' lives.

Not content to embarrass or scare off the "demand" for prostitution, Lt. Prine and her Core Group worked also on the "supply side." A valuable technique proved to be "mapping."[9] The team won the support of the Pinellas County chief judge for the tactic of denying convicted

---

[8] A comparably imaginative and useful mass communications effort is the Charlotte-Mecklenburg Police Department's "Police Beat Live" monthly cable TV show. It is co-hosted by Police Dennis Nowicki and an experienced TV moderator employed by the local government's audio-video office.

[9] The term "mapping" today frequently is used in connection with computer programs that generate maps of crime problems and factors that may contribute to or reduce the problems (see Rich 1995).

prostitutes access to the areas where they had been plying their trade. The arresting officer attaches a map to the arrest papers, with the street where the woman was picked up clearly marked. When the prostitute is convicted, the judge orders her to stay out of this defined area as a condition of probation. If she's picked up for any reason in her mapped area, she can be sent to jail for violating her probation.

Debbie Prine and her officers also discovered and deployed a seldom-used state statute. It allows the 18-month revocation of the driver's license of those convicted of a crime. License revocation, although generating some public controversy, has proven to be an effective deterrent to johns, most of whom drive into specific prostitute-laden corridors from other parts of the city. The message to johns is, "If you're

St. Petersburg's "Dear John" letter tactic is different in interesting ways from a "Dear John" letter, sent by a lawyer and two community groups in Peoria, Illinois, to patrons of local prostitutes. The Peoria letter, characterized unapologetically by its authors as "legalized extortion," threatens a civil suit against the johns for "damag[ing] the peace and security of the neighborhood." The letter goes on to suggest that, if the johns wish to settle out of court, they can make a $1,000 contribution to the "Averyville Improvement Association and the Northside Action Council, groups representing areas with drug and prostitution problems" (Associated Press 1995).

caught illegally strolling, your car will no longer be legally rolling. At least not with you behind the wheel!" The Core Group opted for the tactic of license revocation after surveys indicated that a strong majority of the prostitution-plagued neighborhood would find this approach acceptable.

In addition to these tactics of public shaming, banishing the offenders from their preferred work areas, and restricting the johns' mobility, the Prostitution Core Group used other, more conventional methods for stemming the supply of and demand for street prostitution. The team conducts about 50 undercover sting operations per year, each lasting three days. The first day is devoted to planning, assigning specific roles to each participant, and operational organization. The second day is an eight- to 12-hour detail, during which the sting is staged and completed. On the third day the team members complete all necessary administrative follow-up and paper work. As of September 1995, only five of the team's last 400 arrests had gone to trial. They lost only two john cases and one prostitute case. The team prides itself on building solid cases that don't expose the Department to charges of entrapment and that avoid negative news media attention and win convictions.

In addition to its zero tolerance enforcement strategies, Lt. Prine's team (like Staff Sergeant Bill Mowbray's team in the Edmonton story we told earlier) recognized that prostitutes are not only offenders—they are also victims who need various kinds of support. "You'll never meet anyone with worse self-esteem than an addicted street prostitute," said Debbie Prine.

"These are pitiful individuals with terrible problems. Almost all of them are on drugs. They have no jobs, no education. They're dealing with guilt. Many have been sexually abused as children and come from dysfunctional families. Many are infected with sexually transmitted diseases."

After an arrest, each prostitute is tested for STDs. But test results are not readily available to the police. This is something the Prostitution Core Group are trying to change because they believe they have a need to know. For example, if a prostitute is arrested for solicitation and she is HIV-positive, the charge becomes a third degree felony instead of a first degree misdemeanor. The information is also vital for officers' personal safety.

Lt. Prine's team also would like to start a residential treatment center for prostitutes in St. Petersburg, modeled after the successful Mary Magdalene Project in southern California. The program would provide emotional, educational, and employment assistance, as well as drug treatment to help women get out of prostitution. The women would be in residence for up to 18 months, at the end of which they would be placed in various jobs paying approximately $10 per hour. If the team succeeds in this effort, it would be the first residential treatment center in the nation started by cops for prostitutes. Currently, the St. Petersburg Police Department has enlisted the support of other nearby police agencies and of a county drug treatment facility to organize and lobby for the establishment of the residential center. Potential funding sources thus far imagined by Debbie Prine and her colleagues include grants secured by the Police Department, fines imposed on johns and support from participating not-for-profit organizations. Prine argues:

> *There are various reasons to believe quality implementation of community problem solving will help secure officer safety on the job. Braiden (1995) suggests, for instance, that by helping officers deal with recurring problems (what he calls "fixing it right the first time"), the middle manager contributes to officer safety because "the officer who is at a place for the fifteenth time is not available to back up the officer who needs help in an emergency."*

> "The average fine for johns right now is around $200. We'd like to see that raised to $1,000, with most of the money earmarked for the residential treatment center for prostitutes. Why shouldn't these johns pay to get these prostitutes back on their feet and into respectable jobs?"

The Prostitution Core Group is also blazing an information-management trail in the Department. The team has recently launched a computer database called "ProstCore." The program tracks all data related to prostitution in St. Petersburg. "We expect to have one of the best databases in the nation specifically on prostitution," says Prine.

> "Reports will list calls, arrests, names of prostitutes, their pimps, their associates and related drug dealers. This will give us a really superb analytical tool to chart our progress. The data have always been out there scattered, but for the first time we'll link it all together."

The database is already attracting attention in other units of the Police Department. Homicide, robbery, narcotics and intelligence detectives regularly visit the Prostitution Core Group to gather leads and information on their cases. Prostitutes are frequently involved in other criminal activity or are associated with other offenders. Some of the Core Group's tactics are also inspiring imaginative problem-solving ideas in other corners of the Department. Narcotics enforcement officers currently are seeking to put the names of drug buyers on TV, in an attempt to shame people who hold respectable jobs and social positions in the community out of their drug abuse.

The officers on Lt. Prine's team feel they are making a difference, as do the people who live and work in the targeted area. The latest of the Core Group's semi-annual public surveys revealed that 79 percent of the respondents believe the Group has made a significant impact on prostitution. As further testament to the public's reaction, when a john was being arrested during a recent sting operation, residents came out of their houses and cheered the officers. One should not minimize the motivational power of a demonstrative, appreciative community for police officers who, with the rest of the public, cast an embarrassed eye at national headlines about police brutality, corruption, and bigotry.

Lt. Prine currently serves in the general patrol unit, but she and all the other members of the Prostitution Core Group continue doing double duty, as they have from the project's inception three years ago. Regardless of their changing assignments, each team member remains committed to and active in the Core Group's anti-prostitution initiatives.

The oldest profession in the world may not be coming to an end any time soon in St. Petersburg or elsewhere. Thanks in large part to the imaginative and committed leadership and support of middle manager Debbie Prine, however, an empowered and skillful team of officers will continue inventing and running an unusual anti-prostitution initiative. The initiative is distinctive for its comprehensiveness, duration, effectiveness, inventiveness within Constitutional limits, and compassion for people who are at once both offenders and victims. Such qualities are the "stuff" of which the best policing in the world's leading democracy must be made.

7. Helping officers harness the community's power

In 1993, the Vera Institute of Justice, under President Michael Smith's leadership, and the New York City Police Department, under the stewardship of Commissioner Raymond Kelly, collaborated to produce two short handbooks about problem-solving for police officers and supervisors. The pamphlets present engaging stories about practical, imaginative, instructive efforts by NYPD members to address complicated neighborhood problems. The complexity stemmed from both the resilience of the problems and from the competing values that would have to be considered and balanced if any headway was to be made.

One such story—"Saturday Night Fever"—nicely illustrates the role of a middle manager, a precinct lieutenant named Daniel Ruffle, in helping his hard-working but frustrated officers overcome a seemingly insurmountable disorder problem. The lieutenant, as we shall see, was able to foment community organizing around the specific disorder problem—a step the officers may not have been comfortable taking themselves at that stage of the NYPD's development with community policing.[10] By removing this barrier to effective problem solving, Lt. Ruffle gave the precinct and the entire Department a success story that can inspire thousands of other officers and community residents who otherwise might not be able to see over the horizon at the possibilities for restoring neighborhood safety through democratic processes. The following account is quoted (with some emendations) from Farrell, et al. (1993a: 36-42).

According to residents of the area, the *parents* of some of the kids causing disorder problems on a half-mile strip along 86th Street in Bensonhurst [in Brooklyn] were doing the same thing 25 years ago. But over the years, radios got louder, drugs had become plentiful, and

---

[10] In a study of community policing implementation efforts in Chicago, Skogan, et al. (1995: 35) report relatively conventional first-line and supervisory officer resistance to considering community organizing and other community-involved initiatives as useful tools in overcoming neighborhood public safety problems.

kids became willing to push the limits harder. Most of all, the crowds got bigger. In the late '70s, fueled by the heat of *Saturday Night Fever*, a popular movie believed to be based on the scene along 86th Street and in nearby discos, the area began to develop more than a local following. And by the late '80s, "it was crazy, a circus," according to Lt. Ruffle of the 62nd Precinct.

At 8:00 on weekend nights, kids would start assembling in their cars, crowding the street under the tracks of the elevated B train. They would stay all night. The early arrivals would "set up" along the curb, quickly taking all the legal parking spaces in the six-to-eight block area. When those spots were filled, more would come and double park on either

The benefits to a department of "running many different experiments in different parts of the organization are...numerous." One is that "officers will see lots of apparently crazy ideas being tried and may, in time, realize that they have some ideas of their own that are slightly less crazy. Perhaps for the first time they will be willing to put their ideas forward, knowing that they will not be summarily dismissed. The resourcefulness of police officers, so long apparent in their unofficial behavior, can at last be put to the service of the department. Creativity blooms in an experimental environment that is tolerant of unusual ideas" (Sparrow 1992: 53).

side of the street, leaving only a single lane free in the middle—the endless, creeping, cruising lane. Other traffic in the area would be immobilized until the next morning. Bus drivers complained constantly to the Transit Authority, describing it as the "worst route in the city...totally gridlocked at 2:00 in the morning." One estimate put driving time between 18th and 25th Avenues along 86th Street at one to one-and-a-half *hours*—a trip that, during the weekday, might take as many minutes. According to Jim Estudo, a local resident:

> "Kids ruled.... There was a total loss of control. It became famous as a hang out all along the East Coast. I'd go out and talk with them. Kids from Baltimore, Boston, Connecticut, Jersey, Long Island. One car-full from Erie, Pennsylvania—they'd tell me how great this was. 'I can't believe they let you do this.' And it just got bigger. By the summer of 1990, I'd go out on the corner by my house and there'd be 100-125 kids just on my corner...on my *side* of the intersection of 21st and 86th—there'd be another 100-125 kids on each of the other corners and traffic immobilized in every direction."

Thousands of kids would assemble on summer nights, strutting their stuff. The sound of the elevated subway train, occasionally passing overhead, was drowned out by the rising noise of music, revving car engines, yells and chatter. Ruffle describes being on duty on 86th one night and seeing the "biggest radio I've ever seen in my life," being pulled on the back of a homemade, oversized tricycle, powered by six 12-volt car batteries.

The most serious attendant crime was burglary, which would increase considerably during these "Saturday Night Fevers." The crowds and the noise provided perfect cover for window and rooftop break-ins. Estudo, a local property owner, describes one burglar who used "a buzz saw" to carve entrances in apartment building rooftops because "nobody could hear it with the racket on 86th." Drugs and prostitution flourished at the periphery.

There was no shortage of residents' complaints about the disorder—the noise and the general chaos—but they were most outraged by kids spilling over into the residential areas just behind the commercial strip on 86th. Like most property owners, Estudo, whose home is a few doors from 86th, just couldn't handle "getting up the next day and finding beer cans and marijuana cigarettes and urine and used condoms in my hallway."

Lt. Ruffle remembers that every spring, the Borough Commander would ask about plans for solving the problem 86th Street had become. In recent years, a whole menu of traditional and nontraditional tactics was tried by the Community Policing Unit and by other 62nd Precinct units: "saturation patrol," roadblocks, massive stop-and-summons operations for moving violations, double parking, tinted windows—everything but speeding. Boom-boxes were pulled and vouchered. ECB (Environmental Control Board) noise summonses were issued. But these labor-intensive tactics could never be sustained for long and, at their best, moved some vehicles and some kids from one part of the strip to another, for a while.

Ruffle and his colleagues analyzed 9-1-1 calls from the area, searching for any notable patterns. They struck out. Estudo recalls "flooding the precinct with telephone calls" during the summer and fall of '89. The next spring, "fed up and afraid" about the prospects of another summer on 86th, he began talking to the kids himself. He tried to disperse them, telling them, "Put yourself in my shoes. I'm just trying to protect my home." On a one-to-one basis, he made some headway. More important, he met neighbors trying to do the same thing. A beat cop they hooked up with on 86th suggested that they start coming regularly to the monthly Precinct Community Council meetings.

Ruffle took Estudo and his neighbors aside after one of these meetings, and they were quickly able to agree that the problem was bigger than anything the police could handle alone. Estudo remembers Ruffle telling him that "to battle this problem, you must organize—for power." He encouraged Estudo's group to get the word out and offered them space at the station for meetings. With advice from a local community assistance agency, Estudo's core group followed a set of simple guidelines for "how to organize a community group." Estudo describes the early organizing efforts as "hit or miss," marked by hard work, and lots of door-to-door appeals to residents and especially merchants.... [T]he first meeting spilled out of the meeting room. Eventually the meetings moved to BRAMA, the Bensonhurst Resident and Merchant Association, where attendance at monthly meetings rose to about 200.

Success came in the spring of 1991, when the power of an organized community was coupled with a simple idea about how to make that stretch of 86th Street unattractive as a gathering place for the disorderly group.

The solution had its roots in a brainstorming session of the Community Policing Unit, back in 1989. The unit supervisor had asked each PO to list five possible strategies for dealing with the 86th Street problem, and PO Goffio's list included the idea of changing the parking regulations to "No Parking" throughout the evening and night—and strictly enforcing them. That, thought Goffio, would prevent the kids from even beginning to gather.

In the spring of 1990, Ruffle, Goffio and other officers submitted to the local Community Board, on precinct letterhead, exactly that proposal. Existing parking regulations allowed meter parking from 7 a.m. to 7 p.m. with no restrictions from 7 p.m. until 7 a.m. The precinct's proposal suggested no changes between 7 a.m. and 10 p.m. but asked the Board to endorse a reversal of the ordinarily sensible rules for the middle of the night, making it illegal to park anywhere on 86th Street between 10 p.m. and 7 a.m.

Discussion of the precinct's proposal at the Community Board meeting was dominated by a local merchants' association, which included many restaurant owners who felt that restrictions on night-time parking would cut into their dinner business. The local residents weren't as well organized, and weren't as well represented in the meeting as the restaurant owners, and the proposal was unanimously defeated.

But the idea stuck in Ruffle's mind and, in the fall of 1990, he encouraged Estudo and the growing membership of the residents' group to turn the idea into a bandwagon, and to get that bandwagon moving. With Ruffle, Estudo and members of the residents' group garnering widespread support among other residents of the area, and with BRAMA gathering endorsements from community and business leaders, the plan was ready for re-presentation to the Community Board in March 1991.

This time, with formal presentations delivered by Ruffle and Estudo, who were backed by more than 50 supporters from the BRAMA membership, the Community Board accepted the plan—for a trial period. Details were worked out with the Department of Transportation in the late spring, and in June, just as the summer scene was developing, new parking signs were posted. "No Parking" was easily and efficiently enforced. With only one or two officers deployed to write $25 summonses, it was possible to create a 100 percent certainty that any vehicle trying to park on this stretch of 86th Street after 10 p.m. would be ticketed immediately. In less than a month, the problem was basically solved. Estudo said, "It was like someone snapped their fingers, and it went away."

"What makes it possible for managers to use...skills [as innovators] for the company's benefit? They work in organizations where the culture fosters collaboration and teamwork and where structures encourage people to 'do what needs to be done.' Moreover, they usually work under top managers who consciously incorporate conditions facilitating innovation and achievement into their companies' structures and operations" (Kanter 1982: 96).

Success in the trial period brought support for the permanent regulations barring night-time parking on 86th, and commitments began flowing in to BRAMA from local politicians. In October of 1991, the Community Board voted to make the regulations permanent. Burglary numbers dropped and, since late 1991, BRAMA leaders have judged the area safe enough for the group to conduct its own civilian patrols. In December of 1992, Ruffle was able to close the Saturday Night Fever file, as the summons activity and the complaints had dwindled to the point that the problem really couldn't be said to exist. (The night-time parking ban did not, as it turned out, cause any of the 86th Street restaurants to close—and one has expanded into larger space.)

Fortunately, most disorderly group problems aren't in the same league with Bensonhurst's Saturday Night Fever. [It occupied] a perennial spot on the Precinct Commander's list of major problems each spring *** [b]ut, in the end, the key to making the location unattractive to the group was simple, elegant and gentle.

It is no puzzle why the Saturday Night Fever problem could not be solved some other way. The strategy of "finding a more attractive alternate activity" held no hope of success—however inspired a PO might be, no one gives a party this good on purpose. And conventional police tactics offered no hope of making the location or the behavior unattractive to the disorderly group: Saturation patrols to suppress public drinking, ECB summonses to reduce the volume of the radios, double parking tickets to contain some of the traffic chaos—these measures could and did annoy kids when they were tried, but were too labor-intensive to be sustained for long periods, and they posed to any individual member of the group no more than a *chance* that the allure of "Saturday Night Fever" would be dulled a bit on any given night. The problem was solved when the police and the community found a way to keep the kids from getting together in the first place, and a way of selling it to the interests that placed commercial value on the conditions that had to be changed.

8. Confronting the conventionalists

The NYPD officers described in the previous story would have made no headway at all if they had supervisors denying them the opportunity to try unconventional approaches. As it turned out, they had a middle manager/leader in Lt. Ruffle who "broke down" a political door that all the Department's battering rams couldn't have dented. He did it simply by getting the local electorate to turn the door knob.

But in some settings there will be police at various ranks—if not middle managers then perhaps first-line supervisors—who cling to inflexibility and rule-oriented management as a way of controlling the work of officers. We have in mind the people who probably would have berated the Bensonhurst beat cops for not writing enough tickets at the Saturday Night Fever gatherings. The following scenes, depicting a middle manager trying to patiently confront a rule-oriented sergeant, could come from almost any squad room in America. We thank former Evanston, Illinois, Police Lieutenant George Scharm for developing these transcripts.

A patrol sergeant conducting roll call had just finished reading a memo from the chief, at which point something like the following transpired:

Sgt.: (to the roll call) Problem solving, right. The chief wants us to make decisions and is aware that we will make mistakes. And as soon as anyone makes a mistake, they'll get shot down like always and get reprimanded. Any questions? Okay, let's hit the street.

Sgt.: (after roll call, to the lieutenant) Lieutenant, I'm going to have to write up Jones. He was involved in a recovery of property, and I found out he put it in his locker and not in the property room. It states clearly in the General Orders that all property will be placed in the property room and will not be put in someone's locker.

Lt.: Did you talk with Jones to find out why he did that?

Sgt.: No, why should I? The order is very clear, and he violated the order. That is all I need to know. Anyway, you know Jones!

Lt.: Sarge, Jones may have put property in his locker, but we need to find out why.

Sgt.: Why should we, he violated a General Order, he violated policy. What is this department coming to?!

Lt.: Sarge, let me explain the difference between a General Order and a rule. A General Order is a guideline for officers to follow under most circumstances. If the officer has a good reason not to follow it, then he has that discretion. It has to be a good reason. On the other hand, a rule is mandated. A rule cannot be deviated from. In this case, Jones diverged from the order, but we need to know why. Why do you want to pursue this without talking to the officer?

Sgt.: It's too hard to decide what is a rule and what is a General Order. You are new on this shift. We have always treated both the same. Someone violates it they get written up, period! We make the rules around here, not them! Who do they think they are anyway? If you don't want me to enforce the law around here then I won't.

Lt.: I do want you to enforce the rules and the General Orders, but I want you to take into consideration the facts and try to understand that not everyone violates General Orders just because they want to. As supervisors, it is our job to help the officers, to get them to do their work. If you write them up every time they make a decision that doesn't fit the norm, eventually they will stop taking risks and stop making decisions.

Sgt.: So, in other words, we have become counselors, mothers.

Lt.: No, Sarge, we are becoming what we should have been all along—someone who lets people think for themselves and make decisions. Let me ask you, how would you feel if every time you came to me with an idea I would quote the General Order book showing you why you could not do something? No book can cover every situation. That is why it is called a *General* Order book.

Sgt.: Okay, so what do you want me to do?

Lt.: Call Officer Jones in, or meet him on the street. Simply ask him to fill you in on what happened. After you get all the facts, make a decision if it was proper or not. Once you find out let me know.

> *"The instruction manual of the West Midlands Police Force, in England, had grown to four volumes, each one over three inches thick, totaling more than 2,000 pages of instructions. In June 1987, under the direction of Chief Constable Geoffrey Dear, they scrapped it. They replaced it with a single-page 'Policy Statement' which gave 11 brief 'commandments.' These commandments spoke more about initiative and 'reasonableness of action' than about rules or regulations. All officers were issued pocket-size laminated copies of this policy statement so that, at any time, they could remind themselves of the basic tenets of their department. The old manual had contained some useful information that could not be found elsewhere. This was extracted, condensed, and preserved in a new, smaller, 'advice manual.' It was only one-third the size of the old manual and, significantly, was distributed with an explicit promise that it would never be used in the course of disciplinary investigations or hearings. The ground-level officers were able to accept it as a valuable resource, whereas they had regarded the old manual as a constant threat.... *** As of 1988, the Metropolitan Police Department (London) [was] in the process of making a similar change, moving away from a comprehensive instruction manual and toward clear, brief statements of the principles for action" (Sparrow 1992: 55).*

* *

Later...

Sgt.: Lieutenant, I spoke with Jones. I guess he tried to do the right thing. He recovered this guy's wallet, and the guy asked if he could pick it up after 6 p.m. If Jones had put it in property the guy would not have been able to get it. There was some money in the wallet so he didn't want to leave it lying around. He put it in his locker and told the guys at the Service Desk when he came in to call Jones off the street. The guy didn't show, so Jones put it in the property room the next day.

Lt.:   So Sarge, what would you like to do?

Sgt.:   Well, I guess under the circumstances... To be honest I still don't understand. He violated an order, and even though I understand why, why put things in writing if we are not going to follow them?

Lt.:   Try to look at General Orders as suggested ways of doing something. If done that way, you know it is legal and sanctioned by the Department. However, if you need to do it another way, and you can articulate why, you may. Rules, on the other hand, are steadfast and must be followed.

* *

Another roll call, a different sergeant talking about problem solving, and another fly-on-the-wall peek at what reform-minded middle managers are up against, day after day, when they try to create a work environment conducive to community policing:

Sgt.:   The next thing on our list of things to talk about is problem solving. Okay, you can do problem solving, but you cannot take too long to do it. You must be back up to handle your calls. We cannot hold any call for more than ten minutes.

P.O.:   Sarge, but what if we get tied up?

Sgt.:   I don't want anyone milking this thing. Just because the chief says we can do problem solving, there is no reason that we can't do it in five to ten minutes like everything else. We're still police officers, we are not social workers.

P.O.:   What if we have to contact someone else to help solve problems, like City Hall? How can we do that in five minutes?

Sgt.:   That's not our job. If you have to contact someone at City Hall, write a memo to me, and I will send it through the channels. That's the job of the command staff. If you think that it will take a long time on a call, I want to know about it. Call me, and I will decide if we have enough time to allow you to continue or if it is too busy. Okay, let's hit the street.

Even with formal authority over subordinates, innovation, "[a]s one manager put it, '...takes more selling than telling.' In most of the innovations we observed [in private manufacturing and service companies], the manager couldn't just order subordinates to get involved. Doing something beyond routine work that involves creativity and cooperation requires the full commitment of subordinates; otherwise the project will not succeed" (Kanter 1982: 100).

* *

Here is an eclectic assortment of steps middle managers in the Evanston Police Department tried to take or facilitate others taking during 1994 in support of Chief Cooper's leadership for community problem solving as the agency's s.o.p. What is most important is not whether all of these efforts produced the desired procedural or cultural changes, but the fact that at least some middle managers were able fairly quickly to read what their new chief wanted and to take his general direction and apply it skillfully in a wide variety of day-to-day department activities.

❑ Changing the way cars are relieved allowed roll calls to be extended for team building, conversations within the shift and across shifts, and training. By holding longer roll calls, they were able to have shift meetings several times a week. Problems could be discussed and situations the officers had handled on the street could be debriefed.

☐ Officers were asked if they would like to exercise (workout) in the Department's weight room while on duty. The answer was an overwhelming yes. An interested officer was assigned to survey all the officers on the shift to see who wanted to work out. Twenty-one out of 23 wanted to. The patrol officer was given full authority to develop a schedule. Not only did he work out a very practical schedule, but he issued a memorandum explaining the rules and limitations. The result was officers exercising, better morale, and "covert" team building (since the members of the shift had to cover beats for one another to allow the exercisers to use the workout room).

☐ Officers were assigned to beats, but told they were not required to remain in those beats their full tour. If they wanted to wander they could, but they would be held responsible for their beat. This allowed officers the freedom to leave their beats legally, without sneaking out. It also gave them permission to call in a street stop or a vehicle stop and become involved in something off their beat without fear of getting in trouble. These officers began taking ownership of their beats and usually did not wander far, out of concern that something might happen in their beat and they wouldn't be close enough to handle it.

> *"It is important that we go back to the days when beat and precinct integrity was the foundation of our patrol techniques. Remember when sergeants would not allow anyone not assigned to their precincts to handle assignments within their area? Now, we ... allow the dispatchers to manage...our workload in that they dispatch the closest available car without much consideration to precinct boundaries or problem-solving initiatives"* (Joachimstaler 1995: 1).

☐ Officers were advised that they would no longer be called in by supervisors and told (based on bean counting) that they were not producing enough. They would be given feedback regarding the sergeant's perceptions of their overall work every three months, but they are adults, they know what they were hired to do, and it is their responsibility to do it. The results were interesting: Officers who had not shown any interest in their work for years began to get involved in the new concept of problem solving.

☐ Officers were asked to come up with ideas for roll call training. They were given the freedom to come up with any topic that they felt the shift would find interesting. Officers were encouraged to do the training themselves.

☐ Patrol officers were asked to serve as "guest roll-call supervisors." Those who accepted would hold the complete roll call from beginning to end. This not only involved them, but let them see the ins and outs, ups and downs, and difficulties in holding a roll call. It also lightened up the roll call while the other patrol officers played along. A sergeant was not happy that the guest supervisors were "making a mockery" of the roll call procedure, even though that was not true. The guest roll-call supervisor usually conducted roll call in a manner different from the supervisors but covered the same material and even came up with different methods that would be useful for the supervisors to try.

☐ When an officer came up with an idea, it was either put into effect or the officer was told as soon as possible why it could not be used. The idea was mentioned at roll call and given a positive slant, and the officer was given credit, even if the idea was not used. Supervisors were urged not to immediately shoot down or discourage ideas just because they sound different or "off-the-wall." If the officers' ideas were weak, it was insisted that officers be helped to turn their ideas into good ones.

☐ Officers were allowed to run with their ideas, contact other city departments, and tackle problems.

☐ Officers were asked to "make waves," to come up with things that would change the status quo. Not just for the sake of change, but to improve their environment and the Department's process for doing things.

A practical suggestion for how chiefs and senior managers can help put middle managers in a frame of mind to focus on improving the organization for the future comes from Chris Braiden (1995): "Challenge middle managers not to turf-guard, not to defend the status quo. Suggest that they look down the road three years. Look at current proposals for change from the point of view that you will be promoted and ask what you will inherit at that time. Build something now that you will be happy to inherit as you move up the ranks." This may not work for middle managers who don't aspire to or have no realistic expectations of promotion. But they can be asked to consider whether, at their current assignments, they look forward two or three years from now to inheriting the results of problems neglected today.

☐ Shift files were opened up. Officers were told they could look at any file they wished (except other officers' files); the shift staff had no secrets.

☐ Open communication and consultation were urged, which encouraged some officers to talk about things they had been reluctant or afraid to speak up about. An effort was made to share information freely in the belief that officers who are not fully informed or not allowed to help make decisions will not take responsibility for the jobs or their actions.

☐ In addition to asking officers, in the classic call-to-order before a shift, to "listen up," the lieutenant asked the supervisors to "listen down." He tried to make it clear among his shift that officers know their job the best. The day-shift leadership considered it extremely important for supervisors and middle managers to listen to officers when they say they know a better way, a more efficient method, or when they say things like "This seems stupid to me."

☐ An agreement was sought among all employees on the shift to eliminate sayings like "We've always done it this way," "We don't have the power to change it," and "It's good enough for government work."

9. *"Kid, DON'T forget everything they taught you in the Academy"*

Most of these thumbnail sketches of value-adding middle managers profile people in *operational* units. But unless the infrastructure—the support system—of a department develops apace, the smart money would not be on community policing surviving very long. Captain Kevin Wittman, a 16-year veteran of the Charlotte-Mecklenburg, North Carolina, Police Department, confides that he was given an important but challenging assignment when newly appointed Police Chief Dennis Nowicki asked Wittman to lead the training academy in August 1994. The Chief's request was that the Captain "do something practical to support problem solving."

Wittman, before being tapped to direct the Academy, had a solid reputation as a trainer, as an implementer of community problem solving, and a man who was willing to buck the system.

Kevin Wittman's initiation as a trainer came in 1985 after, as he says, "I shot off my mouth." He was working as a homicide investigator and responded to a major crime scene, involving an officer-involved shooting. "Several assistant chiefs *invaded* the crime scene," he recounts, "and pretty well screwed up the integrity of the evidence." When the evidentiary problems began to surface, one of the assistant chiefs sought to blame Investigator Wittman for the mistakes. Wittman went to a superior and declared: "I have pride in my competence and reputation for integrity. Either you confront the assistant chief about this false accusation or I will." Wittman's boss did the right thing and got the assistant chief to back down. The next thing Wittman knew, a memo came around saying a need had been detected for some refresher training for senior commanders in how to safeguard major crime scenes. And Wittman was asked to come to the Academy to teach the refresher class.

In the Edmonton Police Department, Superintendent Chris Braiden gave Staff Sergeant (the equivalent of an American lieutenant) P.J. Duggan "a chance to strut his stuff—to show what he could do as an individual. P.J.'s contribution was standing up to the bosses and taking them on. He was a champion of the 'grunts.' He really understood their jobs. He would constantly hammer home to the upper level managers what the grunts needed" (Braiden 1995).

"I had never taught anything before, and I had no idea how to do it," he says. But he did it, and did it well. He continued to teach part time at the Academy for the next nine years, while maintaining his operational responsibilities as he rose through the ranks from investigator to sergeant to captain. (The Police Department had eliminated the lieutenant rank in the 1970s after the City directed that no municipal agency should have more than five tiers in its table of organization.)

Kevin Wittman's hands-on experience with community problem solving came as he led the "Adam-3" patrol district for several years prior to being named to direct the Academy. There, officers filled three notebooks with community policing projects, a number of them considered highly successful and widely admired in the Department. A notable illustration was cleaning up an aggressive street prostitution problem on a commercial strip. "If the driver didn't stop his car to listen to the proposition, the prostitutes would spit on the windshield—even if the man's wife or girlfriend was in the car," Wittman reports. Steadfast deployment of a variety of relatively conventional enforcement tactics succeeded in driving the prostitutes out of the area and keeping them away. At least as important as coming away from the Adam-3 District with some good local success stories about community problem solving, however, was Captain Wittman's rich appreciation of how hard problem solving can be for first-line officers. Wittman arrived at the Academy armed with current, detailed information about the kinds of knowledge, skills and abilities that Charlotte-Mecklenburg personnel would need to develop if widespread, successful problem solving would ever be realized.

After being named to head the Academy, Wittman began trying to figure out with his staff how to respond to the Chief's deceptively simple challenge to do something practical to support problem solving. This was a team exploration, and Wittman was empowered to shape his key staff. He recruited from around the Department several officers whom he considered to be both role models of innovative problem solvers and talented trainers; and he transferred out of the Academy an influential training supervisor who the Captain determined was proving to be an insurmountable obstacle to shifting the organizational culture and developing a first-class training program.

Despite his own and his staff's imagination and boldness in challenging conventional approaches, the Captain still recognized that he had been asked to lead a difficult expedition with what he considered a pretty general map. The chief had purposely given Wittman clear *general* direction with wide latitude to discover and determine the particulars. Chief Nowicki, like a number of the nation's other effective strategic change agents, was proceeding from the premise that spelling things out in minute detail would have undermined an opportunity for his new training director to breathe life into the concept of managerial empowerment.

But sometimes middle managers—especially those who have grown up in departments with strong, top-down, command-and-control governance—take a little while to understand that a new chief is really sincere about empowerment. They can be forgiven, of course, because the truth is that not all chiefs who talk empowerment walk empowerment. So middle managers and the rest of the police employees need some time to figure out if their new boss is for real.

"I liked my legs and head pretty much where they are," Wittman recalls. "I didn't want them chopped off as I started trying to keep what worked but replace the rest with better approaches in the Academy. Career suicide was not in my plans." Captain Wittman has since come to understand that his head and legs were never in jeopardy

> *"My management style is to direct people toward an idea and let them develop the how-to. One, they can do it better than I can do it, and two, then they have owner-ship. The ownership's got to happen, and if they're just following orders it's not go-ing to happen, or only with great difficulty"* (Neil Behan, former chief of the Baltimore County Police Department, quoted in Kelling and Bratton 1993: 7).

under his new chief, but a fortuity proved critically important in giving Wittman the early encouragement he sought. He had ready and frequent access to Chief Nowicki who, having come from out of state, was at the Academy for several weeks going through mandatory basic training for certification as a North Carolina peace officer. As the Chief recalls, "During breaks in the class I would wander down to Kevin's office to see how he was doing. We'd be involved in an intense discussion of changes he was considering making at the Academy and I'd look at my watch and tell him the class break was over and I had to get back. 'Don't worry about it,' he'd say. '*I'm* the head of the Academy and I give you permission to cut class for a few more minutes!'"

"It really helped me," Wittman recalls, "to be able to frequently test my ideas with the Chief." Buoyed by the support the Chief was providing, Wittman and his team began to immerse themselves in the adult education and problem-solving literature, to visit admired problem-solving police departments, and to listen critically to a succession of sales pitches from training vendors hoping to be hired by the Academy. Wittman also sent out clear messages to the rest of the command staff that they were at least as responsible as the Academy staff for identifying the Department's training needs.

Based on all this input, Wittman was particularly drawn to a variety of experiential learning methods. Several of them involved team building and group problem solving. Two used rope exercises first developed in the 1960s by adherents of the Outward Bound movement (Wall, et al. 1991: 3; Charlotte-Mecklenburg Police Department 1995). One—a "high ropes" course which *every* employee of the Department, including the Chief's veteran secretary, went through—involved walking on a fairly shaky elevated rope bridge. "It was great," the Captain says, "watching the other members of the trainee team counseling one another on how to do it safely and cheering for their teammates."

> *For empowerment to be valuable, "people need direction (key result areas, goals, measurements), knowledge (skills, training, information, goals), resources (tools, materials, facilities, money), [and] support (approval, coaching, feedback, encouragement)" (Byham and Cox 1988: 126).*

Another exercise, a "low ropes initiative game," required the team to get from one side to the other of a giant rope "spider web." The web contained 16 holes of different sizes and at different heights from the ground. The team collectively had to go through every hole. The challenge was to do so without touching any part of the rope mesh, which was treated as if it was an electrified fence. At first, there was very little teamwork and planning. The first people to the web would go through the easiest holes. The less agile, more fragile, or heftier members of the team couldn't get through the holes that hadn't yet been used, and the team had the "shock" of flunking the exercise. But it didn't take long for the teams to begin planning how they could approach the web to accommodate the needs and talents of each member. "It really helped lay a foundation for problem solving," Captain Wittman reported with obvious pride.

That the Captain is not a pastel wallflower became evident again shortly after he arrived to head the Academy. As part of the Departmental reorganization, higher-ups were considering placing a major in the chain of command between him and his deputy chief. Wittman enjoyed an excellent formal and informal working relationship with the deputy chief and did not want to jeopardize the free flow of ideas and support with an intervening command staffer. The day after Captain Wittman got wind of the planned heightening of his chain of command, at 7:15 a.m. he "was camped outside [his] deputy chief's office door." The captain, along with a colleague who would also have reported to the proposed new major, argued their case for greater efficiencies and effectiveness in building community problem solving in the Department if they could report directly to the deputy chief. The result: there is no major in their chain of command. Wittman's willingness over the years to speak up respectfully but frankly to challenge superior officers does not strike everyone in the agency as proper etiquette, of course, but it comports with his Chief's—and several other senior commanders'—sense of what *loyalty to mission* is really about.

Part of the secret to this middle manager's success in building the training portion of the Department's infrastructure is that he is *results*-oriented. That is, his mission does not stop with the "outputs" of running recruits and veteran personnel through instructional programs and stamping them, like a meat inspector, "trained." Rather, he conceives his mission as continually supporting Charlotte-Mecklenburg police employees in whatever ways they individually need to meet the Department's problem-solving challenges.

Captain Wittman also tries not to invent problems in the Academy that will later haunt operations. For instance, he realized that an overemphasis on unquestioning obedience to authority and discipline too early in recruit training would probably thwart the chances of developing "thinking," problem-solving officers. So while "I respect discipline and believe it is important," Wittman says, "we are careful not to overdo it. In the past, the recruits would have to snap to attention when their trainers entered the room. We were running the Academy like a boot camp. That didn't help the recruits hone their creative, questioning abilities for problem solving."

Wittman and his team also try to meet the actual needs of entry-level personnel by acknowledging frankly that one of the first things a fresh recruit historically had been told by his or her field training officer upon

Having even a single captain like Kevin Wittman on one's management team would be a dream for many police chiefs. Charlotte-Mecklenburg Chief Dennis Nowicki has begun to realize his dream many times over. Two other captains, Craig Huneycutt and James Felder, are illustrative. These middle managers are leading the way—locally and nationally—for enthusiastic, wide-ranging exploration of the problem-solving power to be found in unconventional partnerships between the police and other government agencies. Captain Huneycutt, as part of a "family preservation" project, is helping a multi-disciplinary team explore how police and the county Department of Social Services might more effectively work together. The shared goal is to keep troubled families in tact and assist those families to develop the skills and knowledge to be safe, functional places for raising healthy children.

Captain Felder, in a challenging child-focused project dubbed "Summoning the Village," has evinced a truly remarkable comfort level concerning the proactive, inventive efforts of Sergeant Ken Perry and Officers Katie Flynn and Larry Matkins. He views their energetic and effective brainstorming not as a threat to his own authority but as a source of pride in his squad. The police (including Captain Huneycutt) are working in a genuine power-sharing partnership with school teachers and administrators, school reform specialists, psychologists, psychiatrists, social workers and others. Their goal is to invent ways to help gifted Cochrane Middle School Principal Ken Simmons establish a school and community atmosphere in which inner-city children can learn more effectively and their teachers can do their important, crime-preventive work more successfully.

graduation from the 16-week basic training program was, "Kid, forget all that stuff they taught you in the Academy. I'll show you how we really do police work in this department." The classic line is hardly unique, of course, to Mecklenburg County. While Captain Wittman recognized that he couldn't guarantee how FTOs would greet their new trainees, he revised the basic training curriculum to try to fortify the officers against the risk of sabotage by FTOs.

"We don't tell the recruits there's one single idea about how to do good police work," he says. "We familiarize them with the different concepts that are being discussed and debated around the country, and we explain why we believe the problem-solving strategy is the best approach." This way, when they hit the streets, if an FTO tells them what "real" policing consists of, the recruits are armed with the knowledge that this is just one person's opinion—and probably not one that will make for the greatest policing effectiveness or career success.

Yet another innovation with which Captain Wittman and his staff are experimenting—at the request of Chief Nowicki—is running an "open Academy." By this they mean that the facility is open to members of the public who are interested in seeing what kind of police training their tax dollars are funding. It will be interesting over time to see what accommodations are made to safeguard portions of police training that require confidentiality and how letting civilians observe classes affects the morale of trainees, public attitudes toward the police, and the content, effectiveness and efficiency of instruction.

While most of middle manager Kevin Wittman's ambitious training challenges lie ahead, he has already begun to lead his training team toward significantly bolstering the collaborative problem-solving skills that Charlotte-Mecklenburg Police employees need to reach ever greater levels of success.

10. The bridges of Will County

A river runs through the hard-working blue-collar community of Joliet, Illinois, and it must have been quite the talk of the town when engineers succeeded many years ago in building bridges to span the river's banks. The "bridges" that one police lieutenant, Bill "Fitz" Fitzgerald, built between the Police Department and the City's Inspections Department are less visible to the naked eye, but they may prove profoundly influential to the town's commerce and character. Our thanks for the following story to "in-house outsider" Sandy Kaminska, who has for several years been the Joliet Police Department's midwife for the birthing of a better way of doing business.

Even before the initial "POP" training sessions had been completed in 1992, someone needed to "run interference" between street-level officers and the head of the Joliet Inspections Department. Under Police Chief Dennis Nowicki (who now heads the Charlotte-Mecklenburg Department), all 200 police employees were trained in problem solving, cultural diversity, and community crime prevention as a foundation for shifting the Department's core strategies for dealing with crime and disorder problems. One day in 1992, at Chief Nowicki's request, a PERF trainer was helping the Department explain what Joliet calls "Neighborhood-Oriented Policing" (NOP) to a group that included both police and other City employees.

The session outlined the utility of a multi-agency, problem-solving approach to long-standing Joliet problems. The commonsense notion of local government collaborations immediately appealed to everyone from the city manager to the most junior Inspections clerk. Most Joliet employees also acknowledged that the police had long been the City's "early warning system" and "front line" regarding emerging crime and disorder problems—even non-law enforcement safety and disorder problems such as backed-up sewers and abandoned buildings. And, at least theoretically, City employees agreed that officers should expect some type of feedback when police inform the appropriate City authorities regarding public works, building, health and other non-police problems. However, as the workshop moved into building true collaborative relationships between the police and other City departments—asking for mutual commitments of time and resources—resistance from some managers in other city agencies became evident.

> *One useful role for middle managers is to meet with their counterparts in other city agencies and to deal with protocols for and obstacles to better problem solving cooperation between the agencies. For example, in the Chicago Police Department, district commanders in the prototype districts met regularly with representatives from other city services for these purposes (Skogan, et al. 1994, executive summary: 15).*

In the classroom (and with a nudge in the right direction from City Manager John Mezera), City workers could agree that a neighborhood's problems can best be solved through coordinated efforts. But classroom preaching seldom stands a chance against conflicting organizational traditions and administrative territoriality. City fathers and mothers in Joliet knew this and, at least within the Police Department, had gone to great pains to make organizational and administrative changes that would facilitate collaborative efforts across ranks and divisions. Some street-level officers had already begun testing the willingness and ability of their supervisors to support problem solving. And, although a few sergeants and lieutenants were quietly and cautiously supportive of their officers' efforts, what proved decisive at this juncture was the conversion of the garrulous and popular Lt. Fitz from outspoken skeptic to effective advocate.

Fitz happened to be in the classroom that day in 1992 when Joliet's Director of Inspectional Services defiantly pointed out that he was not about to "have police officers running in and out of his office all day telling him what to do" with the Department of Inspectional Services. Having recently dealt with the trauma of having his officers tell him what tactics they thought were appropriate to their neighborhoods, Fitz was sympathetic to the director's concerns. Given the volume of problems officers might wish to work on with Inspectional Services, Fitz also realized that interagency problem solving would require more structure than anticipated. But structure, in the form of more paperwork and more procedures, no matter how "streamlined," were just what fledgling problem solvers didn't need. So Fitz volunteered to be the liaison between the police and Inspectional Services. And the Director, knowing Fitz (and Fitz's brother Tom, who, at the time, was the Will County Sheriff), agreed.

Fitz-as-liaison began with a relatively formal air: If an officer thought his problem-solving project could involve Inspectional Services, the officer would contact Fitz. Periodically, Fitz or Fitz and the officer(s) would then meet with Inspectional Services and present their specific requests. As Fitz went through the Department's "wish list," Inspections would let him know what they could and could not do or, in some cases, suggested alternative approaches. Fitz and the officers learned from inspectors' suggestions and responses and soon became adept at presenting convincing action plans to Inspections. The inspectors, in turn, grew increasingly willing to act on well-thought-out plans of the Police Department.

After a joint Police-Inspections effort resulted in the closing of a sleazy, crime- and disorder-ridden motel, Inspections Director Richard Bazzarone offered to make a video that could be used to help instruct officers in how to do basic inspections. Although such instruction could not empower police officers to perform inspections, officers did become useful and time-saving "watchdogs" for Inspectional Services. And, after a few more successful collaborative projects and the unflagging encouragement of City Manager Mezera, the formal Fitz-as-liaison system fell by the wayside.

Today, three years after that tense training session in 1992, officers and inspectors regularly work together—spurred by the leadership of Chief Joseph Beazley, a close friend and former Chicago Police Department colleague of Dennis Nowicki's. In most cases the relationship has become so informal that written follow-up to the officers' and inspectors' respective supervisors is usually expected only when a project is completed. Inspectional Services Director Bazzarone is so involved with community-based problem solving that he regularly volunteers his services to such education and employment opportunity programs as Youth Builders. The City of Joliet and Joliet Police Department learned that, given time and mutual willingness to take a chance, true collaborative relationships can be established and organizational cultures can be changed. And Lt. Fitz? He and Sgt. David Starcevich (one of the original NOP officers) will soon be "running interference" with the local school board in a new collaborative effort to identify and address "at-risk" children at the elementary and middle school level. And Fitz is in high demand as a problem-oriented policing trainer for police departments throughout the Midwest.

11. *Don't tell her it's not her job*

Former Fort Pierce, Florida, Police Lieutenant Michele Reilly in April 1994 shared the following insights into the many roles that a middle manager dedicated to organizational change may play:

In April of 1992, the Department divided into districts, with officers and sergeants assigned to a beat for a minimum of two years. Every officer was responsible for problem identification in his or her beat. Sergeants had day-to-day responsibility for monitoring officers' problem-solving efforts. The District Commander (lieutenant) was responsible for overseeing all of this activity within his or her geographical area of responsibility. Lt. Reilly served as the District 1 Commander.

Why is it that in the private business world a number of middle managers behave in ways that are defensive and destructive to innovation? One suggestion, from the belly of the beast, comes from corporate employee Bill Fischer (1995): "Many middle managers are good technical people who got promoted to positions they were not properly prepared for by their companies, and so they don't perform well in those new slots."

Initially, even though the Department had trained extensively and planned for many months for the transition [from a small problem-oriented policing unit to agency-wide implementation], it seemed that few people had a good understanding about how to put all of our theories into practice. Michele Reilly found herself performing duties that procedural guidelines suggested should have been done by a captain, sergeant or officer at any given time.

The agency has three district commanders, a lieutenant in charge of criminal investigations, and a lieutenant in charge of vice and narcotics. "I knew that it was crucial that we were seen as a cohesive team working together," reports Reilly.

"It was difficult for some people to set aside competitive feelings that had existed for many years. Our captain, reared in the 'traditional' police environment, found it difficult to encourage the team approach. Consequently very often I found myself acting as the facilitator for conflict resolution."

District commanders were formally tasked with the preparation of their district budget, scheduling within the district, identification of training needs, speaking to community groups and monitoring day-to-day call-for-service issues. "As we got more involved in the district process," says Lt. Reilly,

> "we found lieutenants doing a variety of duties dependent upon ability and motivation. I rode with every officer at least once during the first six months of his or her district assignment. I did this to reinforce issues that had been discussed at training and our district meeting and for them to get to know me as a person. (I had been out of patrol for quite some time.) We talked about expectations for the district as well as personal aspirations."

In the Madison, Wisconsin, Police Department's experimental police district, everyone helped out as needed. "To help make time for [officers'] problem-solving and shift meetings, the sergeants, the lieutenant, and even the captain work the streets from time to time. This has the added benefit of giving managers a better sense of the types of data and other resources their officers need in order to identify and address neighborhood problems. The...managers tend to think of this as management participation versus participatory management. By occasionally working the streets to allow officers time for other activities, the managers add to the sense of teamwork among [district] employees" (Wycoff and Skogan 1993: 27).

By the time Michele Reilly was able to ride with one officer, both had been in the district approximately four months. They were comfortable with one another because they had worked together in the detective bureau for several years. "He had not been a very good detective," confides the lieutenant.

> "He seemed to be pressured by the steady flow of cases and had often utilized sick time when it became too intense. When I got in the car to ride with him he seemed relaxed, and he told me he 'had some people for me to meet.' He proceeded to take me to most of the businesses on his beat and took great pride in the fact that the business owners knew him by name."

On March 14, 1994, a woman who worked in a convenience store in this officer's beat was murdered during a robbery. The news article begins, "Despondent over the slaying of a friend he had made in his beat, Ft. Pierce Police Officer Richard Farnell...."

"Ideally," in Reilly's view, "a sergeant should be the person who rides with the officers most often and gives them this informal support and encouragement. However, when you have officers who are doing well, it is the responsibility of whomever sees this positive action to reinforce it."

In a recent problem-solving effort by a team of officers working in a beat, Lt. Reilly played a major role in getting it started. The Department had received several complaints in a neighborhood of prostitutes and drug dealers hanging out. The sergeant for that beat was not immediately available, so Reilly grabbed one of the beat officers and said, "Let's go talk to these people."

They talked with the owner of an apartment complex who had several undesirable tenants, with the owner of a local 7-11 which had a loitering problem, and with others who told the police about drug dealers hanging out in the area. "I stayed with the officer while he [conducted these interviews] and helped guide him through some possible immediate solutions," says the lieutenant.

> "We developed a list of additional information we might need and other people we needed to contact. I advised his sergeant as to what had transpired and encouraged the sergeant (asked him about it every time I saw him!) to spend time with the officer, reviewing his progress."

The team was able to determine that an area extending one block east and west of a major thoroughfare was experiencing similar problems. The main road was predominantly commercial, while the blocks east and west were low income residential. Reilly spoke with the sergeant about getting the business owners involved. She and the sergeant developed a workplan in conjunction with the beat officers. Reports Lt. Reilly:

> "If I drove through the target area in question and observed trash in the area, I shared that information with the beat officer and sergeant, with a suggestion that we might want to see that taken care of. When I noticed the city crews cutting weeds in a vacant lot, I stopped and asked the foreman who had made the referral to get them there. When I found out it was one of our officers I congratulated the officer and sergeant, recognizing how difficult it is to get cooperation from other city departments. When I saw that all the abandoned vehicles had been towed from a closed gas station and a fence erected around the property, I made an effort to find out which officer was responsible and to tell him what a good job he had done."

> *"During the action phase [of an innovative project led by a middle manager], the technical details of the project and the actual work directed toward project goals are now in the hands of the action team. Managers may contribute ideas or even get involved in hands-on experimentation, but their primary functions are still largely external and organizational, centered around maintaining the boundaries and integrity of the project"* **(Kanter 1982: 101).**

Michele Reilly believes that "if you are a competent, enthusiastic middle manager with a good understanding of problem solving, there is not an agency in the country in which you would not have plenty to do."[11] The Fort Pierce Police Department began its transition to

---

[11] Middle manager Michele Reilly's words were prescient, for she is now serving in another agency—with plenty to do. As deputy chief of the Lauderhill, Florida, Department (adjacent to Fort Lauderdale), she is helping Chief Michael Scott—a protege of Herman Goldstein, a nationally esteemed "POP" maven in his own right, and a former

problem solving in 1990. "There are still officers, sergeants and senior administrators who need guidance, reinforcement and encouragement where problem solving is concerned," confides Michele Reilly. She offers that it may require that a lieutenant meet with an officer and say, "Hey, let's park the cars and walk for a while." Is that a lieutenant's function? Should that be the responsibility of the sergeant? "I believe," Reilly declares,

> "that if you have supervisors who either cannot or will not assume their responsibilities in reference to problem solving, the supervisors and managers who can identify the needs of officers or others have an obligation to try to meet those needs. This means that those competent supervisors and managers will end up doing a lot of work and those less than competent (or less than motivated) will not do as much. It is probably not fair. But, when you have officers who are capable and who are trying to make a difference, we must do all that we can to support their efforts."

---

colleague of Reilly's in Fort Pierce—establish a brand new police department. With the local government having decided to establish a new local police department instead of having the county maintain responsibility for policing the area, Reilly, Scott and their many collaborators are inventing an agency which has had problem-solving as its undisputed core strategy from the day the department opened its doors.

V. Some Thoughts About How to Help Middle Managers Facilitate Strategic Innovation

So despite the expert predictions of widespread opposition to strategic change from the police mid-ranks, we have reasons for cautious optimism. A fair number of police middle managers, it seems, "didn't get the memo." Perhaps they don't realize they are not supposed to be playing so vital a role in implementing community policing. We do not mean to diminish the reality of opposition from many incumbent middle managers, of course. Otherwise, this book's concluding chapter would be far shorter than it is. But nothing succeeds like success, and the fact that the police industry has produced scores, if not hundreds, of exemplars of mid-rank effectiveness in facilitating community problem solving is an asset that change agents should welcome and deploy even more fully than they have.[12]

We do not wish, and hope the reader will not wish us, to accept the burden of propounding in this chapter only "proven" ideas. That would shorten this chapter considerably! We simply don't believe the field is yet smart enough, and surely we are not, to say with confidence how to maximize

"Here's my idea, it's so simple: If evil men can work together to get what they want, so can good men" [and women!] (Tolstoy, in War and Peace).

the potential positive contributions of existing or new middle managers in community problem-solving regimens. All that is known today about what does—and does *not*—work in policing and in public administration still seems to be just the tip of an iceberg of lessons waiting to be learned (see, e.g., Sherman 1980; Moore 1992, 1994; Travis 1995). As the Vera Institute of Justice pointed out in a superb compilation of ideas from New York City cops about how to deal with various disorder problems,

> "it is too soon to draw conclusions about what's 'best' in the emerging practice of problem-solving community police work. The stories [about addressing disorderly groups] are presented to provoke thought, to be improved upon, and to alert all members of the Department to what is being done and what is being learned on the beat" (Farrell, et al. 1993a: 2).

Similarly, the following speculations and recommendations invite the reader's critical appraisal, the researcher's further inquiry, and the practitioner's efforts—where the ideas seem sound—to test and improve on them in practice.

The premise of this concluding chapter is that there are many really significant contributions middle managers might make to the successful implementation of community

---

[12] We're tempted to publish a mailing list of first-class police middle managers! The Police Foundation some years ago launched the Police Management Association, under Roberta Lesh's leadership, which was an important, albeit not enduring, first effort to bring promising middle managers together for mutual assistance and professional development. The Police Executive Research Forum currently fills a small piece of the gap left by the demise of the PMA with its Senior Management Institute for Police and the SMIP alumni association. PERF hopes in years to come to advance the ball first dribbled by Roberta Lesh at the PMA.

policing. There is much to do to make community policing work and not always enough people available to do it. It is conceivable that too many middle managers having too little of *real value* to do is a pervasive problem in policing. If so, this degradation may feed a pervasive reluctance by middle managers to do the hard work of trying to change the system. But we would distinguish too many mid-managers with too little of importance to do from the problem of inherent and immutable resistance to change. We are doubtful that police middle managers would pose protracted, substantial barriers to change if they had really valuable roles to play in bringing it about (Kelling and Bratton 1993: 2). Thus, our starting point in how to help middle managers meaningfully contribute to community policing is with our definition of what we're up against.

□ *Don't accept "middle managers' resistance to change" as the definition of the organization's problem.* Peter Drucker (1974: 797) two decades ago declared:

> "[T]o focus on resistance to change is to misdefine the problem in a way that makes it less, rather than more, tractable. The right way to define the problem so as to make it capable of resolution is as a challenge to create, build, and maintain the innovative organization, the organization for which change is norm rather than exception, and opportunity rather than threat" (quoted in Kelling and Bratton 1993: 10; see also p. 7).

Former Evanston, Illinois, Police middle manager George Scharm (1994: 5) made much the same point, in response to our inquiry about examples of police personnel *constructively violating* agency conventions:

> "You asked about violating tradition—how it helps make changes. I do not feel so much that it is violating tradition as it is always looking for ways to make improvements. Violating tradition sounds negative, and 'tradition' to one person may mean sacred ways of doing things and to someone else it means just old-fashioned or out-of-date."

For the better part of its six-year life, the Harvard Executive Session on Community Policing, which convened thoughtful police chiefs and researchers every six months to deliberate questions concerning the design and implementation of this new style of policing, struggled with defining a relationship between traditional policing and the emerging strategy. It turned out, not surprisingly perhaps, that the fight was as much about *respect* for past career efforts as it was about praising or critiquing individual tactics and strategies. For instance, O.W. Wilson's "professional model" of policing may have produced unintended consequences in driving a wedge between patrol officers and the public, but at least, Daryl Gates and others at the Executive Session would demand, give the man his due; his solutions were right for his time and helped advance policing.

Eventually, the respect point was substantially resolved through Mark Moore's diplomacy, who tendered the notion at one meeting: Let us openly acknowledge that any progress we might make in fostering police effectiveness will necessarily involve standing on the shoulders of the dedicated practitioners who preceded us. By shifting the definition of the "problem" from whether to reject tradition to how to honor it as we move forward, Moore quieted tempers and facilitated continued progress. (Had someone less vertically challenged than Mark been the diplomat of the moment, it is conceivable that the peace-making metaphor chosen would have entailed something other than *standing on someone else's shoulders*.)

Leaders in other fields have also made the point that it makes little sense to battle over whether traditional, essential tasks or innovative, essential tasks should be honored more highly. As a human services reform advocate said to his traditionalist colleagues,

> "Saying, 'My service is better than your service' isn't the important discussion.... All these services are important. We need to ask, 'How can we use all these services in a way that will make the most sense to people who need help?'" (David Haapala of Homebuilders, quoted in Barthel 1992: 77).

"You just do what you can, and then when you go, the next generation carries on. I mean, I'm standing on the shoulders of...the people who fought for [humane treatment of animals] in the previous generation. Their period of life on earth is gone, but people carry on their work.... [M]y husband and I stood on their shoulders, but there are lots who will stand on our shoulders" (Muriel, the Lady Dowding, quoted in Berry 1993: 151).

As in any ambitious inquiry or advocacy effort, often winning the battle over what the *question* is brings us much closer to insight and victory. Asking the *wrong* question in a scholarly study or R&D inquiry (e.g., How much larger do police forces have to become—or how much wider do cities' main streets have to be—to further reduce police "response time" to the scenes of reported crime?) will produce ineffectual reforms. Asking the *right* question (e.g., How can we get members of the public to call the police instantly when they see a crime in progress—or safely get a snapshot or video recording of the suspect—instead of waiting to do anything until after the perpetrator has fled the scene?) might yield truly beneficial programmatic and procedural ideas. It's not that the *wrong* question is always incapable of being answered; it's that the investment (which may be substantial) in answering it can produce irrelevant or socially harmful conclusions and policy decisions. Admittedly, there are few delineations of "right" and "wrong" questions that will meet with universal agreement. Values, political and economic interests and other considerations can lead to opposite conclusions about the utility of a particular inquiry. A road construction contractor might relish the idea of cities deciding to invest immense sums over time in "Rapid Response" projects that modify main streets by creating special lanes accessible only to public safety vehicles. Such a business might well believe, for personal pecuniary reasons, that the question of how to shorten police response time through road design was a *right* question to ask.

There are so many *wrong* public policy and operational questions asked in the criminal justice field, in our view, that perhaps a bit more elaboration of this point would be helpful. What kind of tactical questions should police have asked in the early 1970s, in the wake of the loss of innocent lives during hostage-barricade incidents? A *wrong* question would have been, How much do we have to invest in R&D to invent lightweight, bionic battering rams that first-responding patrol officers can hang on their belts and use to force immediate entry into buildings where the hostage taker has fled with his captive? Fortunately, one of the *right* questions the New York City Police Department did ask at that time was, How can we use *time* as a "weapon" in hostage-barricade situations? The consequence of the NYPD imaginatively answering that question, of course, has been remarkable success rates for hostage-barricade police teams around the nation over the ensuing decades. These successes have been measured in high arrest rates and very low rates of injury or loss of life to public safety workers, hostages, and offenders (Geller and Scott 1992).

Or consider the problem that sometimes reported crime rates rise during a highly successful community-policing implementation. A *wrong* question might be, How can we reverse the crime rates? Among the *right* questions to ask might be, Are the crime *victimization* rates going up? If not, are we getting higher rates of reporting because the community now believes the police are more willing and able to do something about the reported crime? If victimization surveys show that actual crime rates are down and public opinion polls show that community confidence in the police is up, how can we place in an understandable and positive context—for consumption by the public at large, the media and especially politicians—the combined knowledge we glean from comparing these crime studies and public opinion polls?

Or, as a final illustration, consider the emerging capacity of medical researchers to identify, through simple blood tests, people who have inherited defective genes that predispose them to dying of specifiable cancers or other as yet untreatable diseases—with probabilities of being accurate in the 85 percent range. A *wrong* question to ask might be, How can communities establish programs of universal genetic testing at birth? Another wrong one might be, How can we most efficiently make such birth tests available to people considering dating or marrying us or selling us insurance or bogus cancer cures that prey on the desperate? A *right*—more socially useful—question might be, How does the arrival on the social landscape of these new bio-fortune tellers position communities to demand universal health and life insurance, or at least the enactment of laws preventing the disclosure to the insurance industry of any genetic screening a patient might choose to have conducted? Again, whether one considers a question correct or incorrect depends heavily on normative and economic considerations.

So, in thinking about how to get maximum value out of middle managers in the community policing implementation challenge, we need to strive to ask the right questions and to define the problem in tractable ways.

> *President John F. Kennedy, on the issue of right questions and wrong questions: "Ask not what your country can do for you. Ask what you can do for your country."*

"[W]hen you're trying to break out of existing models, the definition of your problem is shaped in conventional terms," argues Michael Hammer, co-author of *Reengineering the Corporation*. "And what you need to do," he suggested,

> "is think creatively about your problem. *** An example...: until the Xerox 914 copier came along, nobody thought they had a convenience/copy problem. If you asked anybody, 'Do you have a problem with copying?', they would have said no, because they didn't think instant copying was possible. Once they saw that they could have instant copies made, everybody said: 'I've been waiting for this all my life'" (quoted in Vogl 1993/1994: 56).

Many additional examples could be envisaged of *ill-conceived* problems, drawing enormous reform resources and energies, concerning American policing. A basic one may be the problem, framed both by police and especially by politicians, How can we get more police so we can cut crime? While we would not denigrate the accomplishments that more police, more soundly directed and assisted, could attain, still we think the better part of wisdom comes from cops like Eric Davis of Chicago. "If the folks in Washington were really serious about fighting crime," he said, "they would ask, How can we take the $30 billion in the Crime Act and put it into education?" At least, we hope, the thousands of new cops being hired and influenced by the federal government's commitment to community policing (and the new guards watching all the new prison cells with occupants who swung and missed for the third time) will be quality people with ingenuity, bravery and a social conscience. We hope these new criminal justice workers will not only do their work in effective ways but will also forcefully ask society, How can we collectively enhance other institutions capable of building more competent, more crime-resistant communities and citizens? It's one of the *right* questions.

     ❑ *Build on middle managers' existing strengths.* In their remarkable parable about high- and low-performing work groups, *Zapp!: The Lightning of Empowerment*, Byham and Cox (1988: 119) make the deceptively simple observation that "people learn faster from successes than failures." If traditional police middle managers are generally good at reminding the organization of all the other things it has promised to do besides the latest initiative, why not honor this strength of theirs and build on it to move forward? "Building on strengths" is also the leading principle employed by Triangle Consulting's Deborah Allen-Baber, a gifted management counselor to a number of America's top companies (also see Spitzer 1995). This does *not* mean to ignore weaknesses, but to find a foundation of *competence*, however modest, on which to begin erecting the desired new structure. Failure to build on such a foundation risks having the pylons sink in the muck. It also presents the risk that people whose past failures are being placed center stage will conclude that their next performance probably also will be a flop.

Building on strengths is a technique widely deployed in many reform settings, from corporate reinvention to family social services. In the family preservation movement, for instance, counselors eschew such established concepts as the "deficit model," in which a family is assessed "in terms of its flaws and failings." Instead, "family preservation focuses on a family's strengths" (Barthel 1992: 13, 25).

> *"I...know for a fact that our sergeant and lieutenant ranks [in the St. Louis Metropolitan Police Department] are filled with our best potential of talent and have witnessed some outstanding management skills when they are given the opportunity to respond to challenges" (Joachimstaler 1995: 2).*

To build on strengths, one must of course identify what they are. In the best circumstances, those strengths will be directly and obviously pertinent to the tasks at hand. Some of these management and leadership attributes can be inferred from the several portraits of high-performing middle managers in the preceding chapter. Those middle managers, to their employers' good fortune, have strengths bearing directly on the strategic reform challenges before them. Where that is *not* the case, then a little more imagination is called for to figure out how to convert possible weaknesses into strengths—how to welcome the lemons to the garden and make world-class lemonade.

The Outdoor Institute, a North Carolina-based team-building resource center, suggests that virtually all people "have all the resources that we need" to meet job challenges. "Remember," they instruct their trainers, "people are not broken, or in need of being fixed. What they require is a way to access the internal resources that they already have, and to find a way to transfer these to a given task. If a person says '*I can't do that*,' your job is to find a time from their past when they felt competent at doing something, and have them pretend that they feel the same way now. You can actually help them to transfer these feelings and beliefs, and this will assist them in behaving more resourcefully in this new situation" (Wall, et al. 1991: 52).

A starting place for building on strengths is having and displaying respect for the people who are being asked to join the innovation team. As St. Paul, Minnesota, Lieutenant Gary Briggs put it, respect in this context includes acknowledging past efforts and the motivators of those efforts:

> "[T]hese changes [community problem solving] that we're talking about are going to be extremely threatening to many, many people. We need to take the time to give them credit for the things they've done well, because most of the things they've done, they've done at our behest and with our direction" (Briggs 1995: 137).

Another elemental stratagem for building on strengths is paying attention to the training that departments have recently provided for middle managers either in-house or at some external training program and trying to capitalize on newly acquired skills and knowledge (Goldstein 1990: 174-75). If the training turned out to be bad or out of sync with the department's values, then of course the department would want to cut its losses and direct employees *not* to apply what they learned. If the training was *good*, however, and the department still thwarts' the trainees' efforts to apply their new expertise to core job challenges, then the department plants the seeds of cynicism and demoralization.

We need to show empathy and support for middle managers who are trying to build on their strengths to climb out of a pit of professional irrelevancy. They fell in that pit when someone told them their career-long efforts to master the current mores and methods of policing were only marginally useful for the new way of doing business. This is the classic breeding ground for a mid-life crisis. As someone defined it, a mid-life crisis is when you finally climb to the top of the ladder, but you find out the ladder is against the wrong wall.

By the time many police employees are experienced enough to be promoted to mid-management posts, they are approaching the age when mid-life crises can strike. How they react to these critical junctures reveals a lot about character. One hopes they might react like Rev. Anne Marsh, who marked her fiftieth birthday by saying, "These days I am less afraid of death than of an empty life" (1995).

Spitzer (1995) reports that managers in many private sector organizations "are outright hostile to training efforts. Instead of encouraging employees to learn, supervisors often view training sessions as interruptions of work. Employees return to their jobs and find that instead of using new skills they are simply pushed to catch up on the backlog." Even if higher-ups don't *actively* resist a trainee's using new learning, they may sit by passively as the organization's "counterculture" inhibits the trainee's initiatives (Reiner 1992: 470). Besides squandering the precious resources of trust and morale, ignoring an employee's eagerness to apply fresh knowledge diverts training money to window dressing rather than investing scare resources in institutional improvement.

Just as middle managers' newly acquired training can be squandered by higher-ups who do not appreciate the training's value to the tasks at hand, so too can middle managers, if they are not attentive, waste the training their subordinates have received. For instance, Officer Cindy Brady of the San Diego Police Department explained:

"The way it works now is that we receive training, and then we go and implement what we've learned. The drawback is that we have to then go back and play catch up with our supervisors; informing them of the concepts we've learned and the things we've tried. I think the solution to this obstacle is simply time. Once supervisors see that the [community policing] concept is being supported, and that it's not going to go away, then, I think, supervisors will be more supportive" (quoted in Community Policing Consortium 1995: 3).

Aside from middle managers' newly acquired talents, there may be appropriate ways to use *traditional, pre-existing* middle-management skills to bolster the untraditional community policing strategy. One way might be to acknowledge how important it is for community policing to be implemented in a fashion that either enhances or at least does not weaken the existing capacities of the police department that everyone knows will continue to be essential in the future. Most obvious among these police organizational obligations is the need to respond rapidly and appropriately to citizens' genuine emergency problems. Other crucial, continuing obligations that require resources are the maintenance of a well-equipped, well-trained, respectably paid, high-integrity workforce.

What are some of the strengths in middle managers that chiefs and other influentials need to identify and deploy? Kanter (1982: 102) described some of the elements of a "participative-collaborative management style" that characterized private-sector middle managers who were successful innovators within their companies:

□ *"Persuading more than ordering, though managers sometimes use pressure as a last resort."*

□ *"Building a team, which entails among other things frequent staff meetings and considerable sharing of information."*

□ *"Seeking inputs from others—that is, asking for ideas about users' needs, soliciting suggestions from subordinates, welcoming peer review, and so forth."*

□ *"Acknowledging others' stake or potential stake in the project—in other words, being politically sensitive."*

□ *"Sharing rewards and recognition willingly."*

If middle managers can help ensure that essential continuing capacities are not weakened—and don't even *appear* to be weakened—during the implementation and maintenance of a community policing regimen, they will be performing an essential role as part of the implementation team. An actual or apparent slippage in organizational capacity to meet the public's need for *emergency* help will kill the strategic reform initiative and may cost the chief and elected officials their jobs. As a deputy police chief from Kansas City, Missouri, told his colleagues at a conference,

"I have no doubt that the Chief's line would light up if we said, 'Ms. Jones we realize that you've got a problem out there, somebody's breaking into your car right now but we're out doing community policing and we'll be by in two days.'

I don't think that Ms. Jones is going to like that and I think that such a response would probably shut down community policing" (Nunn 1995: 132).

So at the very least, middle managers can be directed to use "best practices" to ensure the continued functioning of traditional and perennial police obligations to the public. (Some modesty about what constitutes "best practices" is in order, for too often in policing what is popular and enduring is simply *assumed* to be worthwhile—see, e.g., Farrell, et al. 1993a: 2.) To be sure, we wish for and believe in the capacity of middle managers to go much further than running old systems as well as possible. We have guarded confidence that, with proper senior leadership, they can become active change agents for the community policing strategy. Moreover, they can help to integrate appropriate aspects of essential, conventional systems into the broader policing strategy. But minimally even the *resistant* middle manager, properly perceived and directed, may be deployed as part of the organization's strength. He or she can protect the department against the accusation from within or outside that the shift to community problem solving is being accomplished at the expense of meeting various other important obligations to the public and to police employees (see Nunn 1995: 131).

In urging police departments to build on their own strengths, we are mindful that headlines throughout 1995 may cause a sizable percentage of the public to wonder with utter sincerity whether some police agencies have significant strengths on which to build. There were the assorted corruption and excessive force scandals in numerous cities. And then there was the nation's most-watched "mini-series" of 1995 (or perhaps of the Century)—the televised O.J. Simpson double murder trial. As "infotainment TV," the saga's ratings probably could have kept it on the air indefinitely, had not the jury, exhausted from its nine-month sequestration, put a swift end to the drama after less than four hours of deliberation by returning not guilty verdicts on October 3, 1995 (Margolick 1995). Police change agents must not ignore the fact that Americans who spent the better part of 1995 mesmerized by the televised trial were fed an almost daily diet of LAPD-bashing—some of it, to be sure, deserved. Very likely (public opinion polling can confirm or refute this) members of the public across the nation generalized to some extent that the weaknesses of the LAPD afflict many other departments as well. To varying degrees, such generalizations would be accurate.

An O.J. trial junkie might sincerely—although, in our view, incorrectly—believe that the LAPD and other departments are so indelibly defiled by the hateful legacy of bigots like retired Detective Mark Fuhrman and by other incompetents on the payrolls that it would be absurd to characterize the departments as having major strengths on which to build. Anyone who has spent time working in or with large, complicated agencies such as the LAPD and met the many outstanding, humanitarian, brave cops who work there knows, of course, that the gross generalizations derived from episodes such as the O.J. trial are harmfully inaccurate. But one ignores public *perceptions* at one's peril, for in a profession such as policing which is committed, among other things, to reducing fear (a perception), the opinions held by the public at large, police officers, and various groups are significant, influential realities independent of whatever the "objective truth" may be.

What, then, could one tell a doubtful public, news media, and politicians about the capacity of even the LAPD to build on its internal strengths in order to gain the operational benefits of strategic innovation? Many answers could be given (see, e.g., Muwakkil 1995). We suspect that the most successful arguments to the general public will not be abstractions or statistics, but frank acknowledgment that lousy cops—even a few of them—can do enormous amounts of public harm, while those men and women who take their oaths of office as personal codes of conduct can be a crime-ridden community's saving grace. Susan Herman (1995), a savvy community organizer and former senior staffer in the NYPD, captured the point eloquently and with characteristic terseness: "There is nothing quite like a good cop. And there is nothing quite like a bad cop."

Police departments, like most other American institutions—hospitals, schools, airlines, civil rights groups, car dealerships, etc.—have a few extremely good and a few extremely bad employees. In our view, the vast majority of workers—in fishbowl jobs like policing and other occupations—are basically good people. It is often difficult, however, to remember this when attention is drawn to a few notorious pockets of problems.

The dilemma is somewhat like a basically healthy person who learns after a routine physical that he has a small cancerous growth. The patient and the doctor rivet their attention on the *problem*, not on the 95 percent of the person's body which is healthy. Until the cancer is properly addressed, it would hardly reassure the patient—any more than it would reassure a community whose police department was discovered to have a virulent brute or bigot in its midst—if the experts insisted that "you have *just a little cancer*." But even a cancerous individual or agency has a powerful survival instinct to move on—to control, contain, and eradicate the malignancy and resume normal functioning. To do so, the organism or organization will have to depend more than ever on its healthy parts—on its strengths—to pull through the ordeal. When systemic problems have caused the cancer, the eradication therapy often is highly risky and can inadvertently destroy perfectly healthy—perfectly innocent—parts of the afflicted body. Any good copy on the LAPD during 1995 can bear witness to this phenomenon.

The news media and others tend, when cancers such as former Detective Mark Fuhrman are diagnosed, to indulge in irresponsible exaggeration about the extent of the cancer's spread among the 650,000 officers who make up the body of American policing. The truth, we believe (recognizing that different people vehemently hold different views on this subject), is that most police departments face considerably *less* severe management problems than undertaking radical cancer therapy. Their challenge—still a stern one—is to guide the vast majority of well-meaning, *average* cops toward better job performance through the incentive and support systems their department has or can create.

As the caretakers and managers of most of a police department's incentive and support systems, middle managers have a golden opportunity to direct these systems to the quest of building on the organization's strengths. They can do this by deploying these systems to find and showcase the really excellent cops on the payroll and to demonstrate to others how to emulate these high-performing colleagues and secure comparable satisfactions (Klockars 1995). These satisfactions include pride in a job well done and the gratitude of a community that, despite the ugliness of an occasional Mark Fuhrman in the ranks, really does wish to find a basis for admiring and supporting the police (Locke 1995; Flanagan and Vaughn 1995).

❑ *Cheerlead—help officers and sergeants believe they can win.* Part of the environment conducive to community policing—which middle managers can help create, but at least must not taint—is one in which those charged with problem solving are encouraged to believe that they can actually put a dent in the problems they are confronting. If someone believes he or she can't accomplish something, they probably can't. The literature of the ages and of the world's many cultures is full of stories and declarations that have proven helpful in bolstering peoples' belief that one person or just a few people with determination can actually make a difference in huge problems (see, e.g., Comer 1988; Schorr 1988). Margaret Mead counseled: "Never doubt that a small group of thoughtful, committed people can change the world; indeed it is the only thing that ever has." Middle managers could be encouraged to develop their own favorite collection of stories about how people have taken on and won difficult fights and to tell these stories to build confidence in their work teams. As most teachers

Try putting a paper drinking straw through a potato, if you can still find a paper straw anymore these days. It can be done, in the same way that a hurricane or tornado will pick up a piece of straw from a field and drive it several inches into a tree trunk. But you cannot put the drinking straw through the potato unless you do it in one swift motion, which is virtually impossible if you are doubtful and hesitate.

know, the best way to learn things yourself is to try to teach them to others. And as in most things, *practice* can improve one's ability to think positively. Pritchett and Pound's (1995: 35) advice to ambitious corporate managers is: "Practice optimism and positive expectancy. Hope is a muscle—develop it."

The importance of *success stories* in fostering faith in a team's potential should not be underestimated (Armstrong 1992). Delattre and Behan (1991: 551) counsel: "To successfully incorporate worthwhile values into the policies and practices of their departments, police managers must simultaneously be both realists and idealists." Some members of police departments may respond best to inspirational, idealistic exhortations to excellence. In our experience, however, the average, good cop in America will be far more inclined to take a chance on departing from conventional methods when presented with realistic, locally credible examples of other officers who have enjoyed success doing precisely what is being proposed.

Though the point may border on simplistic, by far the most convincing way to instill confidence that difficult missions *can be* accomplished is to *get* difficult missions accomplished. Those examples will inspire others' efforts. Talking and cajoling *ad nauseam* about whether a challenge can be met is an affliction of many work groups. If only such units or teams can be helped to move beyond the blather to getting something practical and worthwhile *done*, they may finally get the taste of success and hunger for more. Where some employees lack what former Chicago Police Deputy Superintendent Mike Spiotto liked to call "finitiative"—finishing what you initiate—the middle manager can advance the overall cause by helping those employees build skills for completing their tasks in a timely fashion.

Whatever pep talks or other motivational techniques a middle manager might personally prefer, it is highly likely that the manager is going to have to reach into his or her bag of tricks at some point in a team's efforts to accomplish the strategic innovations represented by community problem solving. As Kanter (1982: 101) observes about the private corporations she has studied, the initial enthusiasm for a bold, visionary initiative may wane when people "face the tedium of the work." At such a time, the manager's key need is for strong "team-building skills." Two ways to keep team spirit high are "by being persistent and keeping the team aware of supportive authorities who are clearly waiting for results. *** [For example, a] letter or a visit from the big boss can remind everyone just how important the project is" (Kanter 1982: 101).

Sparrow (1992: 50) offers a comforting metaphor for those just embarking on the long voyage toward radical reinvention of American policing: While it takes a long time to turn a large ship, especially if it has great momentum, "a huge ship can nevertheless be turned by a small rudder. It just takes time, and it requires the rudder to be set steadfastly for the turn throughout the whole turning period." Still, he reminds us that the rudder set against the current direction will not enjoy tranquility:

> "[T]here will be constant turbulence around a rudder when it is turning the ship—and no turbulence at all when it is not. [I]f the office of the chief executive is seen as the rudder responsible for turning the whole organization...the lessons are simple. First, the bigger the organization the longer it will take to change. Second, throughout the period of change the office of the chief executive is going to be surrounded by turbulence, like it or not. It will require personal leadership of considerable strength and perseverance" (Sparrow 1992: 50).

Where middle managers join the chief in shouldering the burden of turning the organization—which *does* happen often and, in our view, *must* happen frequently for widespread adoption of community policing—they too must recognize that the waters churning about them will test their fortitude. Where do they find the courage to persevere? Some take inspiration from the bravery of colleagues elsewhere who have cast caution to the wind in order to leave American policing better than they found it. Others may look to a higher authority for the faith to keep on keeping on. "Courage," the saying goes, "is only fear that has said its prayers." And still others have figured out how to psyche themselves up play long-shots. As a sign on the credenza in St. Louis Police Chief Clarence Harmon's office proclaims, "The courageous man has no illusions about the consequences of his acts. He expects the worst" (attributed to Heinrich Heine).

Cheerleading is inherently an act of faith, which by definition means rooting for one's compatriots and believing they can succeed even when we know they may fail. There is plenty of room for realism, sufficient space for skepticism, little room for pessimism, and no place for cynicism in the mind of the cheerleader. In a book review criticizing community policing advocates for being excessively optimistic, Mastrofski (1993: 1) quoted a familiar poem: "'Twixt the optimist and pessimist/The difference is droll:/The optimist sees the doughnut/But the pessimist sees the hole." True enough, if one insists on thinking dichotomously. The well-informed realist, however, knows that his options today include buying doughnut holes!

One of the "worst" circumstances a progressive middle manager may confront is when superiors, including perhaps the chief, merely pay lip service to community policing as a core operating strategy. Where this happens, and the middle managers are themselves the most senior champions for organizational reform within their departments, the middle managers may still be able to make some headway. But there is likely to be a huge amount of white water by *their* rudders. In her empirical study of various kinds of private-sector companies, Kanter (1982: 104) found that some had organizational cultures and structures and senior managers highly conducive to middle-management innovativeness, while others were much more hostile to the "entrepreneurial" middle manager. But even in the latter kinds of companies, she discovered, middle managers completed ambitious, innovative projects, that "seemed to be successful *despite* the system" (emphasis in original; see also Sparrow, et al. 1990: 223).

In their seminal study of problem-oriented policing in Newport News, Virginia, Eck and Spelman (1987: 105) attributed significant consequences to the cheerleading of lieutenants and sergeants:

"[T]hose...who encouraged their officers to look for problems, conduct careful analysis, and look for new and different responses had many officers solving problems. Supervisors who showed no interest in problem solving had fewer officers addressing problems. This seemed to be true regardless of the seniority of the officers involved."

When cheering on officers toward difficult goals, a middle manager can do all stakeholders a great favor by being responsible about the size of the challenge undertaken. Biting off too much of a problem too soon will almost guarantee failure in the immediate problem-solving effort and may demoralize the problem solvers for their next encounter with community problems. Middle managers can help officers and sergeants strike a workable balance in problem selection. The goal is to pick *real but tractable* problems, whose solution will be noticed and useful to those afflicted and to take a pass on *huge* problems that no mortal can get his or her arms around. Humility and pride in making a small difference—leaving the world a *little* better than we found it—are part of the secret to sustainable problem-solving enthusiasm for most police officers whom we know. As Douglas Nelson, executive director of the Annie E. Casey Foundation, said about a human service reform struggle: "It's a narrow band of change that we're looking for, and I think it's crucial that people understand that all the enthusiasm for this program rests—and should rest—on its ability to do this narrow and modest *but critical* thing" (Barthel 1992: 46). Author Jonathan Kozol's counsel about problem selection strikes us as just right: "Pick battles big enough to matter, small enough to win" (quoted in Pritchett and Pound 1995: 26).

❑ *Clarify first-line officers', supervisors', and managers' new roles and reduce mixed messages from the top about those roles*. It is crucial that middle managers *not* believe they are serving the bosses' interests by preserving the status quo. To break from the status quo, officers will become the problem solvers. Their focus will be on action and will be results-oriented. The supervisors will be the coaches. Providing direction, skills development, motivation, and reinforcement will be their calling. The lieutenants are to be the gatekeepers. They must develop the system, resources, and support mechanisms to ensure that the officers/detectives (players) and the supervisors (coaches) can perform to achieve the best results. The officers and supervisors cannot perform without the necessary equipment, resources, and reinforcement.

Such generalized role delineations for various police employees in a community problem-solving regimen can be useful summaries, but a great deal more clarity will be required in order to translate conceptualizations of new roles into operating systems and functional relationships. Somewhat more detail about the roles and characteristics of good problem-oriented supervisors was developed by former Police Executive Research Forum staffers Mike Scott (now chief in Lauderhill, Florida) and Rana Sampson (who went on to serve as a White House Fellow and then as a community policing consultant), in collaboration with Reno, Nevada Deputy Police Chief Ron Glensor (Stephens 1995a: 3). Their delineation has been disseminated by PERF and incorporated in some departmental training curricula (e.g., San Diego Police Department 1994: 39-40 and Charlotte-Mecklenburg Police Department 1995; see also Goldstein 1990: 158; Eck and Spelman 1987: 104-05). A quality POP supervisor, they suggested,

☞ Allows officers freedom to experiment with new approaches.

☞ Insists on good, accurate analysis of problems.

☞ Grants flexibility in work schedules when requests are proper.

☞ Allows officers to make most contacts directly and paves the way when they're having trouble getting cooperation.

☞ Protects officers from pressures within the department to revert to traditional methods.

☞ Runs interference for officers to secure resources, protect them from undue criticism, etc.

☞ Knows what problems officers are working on and whether the problems are real.

☞ Knows officers' beats and important citizens in them and expects officers to know them even better.

☞ Coaches officers through the problem solving process, gives advice, helps them manage their time, and helps them develop workplans.

☞ Monitors officers' progress on workplans and makes adjustments, prods them along, slows them down, etc.

One of the simplest ways for a chief to figure out how to use middle managers to advance community policing would be to think of the imaginative ways such managers could be used if their sole mission in life were to block the successful adoption of community policing—and then simply stop using them in as many of those ways as possible! Eck (1992), tongue firmly in cheek, wrote a handy pamphlet advising the "tradition-bound chief" of "ten things you can do to undermine community policing." The list: "Oversell it *** Don't be specific *** Create a special unit or group *** Create a soft image *** Leave the impression that community policing is only for minority neighborhoods *** Divorce community policing officers from 'regular' police work *** Obfuscate means and ends *** Present community members with problems and plans *** Never try to understand why problems occur *** [and] Never publicize a success."

☞ Supports officers even if their strategies fail, as long as something useful is learned in the process, and the strategy was well thought through.

☞ Manages problem-solving efforts over a long period of time; doesn't allow effort to die just because it gets sidetracked by competing demands for time and attention.

☞ Gives credit to officers and lets others know about their good work.

☞ Allows officers to talk with visitors or at conferences about their work.

☞ Identifies new resources and contacts for officers and makes them check them out.

☞ Coordinates efforts across shifts, beats, and outside units and agencies.

☞ Identifies emerging problems by monitoring calls for service and crime patterns and community concerns.

☞ Assesses the activities and performance of officers in relation to identified problems rather than by boiler-plate measures.

☞ Expects officers to account for their time and activities while giving them a greater range of freedom.

☞ Provides officers with examples of good problem solving so they know generally what is expected.

☞ Provides more positive reinforcement for good work than negative for bad work.

☞ Realizes that this style of police work cannot simply be ordered; officers and detectives must come to believe in it" (Glensor 1994: 8).

Goldstein (1990: 158) offers a similar desiderata. He suggests that "the adjustments [supervisors] have...made in their supervisory methods" to propel community problem solving forward include the following unconventional activities:

"They run interference for their subordinates. They shield them from peer pressure to revert to traditional policing. They arrange for them to have time to work on problems by freeing them from some tasks, providing substitutes, and authorizing flexible hours. They develop familiarity with an officer's beat and the incidents officers are required to handle so that, through frequent discussions, problems that lend themselves to analysis and more effective treatment will be identified. They encourage officers to think in terms of handling problems as the primary unit of work. The most successful encourage officers to plan their daily activities in much the same way as a school teacher develops a lesson plan, asking what problems they are working on and what they are doing about them. They provide officers with the freedom to make broad inquiries—to contact residents, officials, and data sources—and they offer suggestions on appropriate contacts. They confer with officers about the results of their inquiries and press them to explore a problem in sufficient depth by raising appropriate questions. They encourage officers to look beyond traditional responses. And, of course, when analyzing or responding to a problem that requires the approval or involvement of other units of the agency, the supervisor has a special role to play as advocate in acquiring such approval or support."

Skogan, et al. (1994: 6/5-6/17) derive from the Chicago Police Department's early struggles to launch community problem solving a list of management approaches that seemed to work well—and others that worked poorly—for the middle managers who headed the five prototype police districts. Among the unhelpful things some district commanders did were punishing an officer for having his hat off during a frantic search for a cop killer; bean-counting performance evaluations; bad-mouthing problem-oriented policing at roll calls; excessive delegation that became a gone-fishing abdication of the commander's responsibility to help officers with their new challenges; the opposite problem of micromanaging officers' efforts and insisting on meddlesome daily meetings that reflected the commanders' excessive

"Examples of what SAPPS [takes power away from] people:

☹ *Confusion*

☹ *Lack of trust*

☹ *Not being listened to*

☹ *No time to solve problems*

☹ *Bureaucratic office politics*

☹ *Someone solving problems for you*

☹ *No time to work on bigger issues*

☹ *Not knowing whether you are succeeding*

☹ *Across-the-board rules and regulations*

☹ *A boss taking credit for others' ideas*

☹ *Not enough resources to do the job well*

☹ *Believing that you can't make a difference*

☹ *A job simplified to the point that it has no meaning*

☹ *People treated exactly the same, like interchangeable parts" (Byham and Cox 1988: 51, 52).*

need for staying informed of minutia; favoritism to certain officers; ruling by rules (that is, seeking cooperation through fear and intimidation); and using certain units as dumping grounds for problem employees. Among the things Skogan and colleagues found various Chicago commanders doing *right* in the early going were displaying confidence in subordinate supervisors; granting problem "ownership" to officers who are responsible and accountable; and allowing employees in conflict with one another to observe one another's predicaments ("It was a real eye opener," said one of the beneficiaries of this approach).

Whether a department selects exactly the role delineations for supervisors and middle managers sketched by Glensor, Goldstein, and Skogan and colleagues or opts for a somewhat different configuration does not much matter. What *does* matter is that whatever sensible role definitions are developed be *effectively and widely communicated* (and, in time, implemented and their effects examined). There are many methods police leaders can use to get the word out to internal and external stakeholders. The starting place for effective communication, it seems to us, is for the communicator to really believe his or her own message. As the experienced actor said to the nervous novice trying out for his first audition: "The trick to acting is *sincerity*, kid. If you can fake that, you've got it made."

"Examples of what ZAPPS [gives power to] people:
- ☺ *Responsibility*
- ☺ *Trust*
- ☺ *Being listened to*
- ☺ *Teams*
- ☺ *Solving problems as a team*
- ☺ *Praise*
- ☺ *Recognition for ideas*
- ☺ *Knowing why you're important to the organization*
- ☺ *Flexible controls*
- ☺ *Direction (clear key result areas, measurements, goals)*
- ☺ *Knowledge (skills, training, information, goals)*
- ☺ *Support (approval, coaching, feedback, encouragement)*
- ☺ *Resources readily available*
- ☺ *Upward and downward communications"* **(Byham and Cox 1988: 56).**

"It is easy to Sapp. It is hard to Zapp" **(Byham and Cox 1988: 61).**

Assuming the sincerity and mixed-message problems don't exist or are under reasonable control, then a key next step is developing a high-quality communications strategy. A bedrock element of any communications designed to impart good values to police employees should be to avoid the hypocrisy of violating those values in how the officers are treated during the communications or training process. "[O]ne of the great ironies of police human-relations training," Goodbody argues (1995: 14), "has been that while recruits are trained in, and are implored to practice, a humanistic style of policing, the recruits are often intimidated, bullied, and treated as 'pond scum' by those who wield authority over them."

A disheartening example of such apparent hypocrisy in public administration comes not from policing but from the schools arena. The leadership of the Chicago public school system in September 1995 excoriated teachers and principals for going to "posh" retreats about how to run schools more effectively. The criticism parroted a local newspaper's piece of jaundiced journalism "exposing" this "scandal" (Rossi 1995). On the face of the newspaper story, there is nothing posh about the retreat (e.g., teachers were damned for engaging in athletic events at the end of the retreat workday, for eating "steak" at dinner, and for failing to sleep two-to-a-room at a moderately priced hotel). How such a school administration expects teachers to enthusiastically embrace the great values inherent in the "small schools movement" when those values are ignored in treating the teachers as if they are thieves is beyond us. If the teachers failed to focus sincerely on school improvement at the retreat (or while in school), *that*, it seems to us, would be legitimate cause for alarm.

If a department has sufficiently aligned its values, goals and procedures to avoid mistreating those it is trying to teach how to treat the public respectfully, then the agency may be well positioned to take advantage of highly sophisticated (and usually somewhat pricey) communications industry experts. One of the police executives who has regularly employed communications specialists to help create internal and external marketing campaigns to support strategic innovation is New York City Police Commissioner Bill Bratton. While heading the New York City Transit Police, the Boston Police Department, and now the NYPD, Bratton launched a number of high-impact communications campaigns with the assistance of Albuquerque-based public relations expert John Linder.

Another police leader who has sought help from a top-flight communications expert is Charlotte-Mecklenburg, North Carolina, Chief Dennis Nowicki. He engaged New Yorker Tony Schwartz to help plan mass communications campaigns in Charlotte. Schwartz's craft insights, which have won him the admiration of such theorists as Marshall McLuhan, as well as virtually every award the advertising industry has to give over the past 50 years, are exemplified in his books (e.g., Schwartz 1973, 1983).

The kind of public relations tactics that thoughtful, socially-concerned public relations experts might help police departments deploy are exemplified by a recent story in the *Washington Post* that has nothing to do with policing. The front page headline read: "At Upscale D.C. Hotels, Suite Deals for Celebrities: Discounts Often Open Door to Publicity." The story indicated that a few of the nicer hotels in D.C., New York, and elsewhere often give film, TV, music, sports and political celebrities steep discounts to stay in their swankiest suites, in exchange for the publicity that the celebs have chosen to stay at the particular hotel. Most of the hotels portrayed in the *Post* story came off as simply making cold dollar-and-sense calculations and not as particularly warm and fuzzy. The implicit message in the piece, calculated to raise the reader's blood pressure, was that it is economic injustice for those who can most afford to pay their way in society to get such freebies. But one hotel out of the several portrayed, the Mayflower, received a disproportionate number of column inches and a very different image. The Mayflower's explanation for the practice of cheap suites for elites went as follows:

> "Jazz musician [Wynton] Marsalis, for instance, pays $99 a night at the Mayflower...where he often stays, for a suite that would regularly rent for $450, the hotel said. The rate is provided because Marsalis occasionally teaches complimentary jazz appreciation classes at the hotel's adopted school, Thomson Elementary in Northwest Washington" (Faiola 1995: A10).

The best (most crafty and most decent) public relations experts should be able to help police departments pull off comparable feats—helping yourself not through greed and direct expressions of self-interest but through socially-responsible generosity that, in turn, prompts goodwill and other, more tangible, benefits.

Before the leaders of organizational reform are ready to use effective communications methods and specialists to explain the new roles they want played, of course, they have to reach some clarity themselves about what those roles should be. Many of the following suggestions bear on this question. By conceiving workable modifications of middle managers' roles, police leaders will vastly enhance the middle managers' ability to help others perform as requested.

□ *Change the emphasis of middle management from controlling to coaching.* Language choices here abound. The shift may be from "enforcer" to "facilitator"; from "sapper" to "zapper" (Byham and Cox 1988); from "boss" to "leader" (Wall, et al. 1991: 50); from "sodding" to "seeding" (Melrose 1995); from "ordering" to "persuading" (Kanter 1982: 102); from "telling" to "selling" (Kanter 1982: 100); from conventional leadership to "servant leadership" in which one leads by serving the empowerment needs of subordinates (Melrose 1995); and so on. The thoroughly modern middle manager can try any of a litany of "hot" approaches to altering the supervisor-subordinate working relationship, including "pep talks, quality circles..., participative management, job enrichment, quality of work life, closer labor-management relationships" and the like (Byham and Cox 1988: 39). The linguistic list is limited only by one's time to consume the latest shelves of popular management literature. What matters, of course, is not primarily the lingo but the conceptual soundness of the role definition. It must be stated clearly that nobody whom we hear calling for appropriate, radical shifts in the way middle managers relate to subordinates means to jettison entirely the option that middle managers be highly directive in proper circumstances. What is at issue is the general relationship between middle managers and officers being asked to do creative, effective, efficient problem solving with the community.

> **What are some of the elements of good coaching?**
> "1. **Explain [the] purpose and importance of what you are trying to teach.**
> 2. **Explain the process to be used.**
> 3. **Show how it's done.**
> 4. **Observe while the person practices the process.**
> 5. **Provide immediate and specific feedback (coach again or reinforce success).**
> 6. **Express confidence in the person's ability to be successful.**
> 7. **Agree on follow-up actions"** (Byham and Cox 1988: 118).

Wycoff and Skogan (1993: 26), studying Madison, Wisconsin's "experimental police district," asked that unit's middle managers about their self image.

> "The captain and lieutenant report seeing themselves as facilitators of officers' efforts to identify and solve problems. Their goals are to become coaches and teachers who allow and encourage creativity and risk-taking among officers. They have given officers substantial latitude to decide their own schedules, determine their work conditions, and decide how to address neighborhood problems. In other matters, the managers consider the input of employees before making decisions."

□ *Talk sense and act sensibly about empowerment.* A few things need to be clarified. First, nobody means to grant people with the authority to use or threaten deadly force *carte blanche* to clean up Dodge City in any way they like. There is still a powerful set of nonnegotiables about what constitutes constitutional, lawful, principled, and sensible police technique (Delattre 1994). If anyone harbored doubts about the appropriateness of maintaining such nonnegotiables, the abuse-of-force, abuse-of-trust, and abuse-of-decency problems that have scandalized police departments in Los Angeles, New York City, New Orleans, Philadelphia, Atlanta and other cities and towns during 1995 should prove instructive (Herbert 1995a, 1995b; Stephens 1995b; Goldberg 1995).

"Many criminal justice personnel have betrayed the public, destroyed their careers, and devastated their families by persuading themselves that serving a good cause is a license to go beyond the law" (Delattre and Behan 1991: 547). Empower them with care.

Second, superior officers (not first-line personnel) have a crucial role—an obligation they cannot abdicate to help rank-and-file officers understand and comply with these nonnegotiables. As Duck (1994: 112) cautioned, "Empowerment doesn't mean abandonment." If we had to pick one sign to hang on the office door of superior officers who are properly empowering their workers, it would be "the doctor is in," not "gone fishing." Former Madison Mayor Joe Sensenbrenner (1991: 69) confesses he learned a lesson the hard way when he asked middle managers throughout his city government to empower their employees but gave insufficient guidance about the managers' on-going responsibilities. The first-line city workers

> "felt their managers...were simply cutting them adrift and thus setting them up for failure and blame. For their part, the managers believed that all they had to do was make an initial statement of support and invite subordinates to 'call if you have a problem.' Employees, of course, took this to mean 'I expect you to take care of it.'"

Third, a foundational element of community policing is the dissemination of authority to the levels at which it can be intelligently exercised. By that we mean the delegation of decisionmaking power to the levels where well-trained and properly motivated workers can see *first hand and in detail* whether specific decisions would advance or impede the organization's mission. Such devolution of authority is often referred to as empowerment. Sensenbrenner (1991: 65), drawing on the insights of statistician and management guru W. Edwards Deming, illuminatingly describes employee empowerment as entailing a *"license* [to] workers to solve problems" (emphasis added). The licensing concept is intriguing because it encompasses expectations that licenses are granted on application by qualified individuals and that such grants of benefits can be revoked if the licensee ceases to deserve the power.

Empowerment is efficient because the person who previously possessed all the authority no longer needs to attend to every request calling for the exercise of that authority. This benefit is illustrated by the old saw that if a man is hungry and you give him a fish, he will eat for a day. But if you teach him how to fish, he will eat all his life. The fish-a-day approach breeds *dependency.* There are limits, to be sure, on first-line officers' decision options. Nobody who cherishes our system of ordered liberty is suggesting that officers be able to wield their considerable coercive powers in illegal, arbitrary, or inequitable ways. Community policing advocates do not, of course, want to produce rogue cops who "take the law into their own hands." Mark Fuhrman is not community policing's poster child.[13]

---

[13] If this book is read after the painful recollection of Mark Fuhrman passes from the reader's memory, he is the former Los Angeles Police Department detective who was a key prosecution witness in the double murder trial of O.J. Simpson. Fuhrman's blatantly racist, sexist, and otherwise bigoted words (and perhaps deeds) rocked the nation when they emerged during Simpson's trial. His hateful comments had been recorded during a series of

Similarly, police empowerment *of the community* for self-protection also has to be done in a thoughtful and monitored fashion to avoid vigilantism. But community empowerment promises great effectiveness and efficiency in crime prevention and order maintenance. The risk that residents will become excessively dependent on a neighborhood beat officer and monopolize time that others need from the officer is one that causes trepidations among many police chiefs and mayors considering starting community policing. Despite conventional wisdom to the contrary, it *is* possible to tell a community in a respectful way that they don't completely *own* an officer who has been assigned to a permanent beat in their midst. Police could take a cue from mental health and social service workers providing family preservation services. They regularly have to tell clients that the intensive support services cannot last forever. A young social worker asked a trainer one day, "Once you're gone, how do you stay gone, if they [family clients] have your home phone number?" The trainer replied: "You say, 'I'm glad I had a chance to work with you, and now I'm working with other families.'... And that's one of the reasons for hooking them up with ongoing services" (Barthel 1992: 38). The police, too, can look for ongoing nonpolice services to assist members of the public after problem-solving officers have remedied specific conditions. That will lessen the need for the police officer to maintain a docket of community problems that expands to the point where the officer becomes overwhelmed and burns out.

Despite the genuine risks of *excessively* expanding power from police policymakers to police street workers without regard to the fitness for responsibility of the personnel, it seems incontestable that more trust and delegation of authority to officers is needed if a grassroots community problem-solving strategy is to work. Such devolution would free these first-line community workers from the incessant, demoralizing, creativity-constraining "mother-may-I" relationship with superiors that characterizes most traditional police departments. Such empowerment means

> "get[ting] rid of the circumstances that we've gotten into with centralization, where you have to ask questions from somebody else and you get an answer, 'yes, it's okay.' If you know the answer is going to be [that it is] okay to do something, then I don't see the need for asking..." (Nunn 1995: 133).

Moore (1994: 286) suggests that we might think about the needed delegation of authority as "'commissioning' street-level officers to initiate community problem solving efforts." That line of thinking builds on Moore's earlier collaborations with Sparrow, et al. (1990) and Meese (1993). At the Harvard Executive Session on Community Policing, former Attorney General Ed Meese argued, as we have indicated earlier, that more fully enabled first-line police officers should be thought of as having the comparable responsibilities and authority to the Air Force or Navy aviators, who pilot billion-dollar aircraft with the capacity to shape world affairs.

---

interviews conducted over several years with Fuhrman by an aspiring screen writer. With Simpson's acquittal of both murder charges in October 1995, some analysts expressed the opinion that the nation was witnessing a phenomenon well known to civil and criminal trial lawyers—jury nullification. This occurs when a jury ignores the facts and the law as they believe them to be in order to send a message about what they consider a larger question of justice and equity. Speculation abounded that the Simpson jury's way of saying "No more Mark Fuhrmans" was by acquitting Simpson (Adams 1995). Other thoughtful commentators and citizens held different views, including of course the conviction that Mr. Simpson neither committed nor knew who committed the murders (Margolick 1995). Some even alleged in the days immediately following the verdict that competent investigation would disclose that the actual killer of Nicole Brown Simpson and Ronald Goldman was a rogue cop.

We shall sidestep here the possible political and psychological debates over whether one person can really grant another power or whether power may only be seized or developed by the empowered. Kanter (1982: 98) is probably right that it's not either/or: "[C]reative managers are not empowered simply by a boss or their job; on their own they seek and find the additional strength it takes to carry out major new initiatives. They are the corporate entrepreneurs."

One of the biggest mistakes we believe some police middle managers make in thinking about officer empowerment is that they view power as a zero-sum game. Power is thought of as a finite resource; for you to get some means I'm left with less. The notion that power is a pie whose slices can only go to so many mouths to us seems flawed. The key, perhaps, entails recognizing the existence of *informal* power. Suppose a lieutenant or captain orders his officers to follow a detailed 15-step plan for developing the legal and community support needed to shut down a notorious crack house.

> *Some might resist officer empowerment—or community empowerment—on the ground that the ties between superiors and officers or between officers and communities that arise from dependency relationships are positive in keeping people in touch with one another. Perhaps, but the argument brings to mind what a humorist, writing about relationships within families, referred to as "the ties that bind—and gag!"*

It would not surprise most experienced observers of policing if several of the officers who were given this assignment only half-heartedly carried out this "missive from the geniuses upstairs." Although the middle manager had *formal* authority to direct that the 15-step plan be implemented, he'd be lucky if all the officers in the squad contributed significantly to the implementation. But if the middle manager either invited officers to discover for themselves such community problems as the crack house or directed attention to the problem but then invited the offices to frame their own solutions—within the bounds of legality and good judgment—the result is more likely to be an enthusiastic effort to address the problem. And the result is more likely to be officers who are grateful for the trust and respect the middle manager has shown them. Such gratitude is "money in the bank" that the middle manager can draw upon when needed. As such, the middle manager has more *functional* power—more capacity to get things done—than he or she did before delegating authority to subordinates.

Consider the classic Jimmy Stewart Christmas movie, *It's a Wonderful Life*. When George Bailey gives the immigrant Martini couple a home mortgage that the Martinis could ill-afford under conventional credit standards, he greatly empowers the new owners. And how does the Martinis' enrichment affect the George Bailey family and their humble savings and loan when financial woes hit the business? The power bounces back, for the grateful Martinis round up the neighborhood to bail out the savings and loan, and the Baileys have their best Christmas ever.

Not only is it likely that savvy middle managers will be able to increase their own power by investing some of it in interest-bearing subordinates, it is also *important* that middle managers maintain a fair amount of power. The reason is that, as Kanter (1982: 97) says, "powerlessness 'corrupts.'" She explains that power is "the capacity to mobilize resources and people to get things done" and the "lack of power...tends to create managers who are more concerned about guarding their territories than about collaborating with others to benefit the organization." According to Gates (1995: 67), President Ronald Reagan's Secretary of the Navy, John Lehman, had a slightly different take on the implications of power: "Power corrupts; but absolute power is really neat." Kanter (1982: 97) brings us back from Washington Wonderland: "To produce results," she wrote, "power—like money—needs to circulate."

Trying to convert middle managers in Philadelphia into facilitators of community policing during the mid-1980s, the police commissioner had to deal with their historical powerlessness. Greene, et al. (1994: 99) explain that there was

"a need to build managerial confidence and competence among subordinate commanders who were used to being told what to do, rather than being self-directed. For years upper- and middle-level police commanders in Philadelphia had been managerially impotent. Decisions were made at the top of the organization. Middle-level managers were not thinkers and policy makers, they simply carried out policy directives."

"How does the traditional management process feel from the receiving (operation) end? Something like this: 'It all comes from headquarters; it is all imposed; it is all what somebody else has thought up—probably somebody who has time to sit and think these things up.' New ideas are never conceived, evaluated, and implemented in the same place, so they are seldom 'owned' or pursued enthusiastically by those in contact with the community" (Sparrow 1992: 54).

Despite that experience in Philadelphia and similar ones in other police agencies, many police middle managers are ready, willing, and able to accept the challenge that they proactively seek and seize power and opportunities to advance the community problem-solving strategy. They concur wholeheartedly that a strategic shift in policing from an incident-oriented to a problem-oriented approach is warranted, and they have imaginative ideas for how to help first-line officers and the service population collaborate for problem solving. A good number of these ideas entail modifying departmental systems and approaches that otherwise would interfere with efficient, effective implementation of reforms.

What these reform-oriented middle managers need from the chief, other senior police managers, and local government leaders is the support and authorization to take bold—and somewhat risky—initiatives. Some departments have long-standing traditions of middle managers devising and modifying systems and procedures. But in most agencies, for middle managers to have clear license to launch such strategic and cultural changes in their bailiwicks, a devolution of authority will be needed from the chief to the middle managers. Bayley (1994: 279) refers to this shifting of power as organizational "adaptation." This, he suggests, "involves command devolution so that precinct and subdivisional commanders can decide how police resources should be mixed in order to meet the needs of specific areas." The authority that needs to be delegated includes the right to critically examine organizational systems and to take such steps as the middle managers deem necessary and proper to adjust these systems. They may and often will seek advice from others in attempting these difficult and sometimes chancy changes.

A few more detailed examples can be offered of the kinds of systemic changes that middle managers might launch. Enabling cross-shift work is one. If community crime, disorder, or fear problems that surface during a midnight police shift require officers to discuss solutions with people who are available primarily during the daytime (e.g., landlords or the *owners* of 24-hour convenience stores), then middle managers need the authority to revise work schedules.

Depending on the nature, pervasiveness, and persistence of the particular problems at issue, a middle manager may decide to authorize officers generally to decide for themselves when they will work their primary shift and when they will work different hours. This need not prove unduly disruptive so long as the officers make suitable arrangements in advance to ensure that their nighttime workload is covered by colleagues from their own or another shift.

Or a mid-manager might instead devise standard operating procedures that entail multi-shift teamwork. Here officers would not only have partners during their own shift but also would have regular "partners" from other shifts who could collaborate in addressing problems requiring work at different hours of the day. Many other approaches might be imagined. But the middle manager functioning as a proactive facilitator of community problem solving would *not* tell officers needing multi-shift effort to just do the best they can within existing time and resource constraints. The middle manager would instead appreciate the importance of connecting disparate departmental and community resources to the officer concerned about a given problem and would seek innovations in organizational arrangements to facilitate these connections.

"Nobody paints a rented house," Chris Braiden is fond of observing. If ownership—a vital stake in and some control over a problem—is crucial in motivating people, then middle managers should not resist allowing *officers* to "own" community public safety problems. Instead, middle managers should put their creativity into figuring out how *officer* ownership can also enhance *middle manager* empowerment.

☐ *Don't give power away for free.* A middle manager who dutifully empowers his or her subordinates cannot always count on their showing gratitude that bounces additional power back to the middle manager. Police departments have their share of ingrates. As a result,

> *"[A]lthough innovation may begin with an assignment, it is usually one...that is couched in general statements of results with the means largely unspecified"* (Kanter 1982: 99). *Consider a collegiate engineering competition in the Spring of 1995, in which the goal was specified but the means were left to the competitors. The objective was to design a prototype automobile that gets exceptionally good gas mileage. The University of Nevada-Las Vegas team "blew the competition away with a car that got more than 3,000 miles per gallon of gas" (National Public Radio news story, June 19, 1995).*
>
> *Such innovations are not the exclusive province of college whiz kids with pencil protectors in their shirt pockets. Consider, for instance, the inventiveness of seventh grade students in George Hoover's "Exploring Technology" class at Cochrane Middle School in Charlotte, North Carolina. Mr. Hoover challenged them to devise and build—entirely without adult assistance—containers or protective housings in which a raw egg could be placed so that when the container was dropped from a height of about four or five feet onto a hard floor the egg would not break. Several of the kids created successful containers from readily available household materials.*
>
> *Patrick Howley (1995) shared a story of similarly imaginative high school students in another city. Their challenge was to find a way to get a tennis ball up and out of a vertical pipe which was closed at the bottom and had an inside diameter just slightly larger than the ball. The only tools they were given were a hammer, a string, and several paper clips. The students were not allowed to puncture the ball or tip the pipe. The most successful team of youngsters employed none of the tools provided. They floated the ball to the top of the pipe. But how did they do that when they had access to neither a water faucet nor any container of fluid? A hint: Remember when you were in high school—what fluid do you think the kids used?!*

managing well requires knowing one's subordinates sufficiently to know how to cut deals, how to barter. Braiden (1995) commented on the notion of negotiated delegation of power: "Giving pieces of power away at every rank allows a department to get more mileage out of the power. Police managers usually have more power than time to use it." Think about that observation for a moment. Suppose police managers hoarded all their power. Would that be useful to the organization or even the managers? Stephen Wright, quoted by Pritchett and Pound (1995: 20) got to the heart of the matter when he asserted: "You can't have everything. Where would you put it?"

So managers can reduce the clutter of unused power by sharing it. "But," Braiden counsels,

> "don't just give power away—*bargain* over what you will get in return from the person who gets a piece of your power. 'I don't just give you power. I want something back. I want passion and good work.' You share power not because it's a *nice* thing to do but because you have other things to accomplish and you need others to exercise your power to get the job done" (1995).

Unused power has a shelf life and can perish. As Kanter (1982: 97) argued: "[W]hen managers hoard potential power and don't invest it in productive action, it atrophies and eventually blocks achievements." In other words, she said, "[W]hen some people have too much unused power and others too little, problems occur" (*ibid.*).

If the power a mid-manager is stockpiling or giving away is beyond his or her *competence* to use in any event, then while devolution may be a solution, executive development—or realignment of power bases in the organization—seem important to consider as well.

☐ *"Democracy is the worst possible system—except for all the alternatives."* It is safe to assume that when Winston Churchill said that, he could not have imagined police departments disseminating authority to the lowest ranks in quite the way it has been done in Madison, Wisconsin. After all, as Goodbody (1995: 14) observed from his vantage point as a first-line supervisor in the New York City Police Department,

> "Worker participation, and the attendant democratic organizational structures it implies, will prove particularly troublesome to the police bureaucracy. The typical police bureaucracy opposes the very notion of worker participation at the most fundamental levels of the organizational process" (compare Angell 1971 and Sherman 1975).

So, too, is worker or citizen empowerment a relatively foreign concept in many municipal administrations. Consider a malapropism recently uttered by Washington, D.C. Mayor Marion Barry—one of such classic proportions it might have come from former Chicago Mayor Richard M. Daley. (Remember, for example, such Daley news conference gems as "Gentlemen, get the thing straight once and for all—the policeman isn't there to *create* disorder, the policeman is there to *preserve* disorder"?—*Newsweek* 1968.) Mayor Barry responded thusly to a reporter's question about public controversy over citizen involvement in screening D.C. police chief candidates: "This is democracy in action," Barry said. "Everyone knows that I'll make the decision" (Thomas-Lester 1995: A24).

The Madison Police Department is not typical. In that agency's "experimental district," first-line personnel, after reviewing essay responses from middle managers who wished to serve in that district, voted on who would serve as their bosses (Wycoff and Skogan 1993: 22; Kelling and Bratton 1993: 7; Couper and Lobitz 1991; Osborne and Gaebler 1993: 261). In a sense, power was ceded by the "electorate" to the successful candidates, as in most democratic elections. Once selected, the experimental district's captain and lieutenant were delegated considerable authority by the chief: "The captain reports to the Department's deputy chief of operations but has substantial flexibility in running the...district" (Wycoff and Skogan 1993: 23). Madison may test a conventionalist's credulity, but it has been a great "teaching hospital," in Mark Moore's metaphor, for numerous police practitioners from around the nation (see Moore 1994).

Madison also won praise from *Reinventing Government* authors David Osborne and Ted Gaebler (1993: 267) for its "employee evaluation of managers. Although not yet widely used," they write, the technique "is a powerful tool. Supervisors in the Madison Police Department developed a Four-Way Check, which solicits feedback from their employees, their peers, their bosses, and themselves" (see also Goldstein 1990: 159; Roberts 1995; Swan 1991; Santora 1992). The notion of subordinates appraising their bosses is similar to what the Center for Creative Leadership, the business management training institute in Greensboro, North Carolina, calls "360 degree feedback."[14]

Another agency which has begun experimenting boldly with bi-directional performance appraisal is the Evanston, Illinois, Police Department. In September 1995, Chief Gerald Cooper asked all employees in the organization for anonymous replies to a fairly detailed, probing questionnaire about the nature and quality of his leadership and management. Although the initial response rate to this (for Evanston) unprecedented survey was low, the Chief took steps to secure more replies by letting people know that he sincerely wanted the feedback. His interest was not so much in giving himself a report card as chief as in enabling the organization to pick up the pace and depth of its strategic and structural improvements by doing more of the helpful things and fewer of the unhelpful. Gerald Cooper, an attorney (and former legal advisor to the Chicago Police Superintendent), bravely and wisely violated the litigator's cardinal rule: never ask a question to which you don't already know the reply. It is a rule our nation proudly violates every time it trusts the public to cast anonymous ballots in elections of public officials.

The degree of democracy that will prove beneficial in running police department problem-solving units remains to be seen over time. Imaginative and courageous experimentation with various power alignments in different departments will help contribute much needed knowledge about the extent to which democratic processes can strengthen police effectiveness and legitimacy.

□ *Recognize the first-line officer as the department's most valued asset so middle managers can feel the importance of working with "valuables."* While former Madison Police Chief David Couper claimed no monopoly on respect for first-line employees, he enjoyed wide esteem for leading his department to police "as though people matter," in Dorothy Guyot's phrase

---

[14] While the Center, which also has facilities in three other cities, serves primarily managers from Fortune 500 companies, the military sends virtually all brigadier generals through the program; another notable army graduate is retired General Norman Schwartzkopf.

(1991). And the people who mattered to Couper *included* the workforce that he asked to treat the *public* as though *they* matter (see Couper and Lobitz 1991: 2, 6; for additional discussion of the first-line officer as the organization's most valuable resource, see Hickman and Silva 1977).

Middle managers can help make the belief that *people matter* a reality. It's not difficult to find *articulations* of the proposition. They can be read in almost any police agency's mission/values statement, which will be nicely framed and hanging in the chief's office and perhaps printed on a wallet card issued to all personnel. If middle managers can help promote the value of the

"Chiefs should set the stage for departmental articulation of fundamental ideals by showing from the outset that when they speak of selfless service and dedication to the public good, they mean it" (Delattre and Behan 1991: 552).

employees whom Chris Braiden affectionately calls "the grunts," then the problem of role definition for middle managers may become somewhat easier. An agency can say and *really* mean that the patrol division is the backbone of the department and that its officers are the most important people on the payroll. If it does, then—and only then—can middle managers rationally conclude that they are doing really important organizational work when they find creative, better ways to safeguard and improve the company's prize assets.

If a department sincerely believes its most important workers are its first-line people, then it will have to go far beyond simply drawing upside down triangles for organizational charts. It will have to scrutinize officers' and first-line civilian employees' working environments to see how they might be made more conducive to good work. Mastrofski (1993: 10) argues:

> "Officers are craft workers who pride themselves in knowing the tricks of the trade. If the chief wants them to change their methods, he or she must convince them that the new methods will work better and not make their work environment less pleasant. The doubters will cease doubting when their personal work experiences suggest that is so."

Skogan, et al. (1994: 4/6-4/7) list an interesting set of the elements that produce police employee satisfaction. Paying attention to these and related aspects of employees' contentment with their jobs might become an important managerial responsibility for lieutenants, captains and civilian mid-managers. They could take as central parts of their mission studying and assessing the reasons for and impediments to officer job satisfaction. The middle manager could consider it a good day's work if he or she had, consistent with the department's core mission and values, removed an obstacle to police officers' enjoyment of their work.

☐ *Recognize that people are unique and allow middle managers to act on this reality.* Middle managers can make a significant contribution to implementing community policing if they see and can be helped to see that first-line officers (and supervisors and managers) have idiosyncratic, diverse, deployable talents. These people are not interchangeable parts in the police department machine. To be sure, common ground, common language, and common skill bases are all important. But honoring individuality may produce more and better *results* for a problem-solving police department than attempting to fit every police officer into the same size uniform to perform the same size functions.

For instance, in Madison, Wisconsin's experimental police district, Wycoff and Skogan (1993: 32) report that the district was managed in a way that honored officers' individualized talents, preferences and strengths:

> "While officers seemed directed by a clear sense of professional propriety, they did not appear bound by a narrow set of rules or expectations about the way in which work would be done. There seemed to be considerable latitude for individual styles. This tolerance for individuality meant there was not a single line of thought about what the job should be or how it should be done; differences in approach resulted in discussion and analysis rather than conflict and hostility."

A good manager recognizes that people have diverse talents and should be encouraged to excel where they can for the good of the team. The following parable has circulated widely among elementary school teachers and administrators since the late 1960s:

THE ANIMAL SCHOOL
A Fable for School People

The Administration of the School Curriculum with Reference to Individual Differences

Once upon a time, the animals decided they must do something heroic to meet the problems of the new world. So they organized a school.

They adopted an activity curriculum consisting of running, climbing, swimming, and flying. To make it easier to administer the curriculum, all the animals took all the subjects.

The duck was excellent in swimming, in fact better than his instructor; but he made only passing grades in flying and was very poor in running. Since he was slow in running, he had to stay after school and also drop swimming in order to practice running. This was kept up until his feet were badly worn and he was only average in swimming. But average was acceptable in school, so nobody worried about that except the duck.

The rabbit started at the top of the class in running, but had a nervous breakdown because of so much make-up work in swimming.

The squirrel was excellent in climbing until he developed frustration in the flying class where his teacher made him start from the ground up instead of from the treetop down. He also developed "charlie horses" from overexertion and then got C in climbing and D in running.

The eagle was a problem child and was disciplined severely. In the climbing class, he beat all the others to the top of the tree, but insisted on using his own way to get there.

At the end of the year, an abnormal eel that could swim exceedingly well, and also run, climb, and fly a little had the highest average and was valedictorian.

The prairie dogs stayed out of school and fought the tax levy because the administration would not add digging and burrowing to the curriculum. They apprenticed their children to a badger and later joined the groundhogs and gophers to start a successful private school.

The celebration of individuality cuts deeply into policing's paramilitary traditions. And, as noted throughout this volume, there are people, occasions, and circumstances which do *not* call for the celebration of individuality. But consider the strengths and resources a police agency could muster if it simply were more aware of the wide-ranging talent bank which its workforce represents. Scientists tell us that human beings over the course of a lifetime use only a fraction of their brain cells—even high-performers like Albert Einstein. How equally true it is that police departments typically are able to access and deploy only a fraction of the skills its employees have developed in their professional and private lives.

For example, suppose a budget slashing local legislature declines the funds needed to upgrade police skills and equipment. Might there not be an individual working for the police department (maybe a civilian records clerk ensconced in some back office) who, investigation would disclose, has all kinds of private-life talents pertinent to the organization's needs? What if the records clerk is president of the PTA in her daughter's elementary school and a savvy community organizer and fundraiser? What if the department wants to pull together a slick newsletter in collaboration with a community group but the budget won't support hiring a competent graphic artist? Maybe one of the department's evidence technicians is both a first-class photographer and a gifted graphic designer. What if training funds for Spanish-speaking classes are nil? Maybe Officer Hernandez can lead the classes in exchange for some appropriate benefits. The list, happily, could go on and on. Sergeant Linda Black of the Evanston, Illinois, Police Department has done some pioneering work in this regard by conducting a talent-bank survey of her colleagues' hobbies and skills.

If a police department is to develop a culture in which each employee is encouraged to do his or her personal best, the organization will have to confront those rules and systems that treat high-performing officers almost the same as those members of the department who do only enough to stay out of trouble. Such approaches often stem from a misguided effort to be equitable. Kurt Vonnegut, Jr. (1961) wrote a parable called "Harrison Bergeron" about a futuristic society dominated by a desire to have everyone *be* equal. This resulted in a high-tech "handicapping" system, run by Big Brother-like controllers ensconced in remote locations. They ensured, for instance, that those people with the greatest jumping ability had to wear leg weights so they could leap no higher than those with average athleticism. Those with the prettiest faces had to wear grotesque masks. Those with the sharpest brains had electrodes implanted that jolted them out of thought anytime they approached a creative idea. A community-problem solving police department will need to jettison the traditional lowest-common-denominator approach to performance standards and management if it is to achieve meaningful successes (see Klockars 1995).

Getting beyond management methods that find mediocrity acceptable will not be easy. It requires setting reasonably ambitious goals and trying to match employees' strengths and *potential* strengths to the tasks at hand (Chicago Police Department 1994: 137). It may help if we illustrate what we mean by matching talent with tasks, which can be very difficult. Imagine a beat with a constant flow of dangerous calls for service. Wouldn't it be wasteful to assign that beat to an officer who is only moderately good at making high-risk house calls but who is especially gifted at networking and researching to identify community-based resources and partners for problem solving? That officer, left free to do what he does best, could come up with problem-solving assets that would help scores of other officers chip away at the problems causing the constant calls for service.

By the same token, if supervisors and middle managers know their employees well enough to realize that, between two female beat cops, for reasons of personal history, one would probably *exacerbate* tensions and the other would very likely be highly *effective* in response to a particular type of family violence call, then wouldn't rational resource deployment suggest that the department should find ways to use the first officer for other tasks at which she excels and send the second officer whenever possible on the domestic assault calls? Admittedly, the logistical challenges could be a nightmare. But the starting place for discussion is the question whether, *if feasible*, such tailoring would make sense in a problem-solving regime.

Toch (1995a) points out that understanding and dealing effectively with such problems as the "violence-prone police officer" depends on appreciating that, usually,

As Klockars (1995) and others have argued, for police agencies to begin to resemble high-performing organizations, they will need to shift from minimal standards (and minimal compliance) to benchmarking high-performing employees and helping others emulate them. In Madison, Wisconsin, one of the Department's "Twelve Principles of Quality Leadership" is to "[m]anage on the behavior of 95 percent of employees and not on the 5 percent who cause problems" (Wycoff and Skogan 1993: 26).

it is the *intersection* of individual proclivities with organizational values, work settings, and specific situational exigencies that results in performance problems. By properly assigning officers so as to match what they are good at doing with what they are likely to be called on to do, police middle managers could reduce problems for all concerned. This does not mean, of course, that remedial skill-building efforts should not be made while a person is put in a productive, suitable assignment. And creativity is called for on the question of where in the department help may be secured in building skills. For instance, Kelling and Kliesmet (1995) discuss the potential for police *unions* to help strengthen the core competencies of first-line officers. We do not mean to imply, of course, that each and every officer can be matched with *useful*, compatible assignments; a few of them would be better off in a different line of work.

It is important, if possible, to match not only employees' *talents* but also their *interests* to tasks. People tend to do a better and more enthusiastic job on things they care about personally. Working on a *solvable* problem but doing so half-heartedly out of disinterest is of little benefit to the community. By the same token, an employee who cares deeply about a problem but simply lacks the know-how to be effective may win the good wishes and appreciation of a beleaguered public, but the community will hardly be served sufficiently. A number of management and organizational consultants have expressed the importance of helping workers find the area of overlap between their "sphere of concern" (the things they care about) and their "sphere of influence" (the things they have the wherewithal to make happen). That area of overlap represents a high-performing person—doing well at what he or she passionately wishes to do. As Sparrow, et al. (1990: 209) observe, "one of the most powerful spurs to innovation seems to be coupling the ability to solve problems with the opportunity to see them firsthand...." And Braiden (1995) adds that one of the easiest places to locate a sphere of concern is in the realm of self-interest: "Police can solve very complex problems when they are personally the beneficiaries of their actions. They have to care about getting it right."

A middle manager who attempts to liberate police problem-solving potential from the shackles of one-size-fits-all thinking about police employees' roles may run into labor-management agreements that specify seniority bidding and other assignment mechanisms (Chicago Police Department 1994: 137). That middle manager could attempt to convince key stakeholders that rank-and-file employees will find renewed job satisfaction if they work on tasks for which they are best suited and work with people with whom they are most compatible. The objective is to unleash great cops to contribute to the full extent of their talents (Kelling and

Kliesmet 1995), but to protect their weaker colleagues from responsibilities and freedoms they are not able to handle. To be sure, we do *not* favor a system of stifling an employee's growth and broader understanding of people and problems with which he or she has not been familiar. Thus, effective learning by officers about communities with diverse socio-economic and racial/ethnic characteristics is part of the basic knowledge needed to do good police work—traditional or unconventional.

When dealing with employees whose patterned lack of skills earns them the label of "problem employees," a good middle manager in a good problem-solving agency should receive high praise for helping such employees build on their strengths to become more productive and valued members of the organization. As a general proposition, little praise should be accorded to "solutions" that consist of restricting problem employees to doing nothing so they won't cause trouble. Sometimes treating employees as unredeemable is necessary because police departments are unable to terminate some truly bad employees,[15] but at least that should be considered a last ditch solution.

To advance community policing as a strategy, middle managers, while they are valuing individuals' unique abilities to contribute to the police mission, also need to be sensitive to the importance of *teamwork*. We will expand on this point in the next segment of this chapter. To be sure, some great problem solving by some great problem solvers best happens as a solo effort—and it should not be squelched. Nevertheless, the experience to date around the country generally suggests that far more good problem analysis and resolution arise out of team efforts.

A final thought on the issue of respecting the diverse (and often untapped) talents of police department employees: Middle managers can provide an important service by being vigilant for *mixed messages* about police employees' potential to contribute uniquely. George Kelling has been very helpful over the years in reminding us, through a series of publications and presentations, about the dangers of being controlled by our own metaphors. Police officers are not "troops" engaged in military battles. They are not fungible, faceless combatants in wars against drugs, gangs, violence or other social ills (Weisburd, et al. 1988: 32). This is one of the reasons why good police leaders generally oppose the use of National Guard and other military units to assist local police with street crime problems. When a well-trained, high-performing police officer gives what President Lincoln called "the last full measure of devotion," the loss is of an individual with special talents, capable of being harnessed in unique ways, for reducing the community's problems.

☐ *Develop powerful incentives for teamwork.* As noted above, teamwork is a core

---

[15] Chicago's latest dilemma is instructive. Headlines in October 1995 reported Police Superintendent Matt Rodriguez's dismay that he can't legally fire cops who he learns are affiliated with Chicago street gangs. In many respects, these gangs are the functional equivalent of the syndicate mobsters of yesteryear. The Department "has always had officers who join for criminal activity," said Chicago Alderman and former cop William Beavers. "As long as we've had the Mafia, we've had members of the Mafia on the Police Department" (Oclander 1995c: 12). The investigative news report claimed the gang allegiance of a few sworn Chicago personnel was so strong that officers connected with rival gangs refused to stand on the same side of the room at roll call in one patrol district (Oclander 1995a, 1995b, 1995c; WBEZ 1995). Goldstein (1995) acknowledged that determining the optimum trade-off between fostering police integrity and safeguarding officers' First Amendment freedom of association is not easy. He warned, however, that more attention needs to be paid to the legal and contractual obstacles that seem to preclude many chiefs from firing truly bad (but not felonious) police officers.

"technology" of community problem solving. Middle managers who wish to contribute powerfully to building organizational infrastructures and work methods that foster effective and efficient problem identification, analysis, and solution will place high priority on describing and demonstrating the benefits of collective action. To Seattle Chief Norm Stamper (1995a), teamwork should not be an *option*—it should be "required as a condition of employment."

The reason Stamper and others insist on team effort is not because teamwork is *nice* or fulfills some other ethereal needs. It is because teamwork is power-enhancing. A well functioning team is stronger than the sum of its parts. As Byham and Cox (1988: 148) put it, "A Zapped team is more productive than a group of Zapped individuals." Some of the ways in which teams gain in efficiency, effectiveness, and legitimacy are illustrated in several of the scenarios presented in the preceding chapter. A number of those teams not only crossed unit boundaries *within* police agencies but encompassed cops and community residents and business people.

Citizens unfamiliar with police culture— and the petty jealousies, turf battles, and other infighting that can occur among employees of the same police department—may be surprised that it is often difficult to get a number of cops across different units of the agency to collaborate on a problem-solving effort. A monolithic view of the police world might presume pervasive concurrence and even conspiracy among cops against outsiders. But those who appreciate how hard intra-agency collaborations can be might resonate to a wisecrack made by Chicago Conspiracy Trial defendant Abbie Hoffman. During his arraignment hearing in the aftermath of the riotous Democratic National Convention, Hoffman looked incredulously at federal Judge Julius Hoffman and declared: "Conspiracy?! We couldn't agree on lunch!"

Middle managers can find a variety of clever ways to help their subordinates understand their interdependence and appreciate one anothers' particular contributions to team efforts. One of the most important ways is for middle managers to practice what they preach. If the model presented is *un*collaborative every time officers and first-line supervisors watch their lieutenant or captain deal with other lieutenants or captains, the "speed" of the boss, as we said earlier, may well become the speed of the crew. Commenting on her study of successful innovation led by private sector middle managers, Kanter (1982: 102) concluded: "The few projects in my study that disintegrated did so because the manager failed to build a coalition of supporters and collaborators." Says Chris Braiden (1995): "We need to need each other. The middle manager must be perpetually bringing the pieces together."

Earlier we allowed the possibility that great problem solving can, at times, be a solo venture. Some people simply do their best, most creative work on their own. While it would be silly and hypocritical for middle managers to encourage officer creativity and then dictate in minute detail the methods to be used in analyzing and dealing with problems, we expect that it will generally be wise for middle managers to counsel collective thinking and action. In private industry, Kanter (1982: 100) argues,

> "the most successful innovations [by middle managers] derive from situations where a number of people from a number of areas make contributions. They provide a kind of checks-and-balances system to an activity that is otherwise nonroutine and, therefore, is not subject to the usual controls."

Middle managers who, through team-building and other techniques, unleash employees' strengths and safeguard their Achilles' heels, foster an environment where workers probably excel at tasks the individual middle manager cannot perform as well. This should pose no problem for a self-confident middle manager who sees no reason to compete with the team members (several of the heroes of the stories in the previous chapter illustrate this point). It is important, if possible, that the middle manager be able to *model* constructive relationships with his or her own *superiors*. In a work environment in which "a lockstep chain of command makes it dangerous for managers to bypass their bosses" (Kanter 1982: 104), the middle manager may not be able to show *through example* that it is acceptable and good, in various ways, for the team to be able to do many things the coach cannot.

☐ *Help subordinates improve by building on their strengths*. Implicit in both of the preceding subsections—treating people as individuals and creating multi-talented teams—is the point that, just as middle managers should be helped to improve through a focus on their strengths, they, in turn, should show the same respect for their sworn and civilian subordinates. This is not just about *kindness*, of course; building on strengths is a sounder *tactic*, in our view, than beginning with deficiencies.

If organizational changes are to be pursued by tactically building on the strengths of first-line personnel and their immediate supervisors, this implies that middle managers' and supervisors' emphases should shift from "catching officers doing things wrong" to helping officers do *useful* things *right* (Weisburd, et al. 1988: 44-45). To catch cops doing things right requires, of course, clarity about what is right. Performing community problem-solving police work *right* means doing things that are effective, efficient (protective of scarce police and community resources), and within values—not necessarily doing business as usual (Kelling and Bratton 1993: 10).

> *"Weak-spot management means that problems, not successes, get attention. Jealousy and competition over turf kill praise from peers and sometimes from bosses"* (Kanter 1982: 104).

If regularly spotting jobs well done is to become part of the middle manager's function, his or her shift in role will be large—as large as the shift required of first-line supervisors, whom commentators have suggested need to come a long way. The conventional expectation is that sergeants in patrol units

> "know where every unit under their supervision is operating. They must check on them personally at least once during a tour (signing the officer's memo book to record the check); report instances in which their behavior deviates from the regulations; monitor the calls to which the officers are dispatched; and respond personally to oversee the police response in a wide range of situations" (Weisburd, et al. 1988: 35).

It is little wonder that the standing joke in New York City for years had been that, when a sergeant encountered a police officer in the field and asked what the officer was doing, the "correct" answer was the reassurance, "Nothing, Sarge, nothing." As Goldstein (1990: 157) puts it, "Most officers do not see their sergeants as sources of guidance and direction, but rather as authority figures to be satisfied.... Given this perspective, the less an officer sees of his or her immediate supervisor, the more pleasant is the job."

There are several reasons to spend significant amounts of time catching cops doing things right. At the outset, it should be clear, however, that the purpose is *not* to stop supervisors from detecting and pointing out subordinates' flaws, mistakes, and needs for improvement.

One basic reason for searching out successful work is that perhaps then people will do more of it. Another reason is that, if an employee needs to improve in some ways, catching him or her excelling at something else is not a bad way to begin the conversation. As a poster hanging over a friend's desk says, "Nothing improves my hearing like praise." Mark Twain announced: "I can live for two months on a good compliment" (quoted in Spitzer 1995). Once a coach has established and acknowledged that officers are doing some specific things well, he or she has identified a solid launching pad for the next leap. The talents the employee has displayed and the manager has praised may help illustrate that the employee is capable of meeting high performance standards. The boss' praise can also help forge a trusting relationship between the manager and subordinate.

One could argue that heavy emphasis on searching for and deploying *strengths* can obscure the importance of capitalizing on employees' "teachable moments." Such moments are relatively rare opportunities for dramatic growth—when people are ready to change or learn something new that they previously would have resisted. In a personal or family counseling context, teachable moments often arise when people realize that their current way of living does not mesh with their basic values—with the "things that are important" to them (Barthel 1992: 22). Or a teachable moment may arise when someone "hits bottom" because he suddenly sees clearly that his approaches to some major personal or occupational obligation simply are *dysfunctional*. Moore and Stephens (1991a: 109-10) discuss why organizations tend to avoid making changes they know are needed until bankruptcy hits: "[T]he expectations and commitments that so long frustrated change are liquidated by the overwhelming fact of failure."

Even if major personal or institutional change requires a significant crisis, however, the path *back* to proficiency from a shattering realization may often still entail identifying what the individual or organization is good at. Again, the tactical reasoning is that the strength(s) provide a place for self-esteem and know-how to get a toehold. Timing is crucial in trying to productively use the window of opportunity opened by a crisis. To take full advantage of a teachable moment, someone has to provide appropriate "technical training" in a timely fashion—before the moment has fleeted (Byham and Cox 1988: 152).

Pointing out cops and civilian employees doing things well (such as people who exhibit expertise and commendable effort in community problem solving) also provides ready exemplars for *other* workers. This is one way for middle managers to illustrate the strengths they will be looking for in their teams. The high-performing employees become the organization's benchmarks for excellence (Klockars 1995; Toch, et al. 1975). Sometimes it is not so obvious how, in aspects of police work traditionally monitored through "weak-spot" approaches (Kanter 1982: 104), middle managers might turn the tables to learn from good behavior. Police misuse of force is an illustration. Normally, *proficient* police decisionmaking concerning whether and how much force to use is a nonevent in the life of a police department—unless it involves a death-defying shootout in which the good guys didn't get shot and the bad guys did. But proficient police decisions about force—including decisions *not* to use it—need not be officially invisible. One might debrief officers who *averted* serious force when the circumstances would have justified its use (Scharf and Binder 1983; Fyfe 1989; Geller 1985; Geller and Scott 1992; Geller and Toch 1995). The obligations to identify and address *substandard* decisions about use of force remain, of course, for a host of good reasons; but we believe a better balance between finding flaws and modeling proficiency would be beneficial to police organizations and their service populations.

How can middle managers help create opportunities for employees to learn from the craft skills of talented problem-solving colleagues? One way is by organizing police officer peer assistance workshops (see Kelling and Kliesmet 1995; Toch 1995a; Toch and Grant 1991; and Toch, et al. 1975). Another approach is less formal "buddy systems" in which peers give one another tips about how to do their work more effectively and more enjoyably. These methods can produce real accomplishments in overcoming skill deficiencies, developing expertise, and emphasizing more generally the organizational value of continuous improvement. If peer mentoring and other interactive learning among first-line workers are done correctly, such activities will help police agencies build on their internal strengths so as to better handle community problems.

In the delicate enterprise of asking officers to candidly discuss their own weaknesses and insecurities (even if behind closed doors with peers), it is crucial that bosses be especially sensitive to sending mixed messages. Although such messages could be sent in myriad ways, one of the simplest and most pervasive ways to instill doubt about the value of the peer assistance process is to conclude the meeting with the stock comment, "OK, now let's get to *work*" (see Spitzer 1995). The time officers have just spent *was* work—and important and hard work at that. Many commentators have pointed out the unhelpful mixed messages sent by classifying officers as "*in* service" while they are randomly patrolling and "*out* of service" while they are helping citizens. Similarly, failing to honor the *work* being done by officers struggling to understand and overcome their professional weaknesses in peer or other types of training is not conducive to the strategic reforms implied by community problem solving.

☐ *The power of trust to inspire trustworthiness.* Full-time professional police forces were established during the mid-1800s in the United States largely because the public had more distrust about their neighbors than time to watch them. So if cops were hired at least partly to be suspicious of members of

> *"Traditional command and control relationships between managers and their employees create suspicion and resentments" (Whitney 1994).*

the community, it is no wonder that modern police forces are staffed amply with untrusting people. But when an officer's active eye for base motives and anti-social behaviors diminishes his or her ability to find the good in people, isn't it harder for the officer to see them as potential allies and collaborators? Middle managers in particular have been saddled with responsibility in many traditional police organizations for assuming or fearing the worst about their subordinates. Under community problem solving—and total quality management (TQM) and other related approaches to treating employees well so they will treat customers well—managers need to know how to use trust of subordinates to encourage them to rise to hoped-for levels of trustworthiness (Weisburd, et al. 1988: 44; Whitney 1994; Yates 1994; Chicago Police Department 1994: 142).

A manifestation of distrust within organizations that has core significance for our present purposes is the presumption by bosses that middle managers are inevitably obstacles to change, which can become a self-fulfilling prophecy (Kelling and Bratton 1993: 6, 7, 10). Don't many people, whether school children, police officers, or voters, often rise or sink to the level key people in their lives expect from them? New York City officers participating in the "CPOP" pilot testing of community policing "indicated that the trust placed in them by the sergeant was a factor in motivating them to behave in a way that justified that trust" (Weisburd, et al. 1988: 44). Said one officer, "We're not going to be screwing up because...it would be a point against [my sergeant]...that he's failing to supervise properly...." (*ibid.*). One of the more dramatic things that some public and private-sector organizations do to try to reverse corporate cultures of distrust is to "throw out the policy manual..., the time clocks and things like approval of expense accounts" (management advisor John O. Whitney, quoted in Yates 1994). "If you can't trust an executive, who must make business decisions worth millions of dollars, to turn in an accurate expense account," opines Whitney, "then something is wrong" (*ibid.*). Similarly, if well-trained, well-armed police officers who necessarily do much of their work beyond the sight of bosses are indiscriminately treated by their employers like untrustworthy kids then, as Whitney says, "something is wrong."

As we have suggested elsewhere in this book, the risk of credulousness—*recklessly* trusting people who are undeserving of trust—is real, and some middle managers will need help in learning how to avert the risk. While they are learning to trust in an informed way (Chicago Police Department 1994: 142), middle managers will make honest mistakes, for which they must be forgiven and from which they must be enabled to learn positive lessons.

Although it may not be fair, the immutable reality seems to be that it is harder to establish trust than to destroy it. Spitzer (1995) suggests that "building trust is like filling up a bucket drop by drop. It takes a lot of time to fill the bucket. However, a single act of dishonesty or perceived dishonesty can overturn the entire bucket and spill out the trust so painfully accumulated."

□ *Give credit where it's due.* This is simple to say but sometimes really hard to do, particularly in an organizational culture where the work of subordinates is subsumed under the ego trips of superiors. When middle managers have genuinely led or facilitated important work by their teams, they deserve and should receive their due share of the kudos. But it is incumbent on the middle

> *To keep a team functioning and loyal to the leader, middle managers can make sure all the team members become "heroes" when the leader explains the team's success to senior officials (Kanter 1982: 95; 1983).*

managers to be sure that higher-ups and other stakeholders (such as the community at large and politicians) understand the credit owed to the particular officers, civilian employees, neighborhood residents and others who did the bulk of the work (Eck and Spelman 1987: 105). "The middle manager's main task," urges Braiden (1995), "is to create heroes." As in other instances, the valuable middle manager will be sensitive to striking a constructive balance between singling out exemplary individual effort and rewarding teamwork and cooperation.

Giving credit to others has tactical as well as virtuous benefits. As we argued in our earlier discussion of empowerment, giving something up (here, credit for attainment) often results in gratitude and enhanced power reflecting back to the source. And there is much truth, we believe, in the sign President Ronald Reagan is said to have placed on his Oval Office desk: "You can accomplish all kinds of things if you don't insist on taking credit for them." (If credit were given for the quote, it would be go Mark Twain—Percy 1995.)

   ☐ *Find a suitable place to file the rule manual.* Lt. Gary Briggs (1995: 138) tells the following tale of his own agency, but he could have been talking about any of thousands of departments. He reports that

> "[t]he St. Paul Police Department manual is 700 pages long.... It's one of those handy documents that the officers throw in their back pocket and take with them out in the squad car so they can answer questions. Nobody reads the damn thing. The only time anybody ever looks at it is when they're taking a promotional exam. What is a 700-page manual going to do for anybody? You know what 90 percent of it is? Ninety percent of it is mistakes that cops made, so we developed a policy so nobody else would ever do it. *** The St. Paul Police Department has probably a half dozen of what I'd call 'serious problem employees,' and we've created a 700-page document to try and control those people, and it doesn't work. *** Why create a document for six people? Why not create a document for the other 524 cops out there to...enable them to become creative and do some interesting things, to provide some guidance and support?"

Where in the office of the prototypic competent, mid-level, community policing change agent would Lt. Brigg's file the rule manual? Where is it in *his* office? Shifting from rule-based, "gotcha" management to value-based, developmental management, while retaining only essential rules, is one of the hardest challenges facing the turn-around

> *Sometimes, faithfulness to core values means letting go of presumptions about the right way of doing business. Or, in the words of a favorite bumper sticker, "My karma ran over my dogma."*

artists in American policing (Kelling, et al. 1988; Wasserman and Moore 1988). Among other things, value-based, continuously improving organizations *expect* and *want* their loyal, talented employees to sometimes break the rules to honor the values (Kelling and Bratton 1993: 10).

   An example or two: If protecting drivers and pedestrians from accidents during religious holidays can be done best by allowing them to park near houses of worship in otherwise illegal parking places, while police stand guard to ensure safety during the services, then bend the rules (Delattre and Behan 1991). If, as Officer Mike Shep of the Evanston Police Department discovered, one can raise funds from local businesses to support an otherwise unaffordable but highly valuable bike patrol program, and if the funding solicitation needs to be written on Department letterhead in order to be credible, then why not, as Gerald Cooper did, bless the unprecedented use of his stationery by a first-line employee? Not all police chiefs *would* approve of officers using their letterhead, of course, and professionals could responsibly disagree about best practices here. The illustration stands for the more general point that the pep talk to officers about breaking rules to honor missions will fall flat if officers see that every time they bend a rule that protects managerial prerogatives they are admonished. Similarly, middle managers will only step up to the challenge of finding and repealing or responsibly disregarding counterproductive rules if they are *thanked* for their organizational loyalty in doing so.

   A voice from the belly of the bureaucracy comments:

"The most difficult task in making the transition to community policing will involve changing the work habits and attitudes of police officers who have learned to adapt to and cope with a punishment-centered bureaucracy. Every new cop has had a veteran tell him, 'Kid, on this job the less you do, the less civilian complaints you get, the less some D.A. is trying to indict you, and the less trouble you get into with the job.' What's disturbing about this, and something police departments should contemplate, is that it's actually pretty good advice—not from a motivational, community service or law enforcement perspective, but from a how-to-survive-being-a-cop perspective. If community policing is to be effective, it will have to confront this attitudinal outgrowth of the police bureaucracy head on" (Goodbody 1995: 12).

Sign on the boss' door: "The flogging will continue until morale improves" (anonymous).

Eschewing a reign-of-terror approach to leadership and management does not, of course, mean that procedural guidelines should all be fed to the paper shredder. (Consider, however, the chain department store, reported by Spitzer 1995, which told its workforce: "Rule number one is to use your good judgment in all situations; there are no additional rules.") The procedure manual, "[i]nstead of an instrument of the disciplinary process, brought into play against wayward officers, ...needs to become a fount of knowledge, guidance, and inspiration for patrol officers: a tool rather than a master" (Sparrow, et al. 1990: 213). This facilitative approach is what many good supervisors and managers have done instinctively even under conventional policing regimens. As Goodbody (1995: 12) notes,

> "the truth is that the most effective supervisors rarely rely on their ability to formally punish people. *** Those who rely on the power to punish as the basis for their authority are usually the least effective at motivating people and accomplishing objectives."

□ *Challenge middle managers to facilitate and assure quality.* There are some who doubt that the words "quality" and "government bureaucracy" belong in the same sentence, unless it's a joke. Former Madison, Wisconsin, Mayor and TQM maven Joseph Sensenbrenner caught the spirit of that skepticism. "Applied to toast," he deadpanned, "the government approach to quality would go, 'You burn, I'll scrape'" (1991: 65).

Jokes aside, quality assurance could be a key middle management role for many essential operational and infrastructural aspects of community problem solving. Obvious examples include quality problem identification, analysis, response, and assessment of results (Couper and Lobitz 1991; Goldstein 1990: 93-94). "One of the best ways I've found to help our middle managers understand what is now expected of them," reports Cheektowaga, New York, Police Chief Bruce Chamberlin, "is to introduce the principles of...TQM." Chamberlain's reasoning is bolstered by Chris Braiden's experience, which is that "most middle managers focus too much on efficiency—have we got the right paper work?—and not on effectiveness—are we delivering quality services to the public?" (Braiden 1995). Acquainting middle managers with the TQM movement, and how the infrastructure of an organization is critical to its producing high-quality services or products, may help middle managers who need to shift their focus from efficiency for its own sake to those efficiencies that advance effectiveness (Wycoff and Skogan 1993).

❑ *Freedom to fail forward.* Many trees have been felled and many barrels of ink squirted to print books on this topic. The tomes counsel managers to tolerate honest mistakes so that subordinates will take chances to invent better ways of doing business. Fans of well-performing organizations and of clean air hope the trees haven't died in vain. Sports fans may want to pause to remember that the best batters in professional baseball get inducted in the Hall of Fame by *striking out* nearly 70 percent of the time. If you don't swing the bat, you don't even stand a chance of getting hits. Lots of key people in the life of a batter can instill doubt or build confidence in his or her ability to swing the bat.

Fort Worth, Texas, Police Captain Randy Ely observes that an administrator has

"to know that there are going to be some mistakes made along the way. What's important is to have a safety net there to catch the officer when he falls, and to remember not to be overly punitive when he makes a mistake. Rest assured that when you empower employees to be problem solvers at the line level, well intentioned mistakes will occur. However, the positive things that are generated by this empowerment will more than offset these errors" (quoted in Community Policing Consortium 1995: 3).

There can be little question, given the high degree of difficulty of many officers' "POP" projects, that the problem solvers "must have the freedom to start over, without fear of censure, when a response does not work" (Eck and Spelman 1987: 104). Middle managers as coaches can do much to help

Sparrow, et al. (1990: 214) suggest that "it is principally middle managers who have routinely quashed new ideas; it is they who must embody the new organizational value 'never kill an idea.'" Never is a bit absolute. Just as we don't wish middle managers to stifle imagination by prematurely ridiculing cops' ideas and suggestions, neither do we think it desirable for middle managers to button their lips if they have good evidence that a recommended course of action is not only silly but potentially costly in human harm, tangible resources and departmental reputation. Under such circumstances, the craft skills called for are diplomatic—thank the person for thinking about how to improve police work but save them from the folly of an ill-conceived idea.

their teams cope with frustration and failure—to see such developments as *temporary setbacks* on the road to success or, as Norm Stamper (1995a) prefers, "as necessary steps to success." The distinction Chief Stamper makes is not merely semantic. If one defines the enterprise, business or work that one does as involving risk taking (e.g., investing in the stock market, publishing books, or providing emergency medical services), then it follows that both success and failure are natural, predictable parts of the job. Edsel stock, lousy book reviews, patients who succumb in the ER and other failures are all regrettable. The only *sure* way to avert them all the time, however, is to stop doing the work. "Progress always involves risks," offered Frederick Wilcox. "You can't steal second base and keep your foot on first" (quoted in Wall, et al. 1991: 2).

One of the hardest things middle managers in police agencies have to do to permit strategic innovation is protect officers from organizational and political recrimination and scapegoating. The ridicule and fingerpointing may well come from the middle managers' bosses, and it may be much easier for a middle manager to stand in the crowd watching a subordinate led to the guillotine than to risk having his or her own neck placed on the block. Sparrow, et al. (1990: 213) assert that "[i]t is *only* [middle managers] who can break the link between failure and recrimination on an organizationwide scale. They must protect their officers from the political effects of legitimate failure" (emphasis added).

To be sure, failing is not inherently virtuous. Indeed, in *policing*, it can be a real problem, for lives, the livability of communities, and liability are at stake. But since failing is *inevitable*, the virtue lies in *learning*—efficiently, effectively, and enduringly—from the setbacks (Kanter 1982: 96; Chicago Police Department 1994: 142). The virtue, as someone said, lies in "failing forward." As Eck and Spelman (1987: 104) suggest, "[r]ecognizing and learning from mistakes [are] the best way[s] to keep from repeating them." It is easy, of course, to say that one should learn from mistakes. But middle managers might do well to reflect on *what* their work teams should learn from particular kinds of errors. Perhaps as important is what lessons they should *not* draw from the same mistakes. Mark Twain captured the last point nicely:

> "We should be careful to get out of an experience only the wisdom that is in it, and stop there, lest we be like the cat that sits down on a hot stove lid. She will never sit down on a hot stove lid again, and this is well; but she will never sit down on a cold one either" (quoted in Wall, et al. 1991: 53).

Police work teams might find it informative and helpful to spend a hour sometime candidly and nonjudgmentally listing some of the more memorable overgeneralizations they have come across during their careers. The exercise might be repaid in more precise, more tactically and strategically useful after-action reviews of efforts to address community crime, disorder, and fear problems.

Rewarding or at least not punishing honest mistakes—and honesty about making them—is centrally important if employees are to take the grant of "freedom to fail" seriously. A manufacturing company in the St. Louis area, Wainwright Industries, makes automobile and airplane parts. It uses huge metal presses to stamp the parts out of a multi-ton roll of quarter-inch thick steel. Letting the roll run out is not a good idea. The press will crash, and the operator will have about an $800,000 mistake on his or her hands. One day on the shop floor a supervisor, who noticed that the operator of one press had let his roll of steel nearly run out asked the press operator: "How do you know when to shut down the press and get a fresh roll of steel?" The press operator replied: "Damned if I know." The supervisor suggested the employee turn off the machine and come with him. What ensued, after the convening of a peer review committee within a day or two, was the committee's decision to give the press operator a minor *award*. It was an award not for ignorance but for honesty. Suppose the punch press operator had said what many cops might have said to a sergeant under analogous circumstance (e.g., the sergeant asks "Officer Jones, do you know how to disarm the Uzi you seized in the drug raid?"). The answer might have been, "No problem boss, I've got it under control," even though nothing could be farther from the truth. By owning up to his lack of knowledge, the Wainwright employee saved the company a costly machine repair and loss of productivity. (Readers interested in further discussion of such analogies may enjoy a story told by Armstrong 1992: 122-24 about a punch press operator in another company.)

Mistakes in the world of people who wear guns and badges may often be more consequential than mistakes by punch press operators, gardeners, house painters, wedding cake bakers and many others. Still, police middle managers must help develop a rational sense of perspective about which mistakes are truly significant—and may require prompt and intense remediation—and which mistakes are minor and can be taken in stride or, even celebrated. As Ed Harris (1995a: 80) suggests, failure to distinguish between the "trivial" and the "tragic" in any human endeavor can cause needless anguish:

> "It is possible to think that long hard winters shouldn't be happening. Or that planes shouldn't be late. That everyone should love you. This is a world of changed schedules, wrecks, accidents, forgotten appointments, broken buttons, and children not doing what they said they would. It's a mistake to think these tragic. Tragic is when you die after living a wasted, unhappy life."

Mother Nature's fury—in hurricanes, earthquakes, floods, droughts—painfully helps us distinguish really important problems from evanescent irritations. The havoc she can wreak makes it unmistakably clear that, almost regardless of mankind does, the forces of nature will have the last word. Or, as Pritchett and Pound (1995: 2) put it, "the world bats last."

For an organization to keep its sense of perspective and "fail forward"—to recognize and learn from grand and small mistakes—there must be some methods by which institutional knowledge is amassed and passed along across work units and over time. Otherwise, everyone is consigned to learning every lesson the hard way, or at least is dependent on unpredictable, *ad hoc* opportunities for learning from others' valuable mistakes. "One difficulty here," observes Sparrow (1992: 55), "is that police officers have to be persuaded that it is helpful, rather than harmful, to record their failures as well as their successes—and for that they will need a lot of reassurance."

Aside from the question of whether officers want the lessons they have learned to be recorded, there is the issue of who is going to do the dreaded paperwork—or data entry. This applies even to recording "good news" stories. Joachimstaler (1995: 5) suggests that a role for middle managers with time on their hands might be to function as "project recorders" for problem-solving officers.

> *"[C]overing up or perpetuating failures must be perceived as a serious breach of responsibility"* (Kelling and Bratton 1993: 10).

❑ *Promote innovation.* If middle managers have helped create an organizational environment in which falling short of ambitious aspirations is understood as a necessary and proper learning opportunity, then these middle managers may have developed the credibility to promote innovation.

"Innovation" is a word tossed around liberally. Whatever it means, we know it's a good thing, and so at every possible juncture we label our efforts and the efforts of people whom we like as "innovative." Kanter (1982, 1983) distinguishes excellence in applying traditional methods within traditional strategies ("basic accomplishments") from "innovative accomplishments." Kelling and Bratton (1993: 7) distinguish project or tactical innovations (within current strategy) from strategic innovations. The Chicago Police Department (1994: 109) noted three of the characteristics it hopes its employees will incorporate as they innovate in furtherance of community policing. To the CPD, a desirable police innovative accomplishment

"(1) produces a substantial improvement for the community;
(2) reduces police workload; or
(3) improves relations with the community."

We might add to that list that the accomplishment—

(4) strengthens the capacity of the police, community, and other collaborators to solve future problems (Kanter 1982, 1983); or
(5) "enriches the work of line officers" (Kelling and Bratton 1993: 9).

It is not essential that every innovation meet each of these standards, of course, but attempting to meet as many as possible helps to ensure that the innovation is not achieved at the expense of other important organizational commitments.

A core technology of innovation is soliciting and making use of suggestions. Middle managers can measurably advance community problem solving if they can persuade officers and sergeants to make frequent, thoughtful suggestions for better ways of policing and of supporting policing. Many organizations in the public and private sectors have had suggestion boxes as long as there have been organizations and boxes. The challenge in filling the box is finding the keys that open the minds and generosity of employees to look for and recommend things that could be done better in the workplace.

"[M]id-managers must be real managers, not overseers. The focus of overseers is control. Overseers know best and their purpose is to ensure that their instructions are followed. Managers view their responsibilities differently. Their task is, or ought to be, to develop personnel who will be free to innovate and adapt—break the rules if necessary on behalf of the values of the organization. Thus, the core competency of managers is to make long-term investments in people, their staff. They teach and create an organizational climate in which persons can experiment; but primarily they present themselves as models for persons in their charge. That is, they coach, lead, protect, inspire, understand mistakes, and tolerate failure" (Kelling and Bratton 1993: 10; Kelling and Wycoff 1991).

An intriguing example is David Robbins' leadership at Wainwright Industries (this is the same company cited in our discussion of how to deal constructively with employee mistakes). A devotee of total quality management, Robbins, co-founder and co-leader of the firm, set his business goals high: He wanted to win the Malcolm Baldridge Award (the highest award America gives its best-run companies) and enjoy all the business successes that award implies. Robbins knew that one of the many ingredients of high-performing, profitable businesses was having robust employee suggestion programs. He surveyed the landscape for exemplars and benchmarks and discovered in the management literature that a Japanese company held the world record for rate of useful employee suggestions (see generally, Spitzer 1995). That record was 50 suggestions *per employee per year*—suggestions that were considered sound enough to actually be implemented by the employing company. That's about one feasible idea per worker per *week*.

Robbins checked his own suggestion box and found that a usable idea was dropped in it at the rate of one recommendation per employee per *year*. How to close the gap? The main thing Robbins did was counterintuitive. He *stopped* paying for suggestions. "I could never afford to pay for the number of suggestions I wanted," he explained. In place of monetary incentives, he did one of the things that any good police detective has to do when investigating crimes—think clearly about what motivates people to do things. "What would *I* want out of a suggestion program if I were one of my employees?" Robbins asked himself.

> **"The overarching condition required for managers to produce innovative achievements is this: they must envision an accomplishment beyond the scope of the job" (Kanter 1982: 98).**

The answer he came up with was, I would want to be taken seriously and I would want timely responses to my recommendations. So Robbins set about establishing what must at the time have seemed like impossibly demanding timetables for responses to employees' suggestions. The drill was that every suggestion made by an employee had to be responded to by that employee's supervisor within *24 hours* of the suggestion being made. Further, if the idea was considered a good one, either it had to be *implemented* or, if implementation would be costly or complicated, the implementation process (R&D work, budgeting, etc.) had to be *commenced* within *72 hours* of the initial suggestion.

That did it. Employees found it exciting to be taken seriously and especially exciting to see that good ideas were translated into real changes—and quickly enough for the employees to benefit from their own suggestions. Within two years, Wainwright Industries jumped from one implemented suggestion per employee per year to 52. Not every idea was of monumental, bottom-line significance. Some were minor improvements in shop-floor efficiency or safety. But other recommendations saved the company huge amounts of money. There was still a small prize program: Periodically the names of employees whose suggestions had been implemented were placed in a hat and those drawn at random got to take their families or friends to a nice dinner courtesy of the boss. By the way, the boss got a prize, too. In late 1994, Vice President Al Gore handed David Robbins a Malcolm Baldridge Award.

What Robbins had demonstrated is that, even if "response time" doesn't much matter when police are summoned to the scene of "cold calls," response time matters a great deal when trying to motivate employees to suggest ways to improve their own organization. For a brief period, what David Robbins knows about how to run organizations and inspire employees inured to the benefit of the St. Louis Metropolitan Police Department, for he was named by the Governor of Missouri to serve a term as president of the St. Louis Board of Police Commissioners. Robbins' legacy to the St. Louis Police was naming Clarence Harmon to lead the Department in the implementation of problem-solving strategies.

Besides eliciting suggestions from employees most familiar with the work, another core prerequisite for innovation is welcoming experimentation. Those who demand absolute proof in advance that an idea will be a winner will probably kill all but the safest experiments. "Only hindsight shows that an innovative idea was bound to be successful" observes Kanter (1982: 97). "Where would the aviation industry be today," asked another sage, "if the Wright Brothers had said, 'We're not jumping off this cliff until you show us a Boeing 707!'?" Or, as celebrated South Central Los Angeles youth advocate Joe Marshall asked an audience of philanthropists on June 1, 1995, at a conference co-sponsored by the federal Office of Juvenile Justice and Delinquency Prevention and the National Council on Crime and Delinquency: "What is the foundation world's fixation with demanding assurance ahead of time that my proposal will succeed? Sometimes I wonder if Harriet Tubman or Martin Luther King could have passed that test and gotten a grant to work on freeing slaves and de-segregating America." Most of the high-performing middle managers we know would rather "go down swinging" against community crime and disorder problems than never dare to step up to the plate.

Sparrow, et al. (1993: 21) counsel similar patience and understanding with the fledgling strategic experiment called community policing. They responded to a critic who complained that their advocacy of community policing in the book *Beyond 911* was a triumph of hope over experience. "[T]he superiority of the new has not yet been scientifically established," the critic carped, and therefore "it is academically irresponsible to promulgate unproven ideas." In defense, Sparrow, Moore, and Kennedy argue:

> "We frequently stress our view that this movement may yet take a decade to reach maturity, and that such irrefutable proof may be a while coming. Meanwhile, there are plenty of promising signs.... For our part we are pleased to offer whatever support we can to pioneering and entrepreneurial practitioners seeking genuine alternatives to what is obviously flawed current practice."

Experimentation in the police field, to be sure, is not the same as experimenting with widgets. Human subjects are involved. This nation takes experimentation with human subjects very seriously, as well it should (Federal Judicial Center 1981). But the police field needs to be candid about the reality that there is a dearth of proof that *conventional* methods are fit for human consumption. As a result, even traditional policing is an ongoing program experiment with human subjects. In any event, it has been and will continue to be possible in police studies to honor the standards required for experimental program innovations that involve human subjects. Some of the most influential studies over the past several decades—which, for example have discredited random motorized patrol as a foundation of crime prevention and brought insight about what works and under what circumstances to reduce public fear of crime and the incidence of spousal violence—have arisen from controlled experiments.

In the private business world, Kanter (1982: 101) suggests, "four central organizational tasks" lie before middle managers during the "action phase" of a team's innovation efforts:
□ *"handle interference" (from outside the project team)*
□ *"maintain momentum and continuity" (handle "interference,...foot-dragging or inactivity" from within the project team)*
□ *"secondary redesign" (infrastructural changes "necessary to keep the project going" such as "a set of new awards and a fresh performance appraisal system for team members and their subordinates;" or "when it seems that a project is bogging down—that is, when everything possible has been done and no more results are on the horizon—managers often change the structure or approach [of the entire project]. Such alterations can cause a redoubling of effort and a renewed attack on the problem.")*
□ *"external communication" (being sure those "peers and key supporters" outside the project team "have an up-to-date impression of the project and its success."*

Four more ways in which middle managers can contribute to building an organizational culture in which innovation is promoted are allocating "entrepreneurial power;" watching the pace of innovation to make sure it doesn't become a runaway stagecoach; providing *enough* direction so that officers don't feel rudderless as they wonder how to get started innovating and what to innovate about; and balancing resources to ensure that new ideas can be tested without forsaking continuing service obligations.

Innovators will typically need both the power already granted to them (standing authority or one-time authority to engage in the innovative project) plus the additional power they can acquire to push the innovation from idea to reality (Kanter 1982: 98). The creative managers are the "corporate entrepreneurs" (Kanter 1982: 98; 1983). In the police context, this means that people with a passion for and a vision of a better way of doing business have to be allowed to find time to ferret out the available organizational authority that is lying dormant or being squandered on useless activity and to deploy this power in support of their innovative efforts.

Middle managers also are in a good position to monitor and adjust the *pace* of innovation to ensure that it neither overwhelms the system and backfires nor fails to challenge employees sufficiently. Organizational change must be guided in a manner that properly balances progress and operational stability. Too little change can cause problems over the long run. But too much sudden change will cause immediate functional problems. Management consultant Michael Robert (1995) counsels that change-agents plan for persistent, incremental innovation, while standing ready to benefit from unanticipated windfalls:

> "Don't count on a home run or big-bang innovation. Innovative companies believe
> in and practice continuous, marginal, incremental innovation in every aspect of
> their businesses. Finding the big-bang idea should be like finding a ten-dollar bill
> on the street. You're glad it's there, and of course you'll use it. But you wouldn't
> head to the supermarket hoping to find one on the way to pay for the groceries."

Problems will arise as well if officers are plunged head first into the innovation ocean without *enough* direction to help them know how to get started and what to focus their innovative talents on accomplishing. Middle managers need to show great sensitivity to the officers who are trying to satisfy the request that they be innovative and who have until recently been accustomed to getting a lot of top-down direction. Untethered and unguided freedom to fail will not be appreciated, is a recipe for disaster, and almost certainly reflects irresponsible management technique. Mid-managers need to balance a "process...in which there [is] a high premium on communication and the willingness to change gears as required by events" with the risk that "all this communication and opportunity for change [will suggest to officers] that the program...[is] without direction." Community policing implementation requires skillful middle managers who are "keenly aware of how this [change] process might appear to the officers on the street" (Skogan, et al. 1994: 7/3).

As guardians of the public purse, middle managers need to manage the resources needed for innovation and for maintenance of essential existing systems. They—and their organizational and political bosses, the media, and the public at large—need to recognize that there will often be trade-offs and that decisions must be made responsibly about those tradeoffs. Allowing middle managers or their subordinates to go after atrophying authority or fiscal resources being used unwisely by the police department in order to provide "venture capital" for proposed strategic innovations does not entail a *carte blanche* grant of permission for first-line employees to curry favor and compete counterproductively with one another for limited slices of the pie. The middle manager often will need to play a valuable advisory role, and sometimes a decisionmaking role, concerning competing demands for resources and power.

For middle managers, the task of managing innovation includes calculating the *results* of change. A focus on *quality* of service delivery can have an impact on the *volume* of workload, without requiring additional resources. An emphasis on frontline experts means challenges to numerous conventional policies and procedures.

While the methods of implementing community policing may vary among different middle managers, the central task is fundamentally the same: With an awareness of what the service population needs, fix the workplace to facilitate policing outputs and outcomes that are more responsive to those needs (Stephens 1995a: 3). Traditionally, the hub of activity for the middle managers has *not* generally been on the external problem-solving activity of the officers, detectives, civilian front-line personnel and all of their immediate supervisors. It has been on the work environment. That focus cannot, of course, be relinquished, but it must be informed by—and priorities must be determined on the basis of—how internal systems support or impede the externally focused efforts of the organization. What is in the way must be removed, and what can help must be developed.

❑ *Recognize that "what we have here is a failure to communicate."* This was the taunt, in the movie *Cool Hand Luke*, at Paul Newman's character by a chain gang boss glowering at him from behind mirrored sunglasses. But the words have been or could be uttered truthfully by the employees of almost any police organization we have observed. Lack of communication is also among the most frequent complaints by private-sector employees who are surveyed by their employers (Spitzer 1995). The complaint in the policing arena is that members of the organization don't communicate well with one another, especially across units and ranks. Even when members of police forces *do* converse, often their communication skills leave something to be desired. How many such conversations end with one or the other party silently asking, in the inimitable words of Lily Tomlin's "Ernestine" the telephone operator, "Have I reached the person to whom I am speaking?"

Where poor communications present a barrier to effective community problem solving, middle managers need to forthrightly take on this obstacle. When officers need the assistance, middle managers should "facilitate communication among different watches [and] arrange for follow-up by specialized units..." (Joachimstaler 1995: 4). Ignoring cross-unit communications problems will doom the department's strategic innovation efforts, since information is the lifeblood of effective policing, and communication blockages within organizations and between them and their external environment thus produce strategic heart attacks.

To foster open and frequent communication within the department and between it and others, the department's general policy should be that officers can talk to anyone who can help address their problems (community groups, business leaders, other officers, other government agencies, national experts, and others) without needing prior approval from high-level police officials (Eck and Spelman 1987: 104).

Maybe they don't even need prior approval from *low*-level bosses. In St. Louis several years ago then-Captain Roy Joachimstaler was proud of one of his officers who took on as a "POP" project a long-standing disorder problem with unsavory people loitering in front of a liquor store. They loitered during a busy police shift, so when the offenders told the responding officers that they were just waiting for a bus (there was a bus stop in front of the liquor store), the officers didn't have the time to wait around and see if that assertion was true. But one officer found the time to make one phone call—to a friend who worked for the city bus company. At the officer's request (made without prior consultation with his supervisor or middle managers), the friend simply arranged through transit authority channels to have the bus stop moved one block away. Problem solved. The men did not loiter at the new bus stop, and they lacked the excuse of the bus stop to allow them to hang out in front of the liquor store. Would *every* middle manager in American policing acquiesce comfortably, as

> *Middle managers need to recognize that information flow within a work team is "the glue that holds your team together" (Chicago Police Department 1994: 138). They also need to ensure that information flows across beats, shifts, and units as needed to keep police who are responsible for aspects of a particular problem current on the status of the problem and responses (ibid.).*

Joachimstaler did, in his officers taking such initiatives to talk with, and collaborate with, external organizations without prior chain-of-command approval? Probably not. But Joachimstaler knew his personnel well enough to know which officers he could trust to take initiatives and check in at their own discretion, and who needed closer supervision in their problem-solving efforts.

Far more basic than interdepartmental communications by first-line officers and horizontal communications across police department units is clearing the way for officers to have open-ended conversations about community problems with the community members who are experiencing the problems. As preposterous as it might seem, because of lowest-common-denominator approaches to stamping out systemic corruption in some police departments, there are formal rules against "unnecessary conversation" between beat officers and citizens (Weisburd, et al. 1988: 36, 38). What was deemed "necessary" under this well-meaning but unartful quest for integrity was only talk about an incident to which the citizen summoned the police. Otherwise, if an officer was caught by a boss talking for ten minutes with a citizen, the boss "figures that's five minutes too long. So he'll give you a 'rip' (disciplinary report) for unnecessary conversation" (New York City officer, quoted in Weisburd, et al. 1988: 38). Where there was no verifiable dispatch as justification for a street corner conversation, proactive chat presumably would have to be justified, if possible, by reference to some condition or incident that officers spotted on their own during their random patrolling.

We do not dismiss the risks of a highly corrupt unit in a department abusing the cover of community policing to talk with shop owners, drug dealers, hookers and others in the neighborhood for extortionate reasons (for an account of Chicago's latest woes with street gang infiltration of the police force, see Oclander 1995a, 1995b). Still, it cannot be that the best way to address this problem is by adopting generalized bans on police-citizen communication. "Such contacts [between CPOP officers and residents of New York City] were important to building good will in the community." Moreover, "those conversations could actually contribute directly to maintaining order in the neighborhood" (Weisburd, et al. 1988: 38).

The image of police trying to understand the community—its nuances and subcultural preferences that could have direct bearing on the effectiveness of various police tactics—*solely* by huddling and talking among themselves and never going directly to helpful community members for information seems illogically inefficient on its face. There's an old story about a Hollywood caretaker of a famous screen-actor German shepherd named Strongheart. Strongheart blazed the trail later trod by Rin Tin Tin, Lassie and other canine stars. The caretaker was puzzled and amazed that Strongheart sometimes seemed able to read his mind and to understand things that animals are not supposed to comprehend. Nobody in Hollywood seemed able to provide any answers. Eventually, the caretaker sought counsel from an eccentric animal expert, a nomadic "desert rat" known as Mojave Dan. Dan made his home in the desert and had an uncanny ability to communicate with his own "family" of dogs and burros and with his extended family of desert wildlife. After listening to the Angeleno's questions about Strongheart one night by the desert campfire, Mojave Dan paused for a long while before answering.

> "Finally, Dan yawned and stretched. Then he spoke, aiming his words at the stars. 'There's facts about dogs,' he said, 'and there's opinions about them. The dogs have the facts, and the humans have opinions. If you want facts about a dog, always get them straight from the dog. If you want opinions, get them from the human'" (Boone 1954: 47-48).

If knowing how to listen and observe carefully can enable a person to more deeply understand man's *best friend*, perhaps those skills could also help police and the rest of us more fully understand our fellow human beings. Just a thought.

Communication is not just sharing facts, of course. It is also fighting, constructively, about what the *facts* are—and about what the problem-solving policies, procedures, and tactics of a department should be. Middle managers need to model the value of debate for those under their charge. This is not easy in a paramilitary organization, as we suggested earlier. But providing a positive example is crucial if a middle manager expects his or her peers and subordinates to participate constructively in debate—and to take constructive criticism in the positive spirit in which it is offered. The mid-manager must engage at appropriate junctures in visible self-criticism and must accept others' constructive critiques (Couper and Lobitz 1991). He or she can establish standard operating procedures that have operational personnel engage in frequent "after action critiques" (debriefings) of management and supervisory performance (Block, undated).

A technique that some middle managers and chiefs have found useful for encouraging constructive controversy in staff meetings entails having a "designated devil's advocate" for the duration of the meeting (with sincere promises that there will be no reprisals afterward!). The boss appoints someone, at the outset of the discussion, whose mission throughout the course of the meeting is to seize every reasonable opportunity to question, test, and challenge out loud the statements that the boss and peers are making. This practice needs to be used in moderation. Anybody who has ever been trapped on the receiving end of a conversation with a young child, who to every one of the adult's answers, asks "but *why?*" can readily appreciate that a little bit of the designated devil's advocacy goes a long way. But as aggravating as the "medicine" may be, consider how much more consequential could be a police department's *failure* to elicit informed disagreement about tactics and strategies.

"Disagree without being disagreeable" (anonymous).

Unquestioning acquiescence in a police agency's way of doing business can lead to the potentially disastrous organizational condition some have called "group think." A superb employee training video on the hazards of group think has been produced by CRM Films of Carlsbad, California. It recreates the background meetings among key engineers at NASA and the government contractors responsible for designing and building the Challenger Space Shuttle.

This is the shuttle that exploded on takeoff, killing all the astronauts on board and stunning the nation, which had become somewhat complacent about the safety record of manned spacecraft. What sends shivers down the spines of police audiences to whom we have shown this video is the *factual* depiction of roundtable meetings among engineers weeks before the ill-fated launch. In several of those meetings, a lone engineer objects strenuously to the launch as planned. He argues that the weather anticipated on the proposed launch date will expose the "O" rings, which seal joints in the space shuttle, to excessive stress. "We've never verified that the 'O' rings will perform adequately under these conditions," he protests. But at this time the entire space shuttle program was behind schedule and being subjected to sniping in the media and on Capitol Hill. So the engineer was shouted down and pressured to withdraw his objections by other members of the contractor's implementation brainstorming committee. "Get with the program," he was told. It's a line police have heard quite often.

☐ *Reinvent the department's infrastructure.* One of the highest callings of middle managers in the pursuit of change that *endures* will be to identify and lobby for modification of organizational procedures and structures to support the desired vision of policing. Earlier we reported the beliefs of insightful analysts that the failure of prior strategic innovations, like team policing, which contained many of the salient features of community problem solving stemmed from inattention to infrastructural changes. The new method of work was a square peg that didn't fit in the inflexible round holes of the conventional police bureaucracy. If the current strategic reform efforts are to succeed, Sparrow, et al. (1990: 214) argue, "midlevel managers [will need] to harness their officers' creative abilities and from them fashion organizational *adaptiveness*" (emphasis added). The list of organizational support systems needing adaptation today in most police departments is a long one—and an increasingly familiar one. Some we have discussed already. The conscientious middle manager—recognizing that he or she cannot do *everything* and thus needing to pick fights strategically—will work with others to promote modifications of organizational approaches to:

> *While the chief creates new ideas and strategies and the officers apply those ideas where the rubber meets the road, institutionalizing change must be done by police managers. In police departments, the chief has laid out the vision and encouragement to engage in community policing. Police officers have responded with a surge of excitement to this new operating philosophy. It is the middle manager, largely viewed as playing a secondary role, who can ensure that community policing is embedded in the police agency as its standard modus operandi.*

- ☞ recruitment
- ☞ hiring
- ☞ training, including peer assistance programs
- ☞ supervision
- ☞ performance appraisal
- ☞ internal affairs procedures
- ☞ R&D and information systems
- ☞ public information and news media relations
- ☞ equipment maintenance
- ☞ procurement processes and standards

☞ procedural and rule books

☞ the tyranny of 9-1-1

☞ work schedules and assignments that impede collaborative problem solving

☞ the balance between specialization and generalization

☞ factors that cause agency units to work at cross purposes

A number of these infrastructural elements merit some additional discussion.

☞ ***Recruitment and hiring.*** Significant modifications of employee recruitment and hiring processes are frequently left on the back burner of reform in many agencies working to accommodate community policing. But this was not the case in Hayward, California, several years ago, where then-Chief Joe Brann put strengthening that department's employee intake processes at the top of his community policing "to-do" list. Traditionally, the Department, like most around the nation, had deferred to the City's personnel staff. The personnel department dutifully found candidates who had the best "weight in proportion to height, ability to read and write basic English, and physical agility" (Brann and Whalley 1992: 72). The police department

> "worked closely with the entrance hiring psychologist to develop a profile of an effective Hayward COPPS [Community Oriented Policing and Problem Solving] officer. This information was then incorporated into the screening criteria for hiring. *** [These criteria] explored a candidate's ability to learn, problem-solve [and] appraise situations for long-term solutions. *** [T]he new recruitment perspective, coupled with mandated traditional policing skills, [began] to glean individuals who possess both a conceptual understanding and applicable skills for problem solving and dealing with the complexities of human behavior" (Brann and Whalley 1992: 72; also see Weisburd, et al. 1988: 43-44 and Nowicki, et al. 1991, for additional discussion of selection issues pertaining to community policing).

☞ ***Training, including peer assistance programs.*** Some people dislike intently the word "training" as applied to human beings, especially adults with average or better intelligence. "You train *animals*," they say, "you *educate* people." We respect the spirit of the complaint, but hope the reader will forgive us if we do not attempt to sanitize the following discussion by avoiding the use of the word "training."

Whether the endeavor be called training, education, or self-actualization, we are sure Herman Goldstein got it right when he complained:

> "[I]t is troubling to find that a department's investment in the reorientation of management and supervisory personnel often consisted of no more than 'a day at the academy'—and sometimes not even that. How much of the frustration in eliciting support from management and supervision stems from the fact that agencies have simply not invested enough in engaging senior officers, in explaining why change is necessary, and in giving these supervisors and managers the freedom required for them to act in their new role" (Goldstein 1993: 5).

Many police agencies use outside trainers to introduce and reinforce principles and tactics of community problem solving to first-line personnel and supervisors. The Hayward, California, Police Department decided to capitalize "on the talent within the department" by having

"the training segments...delivered by in-house personnel who could effectively translate this philosophy into the manner that would meet the unique needs of the employees and the community of Hayward. A clear benefit of utilizing in-house instructors was that employees were able to hear command personnel sincerely support the concepts of *decentralization of authority* and *risk taking*" (Brann and Whalley 1992: 74).

Thus, in-service and recruit training can become a significant responsibility for middle managers in the processes of implementing and continuously improving community policing (see Zhao, et al. 1995: 17-18).

"We have to change completely how we train people, both at the entrance level and also in-service. *** We have to unprogram people from where they are and reprogram them to where we're going. The cops are doing now what we've taught them to do, what we've trained them to do. They don't know anything different. Under our traditional training, we spend 90% of our time training officers to do what they spend 15% of their time doing, that is, making arrests, enforcing the law" (Lee Brown, quoted in Webber 1992: 31; see also Stephens 1993: 3).

After an unhappy early experience with using agency outsiders as supervisory trainers, the Chicago Police Department, in 1994, garnered much more favorable reviews from mid-manager trainees to the use of in-house experts (Skogan, et al. 1995: 17-18). The most important difference cited between the two waves of training was that the successful trainers knew the managers' jobs. "Last year," said one lieutenant, "they [the trainees] ate the civilians alive. They took exception to everything the (civilian) trainers said" (*ibid*.: 18). Another difference was that the first year's trainers were "a little abstract.... [T]hey asked questions like 'would you rather be a tree or a forest?'" (*ibid*.). Undoubtedly, the unspoken answer was, "I'd rather be fishing." Mastrofski (1993: 11), too, pulled no punches. As things look from his perspective, it appears that community policing training programs could be improved

"by *not* inviting armchair theorists, gurus, consultants, and other 'experts' to drone on incessantly about the 'philosophy' of community policing. A frequent complaint from the trainees is that these sessions lack the substance or concreteness that officers require to come to grips with real problems."

☞ *Supervision.* We have addressed throughout this chapter many of the modifications that community problem solving needs by way of first-line supervision, and we need not reiterate those discussions here. In sum, central issues include shifting from primarily "directing" to primarily "coaching" problem-solving efforts, maintaining a capacity for highly directive leadership and oversight when the tactical problems or the employees at hand require that approach; building on strengths (including "catching" cops doing things *right*); and related changes.

Middle managers can foster first-line supervision that, in turn, fosters quality problem solving by helping *sergeants* enhance their credibility with officers concerning community problem solving. This may not be necessary in departments that have been involved in community policing for some years, or in those even rarer agencies that hire through lateral entry sergeants who are experienced problem solvers from other departments. But in most agencies and for most sergeants, the reality will be that these first-line supervisors are being asked to coach a type of work they have never done themselves. That, of course, can produce significant credibility problems among the rank-and-file officers. One could—and probably should—argue with the belief that a person can *only* supervise or coach tactics that they themselves can do well. Professional sports coaches and players are an obvious analogy. Does Chicago Bulls coach Phil Jackson have anything useful to tell Michael Jordan? We think so, even if Phil can't be like Mike.

The coach ought to know *something* about the topic, however. In Meredith Wilson's musical, *The Music Man*, "Professor" Harold Hill promised to give music lessons to a bunch of young rubes whose parents he suckered into buying instruments so they could form the River City Boys Band. When the children ask him to demonstrate how each instrument works, Hill mocks astonishment and declares that he has a far superior method for them to learn to play—the "think" system. "Just pick up your instruments, really concentrate, and *think* the 'Minuet in G,' boys! *Think!*" But cops don't con so easily. And, rightly or wrongly, they tend to expect their bosses to be "*cops* with big jobs," fully capable of doing their *own* direct service policing if necessary. In the community policing context, this means the sergeants—and middle managers—will be more credible to first-line officers if they are very conversant with and adept at using the problem identification, analysis, response, and monitoring methods they are going to supervise. Otherwise, supervisors' efforts may well be viewed (perhaps accurately) by officers as the meddling of uninformed bosses.

☞ *Performance appraisal.* Middle managers can make a monumental contribution to retooling their organizations' infrastructure if they develop comprehensive new packages for assessing the quality and quantity of work done by first-line police employees and their immediate supervisors. The *post mortems* on team policing and other strategic innovations that failed to stick emphasized that the fledgling efforts were misfits in the departments' traditional incentive systems. Performance appraisal is one of those basic incentive systems.

Middle managers conventionally have borne some responsibility to review the "alerts" sent out by "early warning" systems designed to detect officers at risk of poor performance because of job-related or personal problems. Such responsibilities still make sense under community problem-solving regimens. It may be, however, that some of the risks and some of the employee *problem-solving* talents and opportunities that may be jeopardized by the risks will be broader than is the case under most current early warning systems.

The core shift in performance appraisal systems that most of the leading visionaries of community problem solving—and of private corporate reinvention—recommend, of course, is from bean counting to measuring results (e.g., Kanter 1982: 101). Who cares how many coffee beans we've got if the java tastes nasty! It will not help, of course, to simply swing the pendulum from glorifying quantity over quality to glorifying quality without regard to quantity. If there were only one problem and one customer for police departments to worry about, making "quality job one" and quantity "job zero" might work. But departments have lots of people and lots of problems to address, and so what is needed is a rational marriage of quality and quantity. We don't want meaningless quantity; we want and need lots of quality work.

Another way to put the challenge of reinventing performance appraisal standards and systems is that police departments need to reward the things that matter. In community problem-solving systems, what matters includes contributing manifestly to community safety and fear reduction through criminal justice and noncriminal justice tactics; providing other emergency services; officers' knowledge of and involvement in the community in various appropriate ways; the adequacy of problem-solving efforts from the point of view of those who live and work in the affected neighborhoods; officers' behavior toward the public; officers' initiative in tackling problems; and so forth (see, e.g., Sparrow, et al. 1990: 226-28; Trojanowicz and Bucqueroux 1990). By contrast, things that don't matter—or are downright harmful—to a community policing implementation effort include *precipitous* and glutinous use of arrest and other criminal justice system resources; meaningless

When he was superintendent in the Edmonton Police Department, Chris Braiden became disgusted with the continuing practice of giving rewards that purported to be for excellence simply on the basis of career longevity. (Similarly, Cohen and Eimicke 1995 ridicule public-sector promotions based solely on time-in-service.) Braiden couldn't—or thought it would be ill-advised to—take on the whole system, but he did develop his own supplemental award within his unit: a bottle of Irish whiskey for a job well done. "Braiden's bottle," as the cops called it, came to be a coveted award among his officers. If Braiden had his way, he'd introduce financial bonuses into policing as an incentive for innovation and hard work. "I'd cut a deal with newly promoted middle managers, giving them a bonus or a loss at the end of the year to motivate performance. I'd give them an employment contract. Money is a motivator" (Braiden 1995).

paperwork and other "CYA" activities; running breathlessly and unthinkingly to every call for service without regard to its nature; and excessive emphasis on officers' attitudes rather than behaviors—since attitudes are likely to change *after* behaviors do (compare Block, undated: 2). Bittner (1983) refers to the desirable grand shift in emphasis under community policing as one from "legality" to "workmanship" (see also Bittner 1995). If that sea change occurs, honoring and encouraging it through performance appraisal systems will require methods and standards quite unlike those used today in most locales.

When he was NYPD Commissioner and president of the International Association of Chiefs of Police, Lee Brown spoke about the importance of developing systems for rewarding things that matter. "In most police agencies," he said,

> "rewards are based on valor. If you're in a shoot-out, if you're shot or you shoot someone else, if you capture a dangerous person, you get special recognition. Usually a lot of danger and excitement go along with achieving a reward. What about rewarding people for thinking and being creative? We recently gave an award to an officer who made a suggestion about licensing unlicensed livery cabs that will save the city a few million dollars in the short run. That officer didn't have to do that. But he was a thinking, creative person. He saw a problem and came up with a solution. Our reward system should recognize people who solve problems, who use their minds, who think" (quoted in Webber 1992: 32).

Developing sound performance appraisal tools is one way to ensure that the medals or other praise a department hands out send the desired messages. In one of our illustrations in the previous chapter of middle managers who are making great contributions to community problem solving, San Diego's Lieutenant Hank Olais developed evaluation tools for his officers' problem-solving reports. Those tools were designed to detect the *impact* of the officers' work far more than the officers' *activities*. Noteworthy efforts by police practitioners and advisors to develop performance appraisal tools more responsive than conventional systems to the needs of community problem solving have been made by Wycoff and Oettmeier (1993), Jordon (1992), and Trojanowicz and Bucqueroux (1992); see also Nowicki, et al. (1991).

> *"A boss who overcontrols Sapps [disempowers] his people. A boss who abandons control Sapps his people. A boss who uses situational control Zapps [empowers] his people. People only respond negatively to controls when they are inappropriate for the situation"* (Byham and Cox 1988: 96).

A difficult challenge in appraising the performance of individual and collaborative community policing efforts is that some of the things to which we most aspire under the new strategies are hard to see and touch. "[T]he ultimate evaluation," Lee Brown suggested in a comment we quoted earlier, "should not be the arrests but the absence of arrests, when there's no crime. If you have no crime on your beat, then you are doing the job you should be doing" (quoted in Webber 1992: 32).

Stepping back momentarily from *individual* employees' performance to the question of appraising overall *organizational* effort, cumulative victimization surveys are a far more reliable vehicle for tracking the presence or absence of crimes (other than homicide) than are the FBI's Uniform Crime Reports. The UCR merely tallies those incidents that are officially reported to police agencies. Other kinds of public opinion polls besides victimization surveys have also proved to be very helpful to community policing organizations (Peak, et al. 1992: 38; Bigham 1993; Skogan, et al. 1995: 89). Such polls are conducted because the departments take community satisfaction to be a defining feature of good organizational performance. Moreover, customer surveys can provide information on topics about which the reported crime stats are generally silent: levels of community fear; particular problems that the respondents believe are causing different kinds of incidents and are spurring fear; and the like.

Some ways need to be found to incorporate customer satisfaction into the performance appraisals of teams of officers and perhaps even the appraisals of individual problem-solving officers. One thing that seems elementary is that any such effort to invent and impose such job evaluation criteria and systems that entirely excludes input from those being evaluated will run a high risk of failure. We earlier noted that in Hayward, California, "recommendations were solicited from managers, supervisors and line personnel" for changing the performance evaluation system. Moreover, the department decided to align its evaluation approach to its operational decentralization. "[A]ll work units [were asked to devise] their own evaluation instruments and processes...designed around the specific services the work unit provides" (Brann and Whalley 1992: 74). Certain *agency-wide* minimal standards and core values, of course, must be connecting threads running through any such decentralized performance assessment systems.

One of the possible advantages to some decentralization in performance appraisal systems is that this approach may make it easier to make performance appraisal context-sensitive (Weisburd, et al. 1988: 45). There is reason to believe that performance is best explained, for most people, as an intersection of individual proclivities with situational exigencies and structural incentives and disincentives (Toch 1995a). Accordingly, the more one can specify the localized structural considerations and the localized situations that police employees will probably encounter, the better. In other words, the underlying theory here is that certain types of people are more likely to perform in desirable or undesirable ways depending on the kinds of work environments and specific people and problems they encounter. A classic example concerns police abuse of force: An officer with a propensity to lose his temper may prove more successful in keeping calm if his department's culture is very service-oriented than if it is a "kick-ass-and-take-names" regimen.

What context-sensitive appraisal may mean as applied to problem solving, for instance, is that it will avail little to blame equally two police officers in two different precincts for failing to take advantage of a problem-solving resource that exists in only one of the precincts. Maybe the underresourced officer should be challenged to invent or spur the invention of the needed resource in her precinct. But that may take some time and considerable assistance, depending on the nature of the resource. In any event, it would simply be unfair to criticize a person for failing to do the unfeasible.

A fundamental question in framing a performance appraisal system is the "five percent" question. Do we write performance standards for the lowest performers on the payroll—the five percent weakest employees? If we use lowest-common-denominator approaches, then how do we capture the wide array of moderate and superlative efforts that other employees are making? Do we write performance standards for the *average* group of employees? Or do we write them, as Klockars (1995) would have police departments do (at least as concerns police use of force issues), for the five percent *best* employees? By benchmarking its "highly skilled officers," the department calls attention to those whose performance falls short of aspirations. So long as this is not done in a pejorative way (for, by definition, most employees will fail to meet the highest standards most of the time), but in order to identify opportunities for continuing professional growth, this approach may be very useful.

Part of what is involved is shifting the emphasis from after-the-fact discipline and reward to providing incentives for *compliance* with obligations and *pursuit* of excellence. As Block (undated: 1) puts it, it is important to "manage the system of consequences so that it's in the best interest of the subordinate to do what's in the agency's best interest." A sound incentive system for continuous improvement by employees would reward honesty by individual workers and teams of workers about their need for self-improvement. We illustrated one way this might be done earlier when we related the Wainwright Industries story about the punch press operator who was given a minor company award for admitting he didn't know how to avert a costly error. Middle managers would help the police industry by exploring such notions with an open mind.

☞ *R&D and information systems.* In a private organization, the research and development unit and its manager "are expected to produce innovations" (Kanter 1982: 97; 1983). Few, if any, police department R&D units do anything resembling either research or development as those activities are commonly understood in the business world and the military (Reiss 1991). The gaping gulf between policing and these other sectors represents how much most police departments to retool their concepts and methods of research and development to advance community problem solving. Even though R&D resources are shrinking in some *private* enterprises, the percentage of annual organizational budgets devoted to inventing better products and services still dwarfs what the police world dedicates to these functions.

It seems only logical, as the Chicago Police Department has done under Superintendent Matt Rodriguez during the mid-1990s, to have an agency's director of research and development play a fundamental, co-managerial role in designing and assessing the operational and infrastructural changes made to accomplish community problem solving. In Chicago, the R&D director was co-manager of the strategic shift with a senior manager of patrol operations.

Whether operated by an R&D unit, a crime analysis unit or some other component of the police agency, enhanced information management and retrieval systems are a bedrock necessity for officers engaged in problem solving policing. At the simplest level, "[w]hen investigating a potential problem, officers and supervisors need to know if others have confronted the same difficulty before" (Eck and Spelman 1987: 105). Middle managers who can significantly strengthen information-processing systems will serve the policing field well. Upgrading information systems to support community policing is considered by many practitioners to be the leading infrastructural need of police and sheriffs' departments committed to strategic reform (McEwen 1995: 9, 11). The typical automated systems, an NIJ survey disclosed, "are not sophisticated enough to support problem solving" (*ibid.*).

☞ *Public information and news media relations.* A *sine qua non* of police-community brainstorming about problems and their solutions is the sharing of information to which each party has access. For the police part, there are powerful traditions in the law enforcement field of treating virtually all information learned within the scope of police work as secret information, which cannot be shared with "the community." To support the operational, problem-solving efforts of their subordinates, middle managers need to lead the way in critically examining the justifiability of confidentiality classifications. It will almost certainly turn out that, just as in the national defense bureaucracy, some categories of information have been needlessly or improperly classified as off limits to the taxpayers.

The problems of information sharing get stickier when the criminal activity of individual *juveniles* is at issue. Two on-going projects in Charlotte, North Carolina, and one in New Haven, Connecticut, are currently tackling the challenge of developing methods for sharing critical information while still respecting the obligations of confidentiality concerning juveniles' criminal records.

One of the Charlotte projects centers on the students and faculty of the Cochrane Middle School. There, Charlotte-Mecklenburg police officers; Cochrane School teachers, administrators, guidance counselors and social workers; parents, community members, psychologists, psychiatrists and others have coalesced to help students learn and teachers teach in a safer, more enriching environment. The other Charlotte-based project has brought police and county Department of Social Services personnel together to cross-train concerning the prospects and protocols that would enable both to help at-risk families by using "family preservation" techniques. Figuring out how to share appropriate information about families which are risky (although not life-threatening) places for children to be raised is a central challenge of this project.

The New Haven-based project, which is about to be replicated in other locales, joins police and mental health workers to intervene to help children avoid becoming psychological victims of violence they have witnessed or experienced. It entails a collaboration between Dr. Steven Marans' clinical team at the Yale University Child Study Center and the New Haven

Police Department. The casebooks, protocols, and training materials that will emanate from all three of these projects, as well as similar efforts around the nation, should move the field forward in grappling with the difficult problem of how to lawfully and ethically share information that will help concerned professionals better protect children's physical, emotional, and reputational well-being.

Insofar as the news media are crucial to the accomplishment of mass communication about crime prevention and problem solving, police middle managers will also want to re-examine the justification for policies and practices which deny problem-solving officers the opportunity to talk directly—and for tactical purposes—to responsible representatives of the news business. A lone, talented public information officer for a department running several ambitious problem-solving projects simultaneously is hardly a sufficient support system for the agency. Coordination and guidance—rather than muzzling of individual officers—in dealing with reporters will prove helpful to problem solving—and it has the virtue of emphasizing that cops, unless they prove otherwise, should be treated as competent, trustworthy people. A public information officer's efforts to absolutely control officers' media contacts, through prior approval of communications, will undermine the flexibility and timeliness often needed to facilitate problem solving.

☞ *Equipment maintenance and procurement processes and standards.* Police need the tools of their trade, and they need them to work well, sometimes under life-and-death conditions. Police have always needed good, reliable tools but sometimes have not been furnished them due to woefully inefficient procurement and maintenance support systems in police agencies or city governments. An example of the unglamorous but crucial quests that middle managers might undertake to reduce the dysfunctionality of bad support systems comes from Madison, Wisconsin. During his mayoralty there, from 1983 to 1989, Joe Sensenbrenner bravely ventured through the Looking Glass and into the surreal world of motor vehicle maintenance. He tells what happened when he showed up one day at the city garage:

> "The manager and mechanics at the First Street Garage were surprised to see the mayor and a top assistant show up to investigate their problems; most previous mayors had shown their faces only when they needed a tankful of gas. Over the next few years I learned again and again the crucial importance of the top executive getting personally and visibly involved on the battlefield of basic change.
>
> For the most part, the crew at the garage were doubters. But when I met Terry Holmes, the president of Laborers International Union of North America, Local 236, I looked him squarely in the eye, pledged my personal involvement, and confirmed his membership's central role. He agreed to participate. We formed a team and gathered data from individual mechanics and from the repair process itself. We found that many delays resulted from the garage not having the right parts in stock. We took that complaint to the parts manager, who said the problem with stocking parts was that the city purchased many different makes and models of equipment virtually every year. We discovered that the fleet included 440 different types, makes, models, and years of equipment. Why the bewildering variety? Because, the parts manager told us, it was city policy to buy whatever vehicle had the lowest sticker price on the day of purchase.
>
> 'It doesn't make any sense,' one mechanic said. 'When you look at all the

equipment downtime, the warranty work that weak suppliers don't cover, the unreliability of cheaper machines, and the lower resale value, buying what's cheapest doesn't save us anything.'

Our next trip was to the parts purchaser. He agreed with the mechanic. 'It would certainly make my job easier to have fewer parts to stock from a few reliable suppliers. But central purchasing won't let me do it.' Onward to central purchasing, where we heard this: 'Boy, I understand what you're saying because I hear it from all over the organization. But there's no way we can change the policy. The comptroller wouldn't let us do it.'

Enter the comptroller. 'You make a very strong case,' he admitted. 'But I can't let you do it because the city attorney won't let me approve such a thing.' On to the city attorney. 'Why, of course you can do that,' he said. 'All you need to do is write the specifications so they include the warranty, the ease of maintenance, the availability of parts, and the resale value over time. Make sure that's clear in advance, and there's no problem. In fact, I assumed you were doing it all along.'

This was a stunning disclosure.

Here was a major failure of a city service whose symptoms, causes, and solution were widely known but that had become chronic because government was not organized to solve it. *** [T]he source of the downtime problem was upstream in the relationship of the city to its suppliers—not downstream where the worker couldn't find a missing part. The problem was a flawed system, not flawed workers" (Sensenbrenner 1991: 65, 68).

Could police middle managers function as "consumer advocates," quality assurance advocates, or ombudsmen on behalf of their employees in dealing with equipment procurement and maintenance units? If so, then the computers, vehicles, weapons and communications devices officers are furnished may be less likely to impede their work against community problems.

Having penetrated the motor maintenance maze and lived to tell about it, Mayor Sensenbrenner enlisted the empowered employees of the Madison Police Department and other city agencies to keep the ball rolling:

More often than not, unwanted conduct by people in organizations comes not from "bad people" but from bad systems—to which people respond in rational, albeit regrettable, ways. The eighth of 12 principles on which the Madison, Wisconsin, Police Department's strategic reformation was grounded by former Chief David Couper "calls for improving systems and examining processes before blaming people" (Goodbody 1995: 14).

"Mechanics...rode along on police patrols and learned that squad cars spend much more time at idling speeds than in the high-speed emergencies mechanics had imagined and planned for in tuning engines. Various city departments—streets, parks, police—helped the First Street mechanics gather data, and we ultimately adopted their proposals, including driver check sheets for vehicle condition, maintenance schedules for each piece of equipment, and an overtime budget to cut down-time and make sure preventive maintenance work was done.

The result of these changes was a reduction in the average vehicle turnaround time from nine days to three and...an annual net savings to the city of Madison of about $700,000" (Sensenbrenner 1991: 68).

☞ *The tyranny of 9-1-1.* Police chiefs don't run police departments, the saying goes, anyone with a quarter does. Actually, the 9-1-1 call in most locales is *free*. As such, the 9-1-1 system was designed to and has succeeded in enabling the least powerful people in society to summon the police. Under "a mechanism of direct, unmediated service distribution...[a] citizen no longer needed pull with the ward boss or his minions to get police service; the cost of a phone call would bring an officer to the doorstep" (Mastrofski 1993: 14). Such democratization of access to government

> **Mastrofski (1993: 6) is critical of the fact that "[t]he 9-1-1 system has become a favorite whipping boy of contemporary reformers." He is doubtful that officer time freed up by differential response programs is actually being devoted to results-producing problem solving. And Mastrofski wonders "if, in concluding that knee-jerk, fire brigade policing is wasteful and ineffective, ...reformers have not overlooked the possibility that productive policing can be done in a reactive context."**

services is not to be denigrated. Many nations of the world have systems far less friendly to the lower classes. What is needed for community problem-solving strategies to succeed, in the United States, however, is some relief from the mindless pattern of sending a reasonably well-paid, sworn police officer every time somebody sounds the alarm bell, regardless of the nature of the call.

Thus, middle managers can advance community problem solving by helping to establish or strengthen differential response systems and by making other modifications in dispatch policy and practice. They can assist as well by devising workable protocols so that officers cover calls for colleagues busy addressing problems. When facilitating flexibility in call-response systems, the middle managers need to be sure the protocols they fashion strive to equitably distribute the burdens and opportunities among officers over time. No such system will achieve equity each and every time, a fact that middle managers may need to encourage officers to accept with a forgiving spirit. But the workload distribution systems should minimize the risks that a few officers will get all the free time, perks, and limelight (Eck and Spelman 1987: 105; Chicago Police Department 1994: 140). Goldstein (1990: 173) reports that when departments protect certain officers or units from the department's full range of work, resentments and ridicule often follow. For instance,

> "[o]fficers in CPOP in New York City, who are insulated from the pressures of daily calls made to the police, are sometimes referred to by other officers as 'the untouchables.' In Baltimore County, officers in COPE are referred to by regularly assigned officers as 'cops on pension early'" (see also Skogan, et al. 1994: 6/3).

Detractors of Houston chiefs Lee Brown's and Betsy Watson's leadership of Neighborhood-Oriented Policing used to snicker that N.O.P. really meant "Nobody On Patrol."[16]

---

[16] Even if one disagrees with the wisecrack (which we do), one has to admit that when cops make fun of something they're often quite clever—brutal, but clever. What if some of the nation's brightest middle managers took on the special challenge of devising incentive systems that would harness this cruel cleverness but turn it in more socially responsible directions? On the CBS-TV *Sixty Minutes* news magazine broadcast of October 8, 1995, curmudgeonly commentator Andy Rooney brazenly offered a reward of $1 million to any person who comes forward in the aftermath of O.J. Simpson's October 3rd acquittal on double murder charges with information that results in the prosecution and conviction of the person(s) who murdered Nicole Brown Simpson and Ronald Goldman. Rooney,

A department exposes itself to complaints from officers and their bosses about inequitable distribution of burdens and benefits when community problem solving is implemented on a special-unit basis rather than agency-wide. Typical of such split-force approaches are deployment patterns in which there are problem-solving officers (who assist with 9-1-1 true emergency calls when needed) and officers still tethered tightly to the 9-1-1 system for their workload. Two examples can be offered of the resentments and jealousies that can develop when the 9-1-1 call burden is not shared evenly across work units. The Baltimore County Police Department's "C.O.P.E." unit, referred to above by Goldstein, did some really important fear-reduction work. The unit was nevertheless criticized by regular patrol officers who didn't get to participate in C.O.P.E.'s work or its glory (Kelling and Bratton 1993: 7). The Madison, Wisconsin, Police Department's "experimental district" was also resented by officers in other districts as a resource drain and for its special privileges (Kelling and Bratton 1993: 7). In looking for reforms in the department's call-handling systems, it is important for middle managers, as much as possible, to take approaches that will be seen as fair and accepted in good spirit by the department's entire workforce.

☞ *Work schedules and assignments that impede collaborative problem solving.* Closely related to the preceding point, community policing will break down reasonably quickly in a department characterized by inflexible work hours or mandatory transfers on arbitrary schedules. These practices could undermine relationships and joint activities between police and the community. Taking an officer off his or her beat after a specified period of time without regard to the nature or quality of work that officer is engaged in risks "abruptly terminating a relationship with a neighborhood that a police officer has worked hard to cultivate just as it is beginning to produce the desired results" (Goldstein 1990: 175). Giving up too soon on an officer's investments in local partnerships may become a self-fulfilling prophecy by the unfaithful that community problem solving doesn't work. Good working relationships *among police personnel* in different units or on different shifts will also suffer from autocratic and unbending management practices.

It is *not* essential that *middle managers* personally take on the logistical burden of juggling the work schedules of dozens or more officers who have problem-solving appointments at all hours of the day or night. One could envision a cartoon of the poor lieutenant or captain hidden at her desk behind a mountain of request slips for work schedule adjustments. Even with the power of modern technology to enter various requests into a computer program that will spit back optimal schedules for an entire work team, why must the middle manager take personal responsibility, except in especially complicated situations, for dealing with basic day-to-day staffing questions?

---

although seriously doubting that his challenge could be met (Kupcinet 1995), implied that such an investment would be cheap if it could help America calm the flames of racial divisiveness that flared after Simpson's acquittal. Rooney made us think about offering our own reward—for anyone who figures out how to engage for positive purposes the enormous creative energies that many of this nation's cops devote to carping and clowning around. The catchy—even poetic—slogans many police utter (or scrawl in stationhouse restrooms) and the devilishly imaginative things they do to satirize the policies, programs, procedures and people they *don't* like often rival as creative accomplishments some of the best and highest-paid work coming out of Madison Avenue advertising firms and other kinds of think tanks. If only we could store up the psychic energy and imagination of the smart, cynical cop in some sort of *Ghostbuster* battery, then reverse the polarity, and plug it into the solution of America's social problems.... What a glorious exercise that could be in building on strengths! Anybody with a million bucks want to underwrite an experiment?

Would it not work just as well, so long as there are enough *competent* officers on a squad or team to cover a shift's call-for-service load, to let *officers* have first crack at collaboratively adjusting their own work schedules? In any work setting, there will be a few people who abuse an honor system. Byham and Cox (1988: 61) report on empowerment being done poorly and backfiring in one corporate setting: "Given the power to make their own decisions, some people had decided to take a break for the rest of the day." Back-up systems to the honor system are a good idea. But engaging those systems to override the honor system too quickly—before people have had a chance to learn from relatively harmless missteps—is risky. As needed, a first-line supervisor could spot-check (audit) a peer-run scheduling system from time to time to make sure it works, giving closer scrutiny to employees whose repetitive conduct proves they need it. The managers could also step in when asked to help resolve difficulties in reaching voluntary agreements.

In Madison, Wisconsin's "experimental police district," officers needing time for problem solving

> "consult other officers and their supervisors to make arrangements for the necessary time and resources to address the problems. (This means ensuring there will be enough people working, enough cars available, etc.) To date, the managers feel this practice has worked well. Officers have worked cooperatively, switching their days off or changing their schedules in other ways to accommodate their colleagues. Managers provide support by facilitating teamwork between shifts and coordinating the efforts of officers wishing to address the same problems" (Wycoff and Skogan 1993: 27).

Similarly, in St. Louis, Major Roy Joachimstaler helps his subordinates free up the deployment system so that teamwork among pairs of officers is easier. "District commanders should be flexible in allowing their lieutenants and sergeants to deadhead cars," he advises, "thus allowing two persons to work on problem-solving projects, if necessary" (Joachimstaler 1995: 4).

There may be great skepticism among experienced police employees that a primarily self-regulating and peer-regulating system of work scheduling, such as that in Madison's experimental district, will suffice to ensure that cops don't abuse their privileges. Consider, however, what happened in Wainwright Industries several years ago after company head David Robbins tore up the rule manual during an employee meeting and told his workers, "You don't need a rule book to tell you to come to work on time and not to fake being ill." Employee attendance for the years since has consistently registered over 99 percent.

Besides the question of scheduling flexibility to accommodate problem-solving activities while still covering essential calls-for-service, there is the matter of assigning police personnel—sworn and civilians—in such a fashion that, as much as possible, talents are matched to tasks. We addressed this point earlier in this chapter in our discussion of "building on strengths" and allowing mid-managers to recognize that people are unique.

☞ *The balance between specialization and generalization.* Excessive specialization is thought by many to be one of the key *structural* impediments to officers doing good community problem solving. The New York City Police Department, for example, had to bend the rules to allow community policing officers to enforce narcotics laws so they would not lose credibility with local residents and businesses (Weisburd, et al. 1988: 40; Kelling and Bratton 1993: 2). That decision assuredly was made by *senior* rather than *middle* managers, but at least it enabled an environment of organizational responsiveness to the needs of communities, officers, and the officers' bosses. In his reengineering plans for the NYPD, Commissioner Bill Bratton numbered among his prime objectives "unleashing the creativity and energy of precinct police officers from the dead hand of bureaucratic procedure which often kept them out of the crime-fighting front lines" (Bratton 1994: 4).

Earlier, in listing reasons why middle managers might feel a pinch from organizational reform, we observed that in departments featuring standardization of function within areas of specialization middle managers become great experts on relatively narrow tasks. A shift away from specialization toward broader involvement in understanding and achieving entire organizational missions may temporarily threaten the middle managers' claim to special know-how.

> *Community policing "will demand adjustments in every area of the service and in every member. It will fundamentally change how and why we do business. The Community Policing philosophy is not another 'add on' or specialized approach. We will move from specialization built around tasks to generalization built around the needs of the community" (McNally 1991: 1).*

It is important to understand why one would want to glorify generalization at the expense of specialization when doing so can engender resistance. A justification is especially in order when one realizes that downplaying specialization will be characterized by some inside and outside the organization as weakening the department and devaluing the special expertise that its employees have spent years developing. The point is not that genuine expertise is no longer esteemed by the organization or its customers. To the contrary, even greater expertise is being sought so as to make greater progress against daunting social problems with a steadily shrinking tax base.

The point of extolling generalization is that, at least for the *interim*, generalist *functioning* will foster generalist *thinking* (thinking about the *entire* organization's mission). This, in turn, will help direct the attention, energies, and goodwill of an organization's most gifted employees and other stakeholders to a crucial question: Which traditional organizational structures and arrangements, examined freshly and honestly, efficiently help accomplish key *overall* police department-community goals (reduce criminal victimization, cut fear, promote community revitalization, and so forth)? The bumper-sticker slogan, "Think globally, act locally," touches this point nicely. Police employees cannot *each* worry at any length about the *entire* police department's needs and opportunities. But if, as they are acting on strengthening the capacities in their particular bailiwicks, they keep in mind what is good for the overall department (and the overall local government) and its service population, the risk of one person's new solutions becoming someone else's new problems is diminished. Avoiding the "rain barrel effect"—in which plugging one hole springs another loose—requires teamwork. It requires keeping a watchful eye on the *whole* barrel.

Michael Hammer, co-author with James Champy of *Reengineering the Corporation*, explained why he believes generalist thinking is essential to help organizations align their methods to their objectives:

"The deep issue [impeding corporate success] is one of functional specialization and fragmentation—the way we've taken work, broken it into pieces, and proceeded with the assumption that if every individual worried about his or her piece of the work, the whole would take care of itself. In fact, everyone does worry about his or her piece, but the whole is going to hell. That seems to be essentially a universal truth.

*** In [the movie *Absence of Malice* with Paul Newman], the Justice Department thinks Newman has information about a crime. He doesn't, but the Justice Department officials believe he does, so they pressure him to release it, ultimately leaking some very embarrassing information about him and a friend. The press prints it, and the friend is so embarrassed that she commits suicide. Last scene in the movie: Paul Newman's there with the Justice Department and the press, and he has a memorable line. He looks around and says: 'Everybody here is smart. Everybody here is doing their job, and my friend is dead.' I tell executives that by changing one word of that sentence, we have something we can engrave over the entrances of their firms. It becomes: 'Everybody here is smart. Everybody here is doing their job, and my company's dead.' Because everybody doing his or her piece leads to disaster. And that's a fundamental premise wired into any enterprise, public or private, large, medium or small. It's a universally held truth, and it's simply a lie" (Vogl 1993/1994: 52).

A police department probably will not make fundamental progress unless significant components of the organization—say, narcotics, gang, general patrol, records and training units—come together around a shared vision of the whole agency's objectives. Nor will it advance appreciably unless these components examine whether some of their autonomous successes actually are working at cross purposes and resulting in a net loss for the service population. We believe there is an important opportunity for middle managers to take a more holistic view of organizational success, so they can avoid the trap of spending most of their time gluing fragmented organizational efforts together. They can help, in other words, to avoid what Hammer calls the "Humpty-Dumpty school of management" (Vogl 1993/1994: 55; see also Bratton 1994: 2).

Some specialization makes sense and will remain an integral part of any high-performing police department, of course. We need not attempt here to itemize what that specialization should be. Departments around the nation are experimenting right now with finding appropriate balances between generalization and specialization, between centralization and decentralization. Their answers will differ depending partly on local factors, as should be the case. Insofar as departments retain special units, middle managers to whom the different units report can collaborate to maximize the smooth and frequent communication across units that will minimize the organizational left hand not knowing what its right hand is doing.

Pigeonholing mid-managers and others in police organizations invites the "pigeons" to get very protective of their cubbyholes, for it's the only real estate they own. By contrast, organizations in which middle managers have shown entrepreneurial initiatives are ones that create work environments conducive to innovation. Kanter (1982: 102) studied various types of private sector organizations and discovered differences in the amounts and quality of innovation that were due partly to organizational attributes:

"This difference in levels of innovative achievement correlates with the extent to which these companies' structures and cultures support middle managers' creativity. Companies producing the most entrepreneurs have cultures that encourage collaboration and teamwork. Moreover, they have complex structures that link people in multiple ways and help them go beyond the confines of their defined jobs to do 'what needs to be done.'"

☞ *Factors that cause agency units to work at cross purposes.* As the foregoing discussion suggests, one of the principal factors that causes people in different segments of an organization to work at cross purposes is poor communication about what each is trying to accomplish, how, and *why*. Although no organization is free from competition between units (indeed, some high-performing organizations *thrive* on it), healthy competition—especially in a public safety agency—does *not* mean succeeding *at the expense of* your internal competitors. Those who pay the highest price from such competition will of course be the community, who can ill afford to have their Neros in blue fiddling around and sniping at one another while cities burn.

How might components of a police department work at cross purposes? For instance, heavy lock-'em-up enforcement tactics by a "gang suppression unit" may create power vacuums on the streets and precipitate bloody turf wars—with innocent children catching the cross fire. Such methods may also undermine the cautious efforts of neighborhood-based officers to quietly negotiate gang truces that cut the bloodshed as well as the illicit activities of the gangs. Among the neighborhood-based prevention programs that may be thwarted by heavy enforcement priorities is "midnight basketball," which, despite the unthinking derision of some Washington politicians, typically provides useful incentives for school attendance and academic success.

Aside from interunit communications breakdowns, middle managers can try to alter a host of other factors that might impede compliance with comprehensive strategic innovations. The truly brave—and successful—middle manager will develop skills for managing his or her boss and helping to upgrade the boss' work. Such inverted management is often needed because *senior* leaders, including the chief, who fail to clearly articulate where the organization is going often cause units to move willy nilly toward inconsistent objectives and, inadvertently, to trample one another's budding successes.

Middle managers might productively help their bosses better articulate not only what changes are desired but *how*—that is, according to what general principles of empowerment and change strategy—those changes should be pursued. As Stephens (1995a: 3) observes, however, there are many strategic changes for which the real "how-to" expertise lies not with senior managers but with the middle managers themselves. The middle managers, he argues, "know the inner workings of the organization and its people; they are in a much better position [than their superiors] to contribute in a useful way to 'how' it might be done."

Many of the other issues discussed throughout this book also bear on the problem of designing away structural difficulties that produce dysfunctional organizations. Each level or unit in the police agency must change to foster continual growth in community policing. But to the extent possible, each must change in a way that, like the physician's credo, "does no harm" to the good efforts of other units to improve their contributions to the overall mission. Where conflicts arise, middle managers who understand the grand scheme can be an excellent first line of defense against organizations imploding. If middle managers fulfill their responsibility to ensure that the professed community policing *values* are *practiced* at each level in each unit, the chances of fundamental conflicts between units over core principles are lessened. There will still be innumerable day-to-day detail conflicts over interpretations of core values and missions and their application to the tasks at hand, but that's the stuff middle managers were invented to deal with—in a competent, efficient manner that continuously builds organizational capacity.

❑ *Middle managers as demographers and ethnographers.* Besides their essential work of selective demolition and rebuilding of the department's infrastructure, middle managers, if they find time to spare, can help forecast challenges, needs, and opportunities that will face the police organization and the community in the near and mid-term. Middle managers, with whatever assistance they need and can secure from within the department and local universities and community organizations, can identify changing aspects of the community and the likely impacts of such changes on crime, disorder and fear problems. For instance, it may be valuable to develop *neighborhood-level* predictions of trends in the proportion of the population in age groups with elevated risks of offending or being victimized. Or forecasting shifts in the community's racial/ethnic mix, or mix of long-time residents and international immigrants, may produce inferences about the need to plan for public and officer education concerning cultural awareness and historic intergroup adversity.

A middle manager might also, for example, help predict and plan preventive measures against crime and disorder risks that could be exacerbated by the opening of a mental health out-patient treatment center in a given neighborhood. Knowledge that "deinstitutionalized" people suffering emotional disorders are likely to congregate in a particular location can be key "order maintenance" intelligence. Middle managers could take on the daunting task of developing expertise in how to handle emotionally disturbed persons—and the easier but still significant challenge of building collaborative relationships with competent mental health field workers—and then pass on their knowledge and resource lists to their work teams through task-oriented training. The result could be manifest improvements in the effectiveness—and the safety—of police order maintenance efforts. Herman Goldstein and Sheldon Kranz observed more than a decade ago, in the American Bar Association's *Urban Police Function* standards, that

> "the heart of policing consists of working with difficult human problems—often at a point of crisis. Police officers must handle a steady stream of the most serious, the most unusual, the most deviant, and the most bizarre in human conduct that reflects personal and interpersonal problems of the most aggravated form. Many such problems come to officers' attention because the problems are beyond the capacity of those who are professionally trained to aid in solving them. Viewed in this manner, it seems preposterous that those who are called on to handle the most difficult of human problems in their most aggravated forms should receive the least amount of training in this area. ***
> If the police are equipped with adequate knowledge regarding different cultures and life-styles, they can enter into...contacts [with neighborhood residents] with confidence and with less need to rely on their authority. It may be that skill in interpersonal relationships may be as important as physical fitness in equipping officers to cope with potentially dangerous situations" (American Bar Association 1979: 1/188-1/189).

It is hoped that community-based officers will develop considerable expertise in finding demographic and ethnographic information that has a direct bearing on their capacity to do collaborative problem solving in their beats. But there may be numerous situations where middle managers can supplement this information and spot emerging demographic trends that individual officers, immersed in their particular POP projects, may not detect. Even observant officers may not detect *gradual* changes in a neighborhood.

> "Like a mother who doesn't notice how much her child has grown until a cousin comments on what a big boy the child has become since his last visit, officers who regularly patrol a neighborhood may not even realize that changes over time have meant, in essence, that they are working in a different place" (Fyfe 1995).

Equally important for police to realize is that their behavior—intervening or refraining from intervening—in community problems may have powerfully contributed to making the neighborhood "a different place." The police can be like lightning. As Willie Tyler says, "The reason lightning doesn't strike twice in the same place is that the same place isn't there the second time" (quoted in Pritchett and Pound 1995: 14).

The implications of a neighborhood being "a different place" for collaborative problem solving and supportive training are not always obvious. Accordingly, police middle managers have a potentially very useful role to play for officers in making sense of important demographic shifts in neighborhoods (Fyfe 1995).

A related issue on which middle managers could be useful is exploring the discrepancy, if any, between various neighborhoods' natural boundaries and the borders of the police work areas that overlap those neighborhoods. Mid-managers may discover that it is beneficial, where possible, to modify the beat, precinct, or district boundaries so they coincide very closely with the neighborhood's domain. In a number of communities, that tactic has facilitated communication, cooperation, and ownership of problems by beat officers and residents (Joachimstaler 1995: 3).

☐ *Middle managers as diplomats.* Community problem solving, as indicated earlier, involves a lot more persuading and negotiating (toward *win-win* solutions, one hopes) than does traditional, my-way-or-the-highway policing. People with superb negotiating and diplomatic skills need to impart those talents to the extent they can be taught to people who carry guns and wear badges. To be sure, police departments normally have a fair number of officers with significant negotiating abilities. They are not just the high-profile people who talk jumpers down from bridges or penthouse window ledges or persuade hostage takers to surrender bloodlessly. They are run-of-the-mill great street cops who have learned that the best tools they have in many situations are their mouth and their wits. The streets have too many opportunities for officers to paint themselves into corners out of which even the Marines couldn't extricate them safely. Most rookie cops have learned in the college of hard knocks the truth of the old homily, "Don't bite off more than you can chew." (The common lockerroom version of that homily deploys imagery involving body parts of alligators and canaries.)

The kind of diplomatic skills we *primarily* have in mind for middle managers to offer their departments, however, are not their gifts for street-level negotiations during incidents in progress. Rather, we have in mind middle managers helping officers conduct what can be very complex and delicate negotiations with particular neighborhoods or blocks outside the context of immediate incidents. Such negotiations might be over the standards of public behavior that will be enforced at specified times and under specified conditions. It would be difficult—and important—enough to begin to develop *generalized* codes of public order.[17] But that may not suffice in most communities' increasingly diverse neighborhoods. What is acceptable public behavior in one locale (e.g., groups of people sitting on a sidewalk playing board games) may be considered disorderly conduct in another (Farrell, et al. 1993a). As the saying goes, "One neighborhood's fun is another's disorder" (Reiner 1992: 480). Or, as communications guru Tony Schwartz points out, "Noise is *unwanted* sound," and what different people want to hear generally—or what the same person wants to hear at different times—will vary. When potentially disruptive behavior crosses boundaries (e.g., boom boxes are transported across states-of-mind on buses or trains), then a generalized code of conduct acceptable to diverse groups will be needed. But if such behavior is confined to a locale whose culture views the conduct as perfectly acceptable, officious suppression by the police could turn a picnic into a riot.

Middle managers wading into diplomatic waters to contend with subcultural public order issues may find quite helpful a small guidebook prepared by the Vera Institute of Justice, under former Vera president Michael Smith's leadership. The pamphlet compiles imaginative ideas for how to deal with "disorderly groups" that were distilled from hours of one-on-one interviews by Vera staff with New York City cops (Farrell, et al. 1993a). The officers' ideas include a range of practical street tactics, and Vera has framed those ideas with a rich discussion of the delicate balancing act our democracy requires between individual rights and responsibilities. Among the cautions contained in the manual is

> "[s]olving such problems requires understanding the offending group's dynamic, knowing the community's standards for orderly behavior, and devising a strategy that brings the group's behavior within those standards or increases the community's tolerance for the group, or both" (Farrell, et al. 1993a: 7).

Another insight offered by the NYPD officers who provided background for the pamphlet:

> "A group may be considered a disorderly one by many residents, but not by others; or the group may be a core part of a community, while some aspect of its behavior is disruptive of the whole. *Conflicting community views about whether a group is disorderly or not often makes it more of a problem, not less of one. These are the problems that escalate into 'wedge issues' that destroy a community's capacity to move against the other problems it confronts*" (Farrell, et al. 1993a: 12) (emphasis added).

Middle managers as diplomats may help communities and cops not only address appropriate definitions of disorder but also reach concurrence about the *means* of enforcement and peacekeeping within the law and applicable values that will be used to control disorder. Such negotiations should take their cue from the department's central values, which almost certainly

---

[17] Herman Goldstein told an American Bar Association committee, meeting in Miami on February 11, 1995, that crafting a Model Code of Public Order was an early, unrealized hope for the ABA's "Criminal Justice Standards" project, which eventually produced the widely influential "Urban Police Function" standards, co-authored in their first edition by Herman Goldstein and Sheldon Kranz.

will say explicitly or implicitly that citizen and police frustration cannot justify use of unlawful or unsavory tactics that will contribute to broader disrespect for law (Weisburd, et al. 1988: 42).

The explicit negotiation with communities of peacekeeping and problem-solving tactics raises significant legal and political issues that middle managers may also be able to help resolve for officers and their collaborators in other government agencies. The core issue, which Herman Goldstein has often suggested needs considerable attention as part of the foundation for problem-oriented policing, is how to specify the legal/political authority for officers using tactics other than arrest to intercede in the lives of citizens. That is, what guidelines, based on what justification, will help structure officer discretion both to empower problem-solving efforts and to clarify limits on the exercise of police power? (See also Weisburd, et al. 1988: 41.)

We do not mean that lieutenants, captains and civilian middle managers can, all by themselves, forge law reform and political clarification of options and limits for officer activity. But by clarifying in vivid terms (grounded in real-life anecdotes) what the areas of undue vagueness are at present and making suggestions for how the public's needs might better be met through changes in the authorizing environment, middle managers may catalyze and shape the change process. In framing discretionary *enforcement* options, middle managers and their collaborators with expertise on legal and political issues should not overlook the fact that police may be able to accomplish useful things at times simply by making *suggestions* that citizens do things that the police are powerless to compel. Braiden (1995) suggested that, "where police don't have authority to take *action* against a problem, they can give *advice*, like a doctor gives it—'If you keep this up, you're going to get sick.'"

In any such effort to helpfully structure officer discretion, care needs to be taken—especially in departments that are still quite rule-bound—that officer discretion is not excessively structured. Too much guidance or direction can be stifling, as police have

> *"The desire to help, when coupled with the desire to control, is totalitarian"* (David Greenberg).

learned for decades under traditional organizational approaches. A desire to be helpful, reflected in very detailed guidance, may have the practical effect of undercutting the grant of discretion. An example comes from Sparrow (1992: 54), who relates a story about a delegation of expanded arrest discretion in the United Kingdom. The grant of broader arrest powers emanated from the Attorney General's office, and the way that some county police agency headquarters in turn communicated the grant of wider discretion to their officers eviscerated the desired discretion:

"The 1984 publication in Britain of the *Attorney General's New Guidelines on Prosecution and Cautioning Practice* provides a useful example [of the tendency for centralized authorities to issue more detailed guidance than local practitioners find necessary or helpful]. The purpose of the guidelines was to introduce the idea that prosecutions should be undertaken when, and only when, prosecution best serves the public interest. As such, the guidelines represent a broadening of police discretion. In the past, police were authorized to caution only juveniles and senior citizens. Under the new guidelines offenders of any age may be cautioned in appropriate circumstances. Unfortunately, the order was issued in some county forces through some 30 pages of detailed, case-by-case, instructions distributed from headquarters. The mass of instructions virtually obscured the fact that broader discretion was being granted" (Sparrow 1992: 54).

☐ *Middle managers as border guards.* One of the more difficult, risky tasks that middle managers may need to perform to assist the implementation of community problem solving is protecting (and seeking help from senior managers in protecting) problem-solving officers from pressures to revert to traditional methods. Those pressures may be imposed by the officers' peers, other managers, sister city agencies, politicians, the media, and others with power. Mastrofski (1993: 11) suggests that the challenge "is in buffering [community policing] experiments from the demands of organizational routine and a public that is not so tolerant of trial and error."

Middle managers who are committed to positive changes in their department can do a great service to their own communities and to the community policing movement, albeit at some personal career risk, if they can find ways to protect good cops from inept or malicious supervisors, managers and other reform obstructionists. Moving a police department is difficult enough without having to entrust too many of the delicate maneuvers to the police world's equivalent of Garrison Keillor's Monback Movers.

Kanter (1982: 100; 1983) describes a border guard role for middle managers, protecting the innovation action team from *external* interference that would undermine or retard progress:

"Whereas managers need to directly counter open challenges and criticism that might result in the flow of power or supplies being cut off, they simply keep other interference outside the boundaries of the project. In effect, the manager defines a protected area for the group's work. He or she goes outside this area to head off critics and to keep people or rules imposed by higher management from disrupting project tasks. While the team itself is sometimes unaware of the manager's contributions, the manager...patrols the boundaries.... Acting as interference filters, managers in my study protected innovative projects by bending rules, transferring funds 'illicitly' from one budget line to another, developing special reward or incentive systems that offered bonuses above company pay rates, and ensuring that *superiors stayed away unless needed*" (Kanter 1982: 101) (emphasis added).

> *When former Superintendent Chris Braiden was placed in charge of a major organizational reform project in Edmonton (evaluating the Department's structure and recommending significant changes), he more than once had to run interference with the chief to protect the project and his team from manipulation or frustration by influential people whom the project made nervous or antagonistic (Braiden 1995).*

Holding superiors at bay, particularly those with micromanagerial tendencies, constitutes a great test of employees' individual bravery and loyalty to mission. But bravery must be tempered with diplomacy, as Seattle Chief Norm Stamper (1995a) observes, for "unless superiors are invested in a project or strategic innovation, they can't or won't support it. They need some association with the effort." Sensenbrenner (1991: 69) adds a caution not to thwart much needed inter-agency partnerships by misguidedly "protecting [the] department from the rest of city government." A manager who has done that, Sensenbrenner opined, "could hardly have devised a better way to nip cooperation in the bud and help problems multiply."

Kanter (1982: 101; 1983) adds another critical role for middle managers: helping to ensure that, while they're watching the borders, no *internal* actor is ruining the project they are protecting from alien forces. Internal interference (resistance within the work group) may arise for any of various reasons, including excessive work loads, doubts about the value of the undertaking, or leaders' ambivalence expressed through mixed messages.

❑ *Middle managers as boundary-spanning agents and resource brokers.* Being a boundary-spanning agent sometimes seems like the opposite of being a border guard. It's somewhat like the distinction between an immigration official who congenially makes it easier for legitimate immigrants to cross their nation's boundaries and the border patrol that concentrates mainly on fending off those who have no legitimate business crossing. Both roles are important, but they can be very different. Properly understood and implemented, these roles are *not conflicting* parts of a comprehensive strategy for helping improve what happens *within* the national or organizational borders. They are *complementary* functions.

Middle managers as boundary-spanning agents can help others move across various kinds of organizational compartments. Some of the walls that need to be scaled are *functional* barriers, such as those between specialized units or between the police and other government agencies (Sensenbrenner 1991: 69). Others are *resource* or *competency* boundaries. In the case of resource barriers, for example, a helpful middle manager can span the gap between expertise about community problems (the officers' and the community's know-how) and pertinent organizational resources needed to address those problems. Sparrow, et al. (1990: 213) observe that

"middle managers separate knowledge from power in the department. Knowledge of the harsh realities of community problems has normally resided at the street level, and power over resources has been carefully preserved at the top. Middle managers must stop being a barrier between the two and start bringing them together."

As a broker between departmental elites and work-a-day problem solvers, the middle manager can help to win organizational acknowledgment (that is, persuade the elites) of the importance of particular problems officers wish to address (Sparrow, et al. 1990: 213). Having done so, the mid-manager can then make the pitch for unusual commitments of resources needed to support the officers and their collaborators. (Presumably, *usual* commitments of resources in a well-designed problem-solving agency can be secured by the first-line problem

Is the middle always an unenviable place to be—stuck between the proverbial rock and a hard place? Tongue in cheek, Braiden (1995) suggests, "In police departments the officers blame the chief for making too many rules that prevent them from thinking for themselves. The chief blames the officers for being too timid to think for themselves. The best place to be is in the middle, because you can blame both ends!"

solvers without intervention from middle managers.) A kind of atypical resource commitment with which officers might need and appreciate their bosses' help is a large amount of time within and outside an officer's normal shift to address problems which are considered complicated but, with enough effort, "solvable." Another special kind of commitment might be extensive and intensive collaboration with agencies outside the police department's service jurisdiction, which might necessitate clearing certain kinds of intergovernmental cooperation hurdles. Still another is simply considerable amounts of money to underwrite expensive efforts that cannot be funded by conventional means.

There are also a host of resource needs that first-line problem-solving officers will have but whose task-relatedness the middle manager might have to fight to establish, especially during a department's early transition into a problem-solving mode. An example might be the opportunity for officers to conduct or commission surveys and get pertinent crime and disorder analyses in a timely fashion (Eck and Spelman 1987: 104). The officer might want the disorder data for addressing an order maintenance problem in its own right or because the disorder provides an incubator in which more serious crimes thrive (see Wilson and Kelling 1983; Kelling 1985; and Skogan 1990). To accommodate such continuing information needs by first-line problem solvers, an organization's infrastructure (particularly crime analysis and R&D units) may need to be substantially upgraded.

With access to organizational elites—or at least better access than first-line employees will normally have—the middle manager can also close information gaps that will enable organizational leaders and influential people outside the department to offer timely praise for exemplary police work by problem-solving teams. This includes praise aimed not only at police department sworn and civilian employees but praise for noteworthy *community* self-improvement and revitalization efforts.

> *Corporate leaders must make it relatively easy for creative, innovative employees to tap the organizational power ("information, resources, and support") needed to implement innovations (Kanter 1982: 98; 1983).*

Another crucial role for the boundary spanner is to ensure that subordinate supervisors and first-line personnel continue to get the training and other professional development opportunities they need. As we have emphasized throughout this book, the work of police officers is in the process of changing in revolutionary (albeit perhaps, to outsiders, in *quietly* revolutionary) ways. For this revolution to succeed will require a monumental commitment to reeducation efforts for those expected to carry out radically unfamiliar functions.

The organizational broker or boundary spanner needs to have sharp scissors—or depending on the extent of bureaucratic underbrush, a huge machete—for cutting organizational red tape. This role contrasts sharply, of course, with the conventional image of the middle manager as slamming doors on subordinates' needs for timely and pertinent organizational support (Chicago Police Department 1994: 142). One can usually spot the sorry subordinate who dared to ask a by-the-book boss to help with the organization's red tape—the employee comes away wrapped in it like a mummy!

☐ *Address the problem of middle managers' distance from the department's customers.* Middle managers need to find "tricks" to keep themselves motivated on such often thankless tasks as cutting bureaucratic red tape. Success in such endeavors is not likely to be the subject of teaser announcements promoting the evening TV news! While glory and 15-minutes of fame are, therefore, unlikely lures to bureaucratic renovation, middle managers can avail themselves of the same "secret" source of inspiration that many first-line officers and police chiefs have discovered. The secret—also known by hundreds of *middle managers* across the country—is direct exposure to the appreciation of satisfied customers. As Moore (1992: 151) puts the challenge for the police CEO restructuring his or her organization, the CEO must "take steps to get officers out from behind the wheels of their cars and midlevel managers out from behind their desks and reports."

> *So long as middle managers are not accountable for community conditions (outcomes), they can afford the luxury of embracing ineffective strategies evaluated only on process elements. Drucker (1986: 200, cited in Kelling and Bratton 1993: 2), observes: "Far too few people, even in high positions with imposing titles, are exposed to the challenge of producing results."*

Opportunities for more contact between middle managers and the community can help advance several objectives. For instance, it can sensitize managers to the community's needs. Such contact can also serve as a reminder that the purpose of *internal* systems is to help officers address *external* service needs. That reminder may help middle managers avoid the problem adverted to earlier where the bus is forbidden to stop and pick up the people lest it fall behind schedule. Direct middle manager-customer interaction may also enable managers to develop an independent assessment of community needs and officers' responses to them for use in evaluating officers' work (see Wycoff and Oettmeier 1993). Moreover, such interaction can more explicitly reveal the *diversity* of problems and community preferences and resources. Armed with these insights, middle managers can take account of this diversity in making and reviewing officer evaluations.

When police employees close the gap between themselves and their customers, powerful lessons can be learned. As an officer in St. Louis observed,

> "My partner and I began holding meetings with the residents of the area trying to find out [their] concerns.... We learned several things. One main thing that we learned was that the good people far outnumbered the bad people. The good people were held captive by the bad people because they were afraid and didn't have confidence in the ability of the police to do anything about the crime problems in the neighborhood. *** Several of the police officers who were assigned to ride the area began to change their perceptions of the residents of the area, realizing that they needed the residents to effectively fight...crime.... The officers were given much information about the criminals in the area, and this was something that was unheard of before."

When he was working as a born-again foot beat officer under former Chief Bill Logan, Evanston cop Dennis Nilsson (now a lieutenant) captured graphically the sharp shift in perspective that police officers often go through when they make the transition from seeing the public as the enemy to seeing them as partners for public safety. Nilsson described to a meeting of the Harvard Executive Session on Drugs and Community Policing how ending a steady diet of criminals and low-lifes in favor of a more balanced exposure to people of all types living and working on his beat changed his outlook on the public. He titled his presentation: "A Community Policing Officer's Changing View of the Community: From Assholes to Assets."

Another clear benefit of frequent and forthright conversation between middle managers and police customers is the opportunity to try to see the police through the eyes of customers and to understand the criteria by which citizens decide how satisfied they are with police service.

Former Madison, Wisconsin, Mayor Joseph Sensenbrenner observed that city residents tend to compare the quality of local or state government service with performance of related tasks by private-sector service industries:

> "'People are making comparisons,' says one quality expert. 'They can call American Express on Monday and get a credit card in the mail by the end of the week, but it takes six weeks to get a lousy driver's license renewed. You might not think the motor vehicles division competes with American Express, but it does in the mind of the customer'" (1991: 64).

If the police make a genuine, informed commitment to open, honest, respectful dealings with their service populations, community involvement in public safety initiatives can be promoted even against the backdrop of stark community-police alienation. New Orleans, for instance, has been plagued over the past several years with police corruption and violence problems that caused some residents to feel it was dangerous to call the police for help (for related problems in certain Chicago neighborhoods, where a few officers allegedly are affiliated with criminal street gangs, see Oclander 1995a, 1995b, 1995c: 12). Yet, a determined commitment by a new chief to changing the culture of the New Orleans Police by confronting the dysfunctionality of corruption has begun to pay some dividends. A resident of one of New Orleans' impoverished public housing communities told an interviewer recently: "With community policing eventually there's a *comfort zone*"—because the gap of ignorance and distrust between the police and community gets narrower (D. Wilson 1995; compare Herbert 1995a, 1995b).

Dealing with middle managers'—and officers'—estrangement from or mere unfamiliarity with a community also can help to sharpen their focus about the underlying causes of time-consuming calls for police service. Innumerable problem-solving stories support this observation. Braiden (1995) illustrates the point: An elderly widow who called the police repeatedly without good reason hoarded lots of police time. The beat officer who took time to talk with her figured out that her variegated pleas for policing were in reality expressions of loneliness and requests for attention. With her permission, he signed her up for a widow's social group. In the ensuing years, she never called the police again on nonsense. As Chris Braiden related this story in a recent community policing workshop for the police and civic leaders in Evanston, Illinois, he asked the assemblage Socratically, "How do police spot such opportunities?" Under her breath, a city manager's staffer in the audience timidly got it right: "Just take the blinders off." Closing the distance between police and their customers is a powerful way to help officers throw off the blinders that have become an invisible but detrimental part of their uniform.

☐ *Address the problem of middle managers' distance from the department's worker bees.* Similarly, a middle manager distant from his or her *internal* customers (subordinates) may lack a vibrant appreciation of their needs and dedication. Without this appreciation, the mid-manager may lack sufficient motivation to strive skillfully to help his or her subordinates. Providing more opportunities for contact between middle managers and officers can help the managers become more familiar with officers' strengths and weaknesses. This knowledge, in turn, can impel the middle manager to help subordinates get what they need from the department and contribute to their full potential.

Regular manager-employee contact may also help improve middle managers' skills in communicating with officers. Of course, there is the risk that familiarity will breed contempt—in either direction. But that risk cannot be allowed to forestall the effort at productive, routine communication. If to know one another is to hate one another, then the manager and/or the subordinate may need some help in improving communication skills, if possible, or some "attitude adjustment." If skill building or opinion changes are not feasible, then it may be necessary (where legal and contractual circumstances make it possible) to reassign or even terminate the offending person(s).

Another reason to foster frequent communication between managers and employees is to establish that *contact* between managers and their subordinates is a *routine, normal, and usually positive* experience rather than a sign that someone is in trouble. If such routine communication includes constructive criticism of department efforts, and the subordinates see that no harm befalls them for tendering honest opinions, this can help avert the problem of "group think" which we mentioned earlier.

Pulitzer Prize-winning journalist and author Hedrick Smith (1995: 12), speaking to the National Press Club, cited a private-sector example of how managers who try to close the physical distance between themselves and first-line employees can improve information flow and worker morale. Recalling his recent walking tour of the Ford Motors South Chicago plant, Smith, author of *Rethinking America*, reported the plant's decision to eliminate "the golf carts that the managers were riding around in. Now, this plant is enormous," Smith recalled,

"and it has concrete floors. ...I walked all over that plant, and...my feet hurt just thinking about walking around that plant. So the managers of course rode around in golf carts, and everybody else walked the concrete floor. Now, two things happen if you ride golf carts in a factory. One is everyone else hates you...because they envy you. And the other thing is the only people you're talking to are the other people in the golf cart. There is no communication going on with the rest of the factory. So the boss there,...named Redge Anson, said, 'We're going to eliminate the golf carts, and the managers, including me, are going to start talking to the people on the assembly line.' [You] have to do more than just make yourself physically available; you've got to be intellectually available. You've got to be open. You've got to be willing to listen. You've got to do what any good reporter does, and that is go ask people what's going on, what's wrong, and

> **HOW NOT TO CLOSE THE GAP BETWEEN MIDDLE MANAGERS AND WORKING COPS:** *Middle managers opposed to a new way of doing business can easily sabotage a reform chief's agenda by complying with the letter but not the spirit of new procedures. For instance, consider the acting weekend duty commander who, following the mandate to get out on the streets and see what the officers and the community are facing, takes a marked squad car out and responds to the scene of various calls for service. What's the problem? He stood at a slight distance from each scene, not helping serve the citizen's needs, not encouraging the officer to do his or her best work, with his arms folded and a scowl on his face. The message rang loud and clear to the officers being observed: "Go on. Make my day. Violate some rule or procedure."*

draw yourself into the process and draw other people into the process. And they began to do that [in the South Chicago plant]" (Smith 1995: 12).

Informal training at roll call or at other times is one of the many settings in which middle managers might close the gap between themselves and first-line personnel. A middle manager might design and deliver such training personally or simply coordinate its preparation by someone else, make the logistical arrangements, and participate in the discussion to gain familiarity about what is on the minds of officers.

An example of such training might be assisting officers with developing expertise in accessing city services, to deal with such problems as "graffiti, pot holes, abandoned buildings, broken street lights, and missing traffic signs" (Skogan, et al. 1994: 7/11). The training might also focus on the "social service resources available to residents in [the officers'] districts and on how the public can access them" (*ibid.*). A middle manager might approach this challenge by teaming with police union representatives to jointly plan and conduct a seminar for police officers and their families concerning the social services available to *them*, should they need the help, in their own neighborhoods of the city. This focus would show concern for the well-being of officers and their career survival and success. In turn, officers who had developed an appreciation for the social services available in or near the beats where they reside could be peer resources to fellow officers assigned to work those beats and who need to make social service referrals to beat residents in the course of their problem-solving police work. There is potentially a triple "win" from such an approach: the department shows respect for the personal health and welfare of officers and their families, colleagues come to see one another as experts, and the union gets to play a positive role in advancing community problem solving (on the latter point, see Kelling and Kliesmet 1995).

❑ *What chiefs, senior police managers, and local government leaders can do to help.* Stated most succinctly, these officials can be useful by facilitating the accomplishment of *everything* that has been recommended previously in this chapter. Moreover, those senior officials would go far toward helping middle managers follow the counsel in this book if the senior officials treated middle managers in the way they would like mid-level employees to treat subordinates. (Kelling and Bratton 1993: 10-11 discuss broadly the kinds of contributions that police executives and government leaders can make to bring middle managers into the fold as organizational problem solvers.) In the balance of this chapter, we shall be more specific about selected items on the "to-do" list of police higher-ups and appointed and elected government officials.

For starters they can articulate a clear, powerful, consistent vision for the kind of department the chief and other key stakeholders want (Kelling and Bratton 1993: 10). When Chris Braiden served as an Edmonton Police Superintendent, for example, the vision he propounded was that the Edmonton Police Department should become "the Mayo Clinic of Policing" (Braiden 1995). Detail was needed, and was supplied, but that was certainly a strikingly powerful vision. Or consider George Kelling's provocative proposal that a community policing department's core mission should be to prevent the *next* crime. Empowered by Charlotte-Mecklenburg Police Chief Dennis Nowicki to reconsider the Department's compact with the community, a task force recently accepted Kelling's challenge. The mission/value statement they fashioned provides:

"The Charlotte-Mecklenburg Police Department will build on problem-solving partnerships with our citizens *to prevent the next crime* and enhance the quality of life throughout our community, always treating people with fairness and respect" (Charlotte-Mecklenburg Police Department 1995) (emphasis in original).

A striking example of a police unit whose dedication to catching crooks overwhelmed its obligation to prevent the next crime is the LAPD's notorious Special Investigations Section. The Department was slapped with law suits by victims of store robberies who alleged that the robberies were observed but not averted by the SIS team. This police unit, hoping to gather evidence against the offenders, recurringly waited until the crimes had been completed and then engaged the culprits in fatal gunfights (Meyer 1994a, 1994b; Martin 1994; Smith 1994). The SIS example has provided a powerful negative lesson to police in many jurisdictions about how better to prioritize their complicated duties to serve and protect.

Powerful stakeholders can also provide a clear mandate to all department employees for the changes they must help achieve. Moreover, the top bosses and outsider leaders can help secure the resources needed to provide adequate planning for the major strategic changes and any needed pilot-testing and subsequent redesign. It should never be forgotten that the full transition from stuck-in-the-mud traditional law enforcement to robust community policing will not be measured in hours or months but in years. It may even be measured in generations. As some sage once suggested, "The things worth accomplishing in life cannot be accomplished in one lifetime." During the transition, the change-agents will need to be resilient, patient, and very tolerant of ambiguity.

Skolnick and Bayley (1988) relate a British joke about how you can tell when the London Metropolitan Police Department is in the midst of the difficult transition from traditional to community policing, with all the ambiguity that metamorphosis creates over expected roles: The bobby, riding his bicycle through the park, spots a strolling pedestrian. The bobby promptly jumps off his bike, throws the pedestrian to the ground, and tells him what time it is.

It wouldn't be funny if it didn't contain at least a grain of truth. The bobby may have been under pressure to produce his daily quota of "positive citizen contacts." If that seems ridiculous, consider a practice criticized by Skogan, et al. (1994: 7/5-7/7) in which a police department determined to launch community policing on a tight, politically driven timetable, issued an edict that all community policing beat officers should have five "nonconfrontational

> *"I know what 'bottom-up' innovation means to most police mid-managers," quipped Evanston, Illinois, lieutenant Dennis Nilsson. "It means the manager's bottom is up and exposed in case something goes wrong!"*

contacts per day with citizens." Even if the result is not alienation of officers from their potential problem-solving partners in the community, such well-intentioned but ill-advised bean counting can be demeaning to the officers and the citizens affected. Engineered friendliness also is likely to lead both parties to ridicule the new strategy as superficial, public-mollifying window dressing.

At times, the practitioner devotees of community policing, driven as much by faith as by "admissible evidence" that this new approach will attain the desired results, must feel like "the blind man trying to guide a stubborn elephant" (Sawyer 1995). Not only must influential people foster an environment tolerant of ambiguity about the details of an emerging police strategy, they need to help many skeptical managers attain some professional comfort with innovation driven from *the bottom up.* As New York City Police Sergeant William Goodbody (1995: 14) explains:

> "One way to change existing organizational practices is to re-evaluate how we view organizational change itself. Traditionally, organizational planning and change have been seen as preconceived activities. In this scenario, enlightened leadership has a battle plan for reform. The very process of change begins at the top of the hierarchy and is implemented downward throughout the department. When we begin to vest decision-making and operational power with the work force, this standard prescription of change becomes less relevant.
>
> ... [Commentators have argued that] a theory that 'assumes goals come first and action comes later is frequently wrong. Human choice behavior is at least as much a process for discovering goals as for acting on them.' While the mission and objectives of policing remain devoted to addressing crime-related issues, defining community problems (quality-of-life issues) and how to combat them...will be a fluid process requiring flexible organizational supports. The organization, and the people involved in the process, will have to look for change and innovation in action and not wait for it to come down from above."

We suspect that a serious study of humankind's innovations over the course of history would reveal that necessity was, indeed, usually the mother of invention; and that necessity typically is first and most clearly perceived by those directly involved in struggling to make something happen.

Top people can and must also grant clear authority to implement the needed changes to the responsible managers. But they can't devolve and disappear. They must show continuing *personal* interest in and support for the mid-manager's efforts to push forward toward the goal. In the private-sector organizational reform setting, for middle managers to be able to carry off successful innovations,

> "a general blessing from the top is clearly necessary to convert potential supporters into a solid team. In one case [of private sector mid-management innovation], top officers simply showed up at a meeting where the proposal was being discussed; their presence ensured that other people couldn't use the 'pocket veto' power of headquarters as an excuse to table the issue. Also, the very presence of a key executive at such a meeting is often a signal of the proposal's importance to the rest of the organization" (Kanter 1982: 100).

Another arena of reform requiring senior administrative and political support entails performance evaluation for *middle managers.* Big bosses must use the same kinds of refashioned performance appraisal and reward tactics on middle managers that we earlier urged the mid-managers to use to motivate their subordinates. Thus there should be a clear linkage of rewards to performance in implementing the desired changes. Deserving middle managers can be rewarded not only with promotions (of which there are precious few available) but also with interesting temporary assignments, travel to conferences, opportunities to step into the limelight (such as at news conferences and high-profile public events or by co-authoring published articles), and other professional development opportunities and perks. Monetary bonuses, which are commonplace in the private sector, may be available in the public sector on a far more limited basis or they may simply be unavailable (Kelling and Bratton 1993: 10). But it is worth keeping in mind two earlier examples: corporate executive David Robbins' forsaking the *pay*-for-suggestions approach as he successfully catapulted his manufacturing company over a couple years from a mediocre rate of implemented employee recommendations to world-class status; and "Braiden's bottle" of Irish whiskey for Edmonton cops who turned in exemplary contributions to community problem solving. The examples may teach us that sometimes *tangible* bonuses work in policing and more *ephemeral* approaches work in the bottom-line-oriented business world.

The example of "Braiden's bottle" brings up another, crucial contribution that police chiefs, politicians and local government administrators must make to enable middle managers to actively and successfully participate on a community policing implementation team. The reader will recall the context in which Superintendent Braiden began his whiskey award—he was disgusted at having to give the same "exemplary conduct" prize, which was really a "longevity" award masquerading as a merit award, to two officers on the same day. One officer was a superlative performer; the other, a laggard. The pertinent point at this juncture is that those people with significant power to influence middle managers must avoid sending the mixed messages that would come from *equally* rewarding obstructionists and contributors (Kelling and Bratton 1993: 10). "Just as parents must convey clear values to their children," Braiden (1995) suggests, "the chief must make a clear statement—through *action*—about who he or she considers a hero and who is not a hero."

> *What departure from traditional practice is intended by giving police territorial responsibility rather than shift responsibility? "At first sight it appears that patrol officers who drive cars on shift work have territorial responsibility; for eight hours a day they each cover an area. In fact, there are two senses in which that particular area is not the officer's professional territory. First, officers know that they may be dispatched to another area at any time, should the need arise. Second, they are not responsible for anything that occurs in their area when they are off duty. *** The fact that a professional territory spans a period of time rather than an area clearly has the effect of forcing the officer's concern to be largely focused on incidents rather than on long-term problems of which the incidents may be symptoms" (Sparrow 1992: 56).*

Police chiefs—and, often, city of county hall officials—will also be needed to help middle managers push through positive changes in *structures* that will facilitate problem solving. An example would be shifting from a centralized, functional system to a decentralized, geographic approach (Kelling and Bratton 1993: 8). Another would be establishing stable beat assignments. And still another would be framing and implementing a system that manages calls for service well enough to allow time for problem solving. In many locales the move into a meaningful differential response system is considered to be political nitroglycerin, and the active assistance of community organizations and others is needed to provide political cover for elected officials and appointees—such as police chiefs—who serve without job security.

Senior police administrators can also make middle managers more credible to their subordinates by visibly involving middle managers in the key planning for change (Kelling and Bratton 1993: 10). Moreover, a consultative relationship by upper-level officials toward mid-managers will motivate middle managers to keep thinking about how to help the top people meet their goals. An obvious example is querying middle managers about the kind of executive development training they need and enjoy when curriculum planners are revising such training (see Zhao, et al. 1995: 17-18). In Savannah, Georgia, for instance, police Major Dan Reynolds needed to upgrade middle management training on how to facilitate community problem solving. He surveyed his upcoming students to ask them what has worked and what could be improved in the community-service efforts of both first-line problem solvers and their middle-management facilitators. Reynolds' questions may be helpful to other agencies. After seeking a description of a "POP" project that the mid-manager or his or her officers have conducted, the survey asked each respondent to:

☐ "Describe your role, as a supervisor, in the completion of the POP project."
☐ "Describe any problems [or] challenges you, or the officer you assisted, encountered in completing this POP project. Explain how you assisted the officer or dealt with the problem."
☐ "Describe specific skills or talents you feel helped you successfully complete the POP project or assist the officer in completing the project."
☐ "Provide any suggestions or comments you have which we should incorporate into future POP training or the POP program" (Reynolds 1994).

Likewise, in revising the Chicago Police Department's in-service supervisor training for community policing, implementation manager Chuck Ramsey, now a deputy superintendent and considered by many to be a rising star, reportedly won the appreciation of mid-managers for consulting them closely on what they liked and disliked about previous rounds of training (Skogan, et al. 1995: 18). Of course, the *sine qua non* of such consultation is that the person asking for the advice must both really want to hear the answers and have the power to do something with them that the respondents will consider useful.

Senior police administrators and local government *personnel* officials who have police hiring authority may need to "weed and seed" the middle management ranks to help cooperative employees and to hinder obstructionists in meeting their objectives. A department may have good reason to select some new middle managers who agree with the new strategy. This infusion of additional talent can create peer pressure on—and a support system for—good incumbent middle managers.

> *"Wherever I go, middle managers are cited as the blockage. We've got to quit seeing police departments as three tiers—the chief, middle managers, and everyone else, where the special talent attributed to the mid-level people is their capacity for resistance. Generally, middle managers will be as good or as bad as their leaders" (Braiden 1995).*

In numerous ways, the police chief and his or her most senior command staff also must go out of their way to "foster a creative environment" (Kanter 1982: 97) in which middle managers can do their finest work and enable others to do theirs. Kanter summarized, based on empirical study, the conditions under which *private-sector* middle managers are best able to innovate. While some of these characteristics may not apply fully to public police agencies, they may stimulate thought concerning the police context. Thus, mid-level employees best innovate in organizations that have

"☐ Multiple reporting relationships and overlapping territories. These force middle managers to carve out their own ideas about appropriate action and to sell peers in neighboring areas or more than one boss.

❑ A free and somewhat random flow of information. Data flow of this kind prods executives to find ideas in unexpected places and pushes them to combine fragments of information.

❑ Many centers of power with some budgetary flexibility. If such centers are easily accessible to middle managers, they will be encouraged to make proposals and acquire resources.

❑ A high proportion of managers in loosely defined positions or with ambiguous assignments. Those without subordinates or line responsibilities who are told to 'solve problems' must argue for a budget or develop their own constituency.

❑ Frequent and smooth cross-functional contact, a tradition of working in teams and sharing credit widely, and emphasis on lateral rather than vertical relationships as a source of resources, information, and support. These circumstances require managers to get peer support for their projects before top officers approve.

❑ A reward system that emphasizes investment in people and projects rather than payment for past services. Such a system encourages executives to move into challenging jobs, gives them budgets to tackle projects, and rewards them after their accomplishments with the chance to take on even bigger projects in the future" (Kanter 1982: 104-05; see also Kanter 1983).

Top organizational officials must also make a serious commitment to educating middle managers well, just as the middle managers must move mountains to help officers and their supervisors secure the knowledge, skills and abilities they need for problem solving and coaching of problem solvers (see Zhao, et al. 1995: 17-18). Little in typical police middle managers' prior experience equips them for their new responsibilities. Indeed, as we have discussed earlier, most of these managers have been rewarded—including by promotion to their current post—for doing well a number of things that run counter to what they will soon be expected to teach and lead others in doing. Accordingly, middle managers' bosses must be tolerant of the managers' transitional problems and offer meaningful assistance to ease their transition. In the midst of creative chaos, a middle manager may need a supportive, empathetic mentor in the organization who can reassure him or her that others are confused too and that there's no shame in being befuddled at times. Pritchett and Pound (1995: 18) report that they opened a fortune cookie which read: "You belong to a small, select group of confused people." Would that the club were an exclusive one!

A harmful error some senior officials make is expecting middle managers to use the same old skills and tools to perform new functions. A car can't go fast in second gear for long without burning up the transmission, but it can't start up well in third or fourth gear if it's pulling a heavy load. So, too, must middle managers have different speeds and different methods for different challenges.

By training middle managers in Houston's Westside district, which Betsy Watson ran under then-Chief Lee Brown (before eventually succeeding him as chief), the Houston Police Department helped address the underlying problem that had prompted resistance from the district's lieutenants: they "simply did not know what was expected of them" (Kelling and Bratton 1993: 8).

Implicit in almost everything that has been said on these pages concerning the positive contributions that middle managers can make to implementing community policing is that this assignment is a *hard* one, requiring very substantial skills. Where police middle managers do not have some of the skills they will need to be facilitators and even leaders of change, their skills must be enhanced on a priority basis. Michael Hammer told an interviewer what he believes typically causes unsuccessful corporate reengineering efforts to fail:

> "[R]engineering is like chess, not like roulette. People lose often in both, but when you lose at roulette, it's fate, chance, odds, bad luck. You don't lose at reengineering because of bad luck. You lose at reengineering out of stupidity. It's sitting down to play the game and not knowing the rules, and the mission of the queen.... It's a combination of not understanding what it is, getting caught up by the term, and having a vague and fuzzy sense, but not having any disciplined technique or tools and/or trying to make it happen without the queen; that is, an intensely committed executive leader. The biggest causes of reengineering failure are ignorance and lack of strong leadership" (quoted in Vogl 1993/1994: 53).

While the skills needed by middle managers and CEOs may differ depending on the tasks, the essential point remains that we can't expect skilled performance from players unschooled in the game.

In the St. Louis Metropolitan Police Department, reports McCrary (1995: 133-34), when community-oriented problem solving was being introduced early in 1991, the agency developed a four-day training program in the academy:

> "The board of police commissioners went through it. The majors, lieutenant colonels and the captains went through it. The department made a mistake and skipped the lieutenant and...sergeant rank, in order to get the program going, and went to the patrolman rank.... Well, what happened was, when these police officers came back from their training to their districts ready to go with their new ideas, they met opposition from the sergeants and lieutenants who hadn't had the training, who hadn't been told what the program was all about, and the initiative...almost stalled. Eventually we got through that and we got the sergeants and lieutenants trained, but it took quite a long time to get to that point."

Is training—especially high-quality training which is tailored to the needs of the trainees—cheap? No. But as Spitzer (1995) observes about private-sector organizations, "More and more companies realize that ignorance is more expensive than training."

Although there is much valuable information that can be transmitted to middle managers during formal academy workshops, there can be no substitute—given that the heart of community problem solving is using judgment wisely to apply general principles to specific issues—for the kind of learning that can only come through mentoring relationships. As Tonry (1995: v), quoting the sage Veraswami, said in dedicating a recent book to criminologist Norval Morris, "So far as I can see, *everyone* who achieves anything of note reports having had a mentor, someone to whose spark of encouragement and teaching he owes his achievement." The wise chief will surround himself or herself with people who can be intelligent consumers of the chief's craftsmanship and vision—and who can teach the chief how to do a better job by continually and candidly asking the hard questions from which all need to learn.[18]

Providing formal education and mentorship to middle managers in what they should do is necessary but hardly sufficient to enable the middle managers to break down bureaucratic walls that will impede community problem solving. Because there will be people pushing back on the other side of many of those walls, top bosses can create a community-wide environment conducive to change by developing powerful external constituencies for change. This can be done partly through the top officials' openness to the news media, the community at large, and community leaders. (Kelling and Bratton 1993: 5 discuss some lessons on this point derived from a failed strategic innovation effort in Dallas.) The senior change-agent in a police department

> *Among the most important things mayors, city managers, city councils, police chiefs and others who can affect a middle manager's work environment must do is establish the predicates for quality in the police organization. Former Madison, Wisconsin, Mayor Joe Sensenbrenner (1991: 69) succinctly described the four TQM pillars on which Madison sought to support its strengthening of city services: "excellence as defined by our customers, respect for employee worth, teamwork, and data-based decisionmaking."*

"may identify pressure groups that he can use to his advantage by eliciting from them public enunciation of particular concerns. He may be able to foster and empower the work of commissions, committees, or inquiries that help to make his organization vulnerable to change. He can then approach his own organization backed by a public mandate—and police of all ranks will, in due course, face questions from the public itself that make life very uncomfortable for them if they cling to old values" (Sparrow 1992: 52; see also Moore 1994: 292; 1990).

The chief or other change agent thinking about employing such inside-outside pressure tactics on an organization can hardly expect to have this playing field entirely to himself or herself. As Moore and Stephens (1991a: 108-09) suggest,

"[I]f it appears that there is turmoil in the department and that the turmoil is being created by an executive who does not understand his job or the mission of the police...then [influential] outsiders will intervene. The intervention will often be to remove the chief so that things can get back to normal.

The insiders know this. They also have relatively easy ways of mobilizing the outsiders. There is often a police union that can complain loudly about the changes planned or occurring within the department. The detectives often have quite easy access to police reporters, who can produce stories about declining

---

[18] Ruben Ortega, currently the police chief in Salt Lake City, seems to have exemplary mentoring abilities. When he was chief in Phoenix, in an experience that, to our knowledge, nobody has yet studied or written about, Ortega fashioned a relationship with (and, presumably, an empowerment of) his five assistant chiefs, which must have been exceptional. It can't be strictly an accident that every single one of these five assistant chiefs went on to become a well-respected police CEO in significant departments around the nation. As Braiden (1995) says, "Ruben Ortega was not lessened by the success of his assistant chiefs. He was magnified by it. His career illustrates the point that the primary power a chief possesses is the power to give others a chance to be great." Perhaps Ortega should be commissioned to reflect on what is being done, and can be done, to help *middle managers* around the landscape do as well for their industry as the five Phoenix phenoms are doing for it.

morale and a loss of professional competence as a result of changes the chief is making. Thus, subordinates, in alliance with outsiders, can oust a chief who demands changes that are unpopular. Indeed, it is probably true that more police executives have been fired by their subordinates than by their mayors."

Facing such a set of challenges in Philadelphia, the police commissioner sought to overcome "an administrative culture designed to resist change" (Greene, et al. 1994: 99). He did so partly by "forming a coalition of upper and middle-level managers with active external business and community support...." In this fashion, he "sought to encourage a linkage among the long-term reform interests of the external community with the long-term capacity of those within the police department likely to be its future" (*ibid.*: 99, 102).

Sometimes the most determined change agents for implementation of police strategic or other reforms will not reside in the police chief's office or even within the police department. This perspective would hardly shock outside interest groups who see this state of affairs as the *rule* rather than the *exception* (see, e.g., Friedman 1994). Under these circumstances, the internal change-agent's task becomes the all-too-familiar one of managing *upwards*. Or an outside pressure group or think tank may be able to influence police leadership. For instance, Szanton (1981: 118-19) relates a story about the Vera Institute of Justice's success, over time, in persuading a New York City Police commissioner in 1964 to reverse a well-entrenched policy. The Vera advocates wanted to ameliorate a long-standing and "well-understood problem."

"The problem was that except for traffic and minor regulatory offenses, all arrests in New York City set off a sequence of events which dislocated the life of the accused, wasted an enormous number of police man-hours, and burdened the criminal justice system. *** Depending on the time of day, the process might take from six to 18 hours. *** The arresting officer, accompanying the accused from scene of crime to station house to court, was unavailable for patrol duties. If the arrest occurred toward the end of the officer's tour, the process meant that he would be hours late getting home—hours for which he would be only partially compensated. Some observers of the New York City Police Department believed those circumstances created a strong disincentive to arrest toward the end of tours. [An *opposite* problem was experienced by the NYPD during the next decade when overtime pay was made available. Then-Commissioner Patrick V. Murphy called the dilemma 'collars for dollars.']

The solution Vera proposed in 1964, for a limited number of crimes and for accused persons who appeared responsible, was to issue simple summonses following arrest, as in traffic offenses. The police commissioner rejected the idea. Vera countered by bringing pressure on him from an important judge and by preparing to try the idea with a suburban police department. The commissioner reluctantly agreed to a trial in one precinct. *** [S]hortly after the favorable preliminary results were in [a Vera staffer] appears to have suggested to the organizers of a national conference on criminal justice that the commissioner be asked to speak, and then to have prepared for the commissioner a talk on police innovation in New York City in which he could claim credit for the early success of the summons experiment."

This is hardly a *novel* story. There are numerous instances involving successful outside vision, R&D, lobbying, support, and yielding the spotlight to the public official who eventually came through. Yet Vera often has been better than most outside organizations in using this strategy in the criminal justice world. There is much in Vera's approach that successful reformers *inside* organizations, including police managers, can and do emulate. Szanton (1981: 120) provides insight into the Vera method (circa 1980):

> "It offers not novelty of concept but assistance in execution, insulation from risks, and good odds on winning a prize more valuable than any other to public officials: public approval. 'They are not a fault-finding organization,' remarked a former New York City police commissioner laconically. The director of Vera's Cincinnati offshoot put it more directly: 'We're in the credit business...[a]nd you've got to be sure there's credit to give. Design the experiment so it works on day one, not on day 90. You may never get to day 90.'"

The last point—that even 90-day wonders may be too politically risky for many public officials—provides troubling counsel to those of us hoping to settle in for the long haul with community problem solving. Perhaps such risks underscore the importance of longevity for such government funding and technical assistance programs as the federal Justice Department's Office of Community Oriented Policing Services. Institutions with the clout and the underwriting of the COPS office may be essential strands in the political, fiscal, and intellectual safety nets that police chiefs and elected officials will need from time to time to help them walk the high wire. Government-underwritten technical assistance, training and other support may help these dedicated local officials get through difficult implementation setbacks and ambiguities so they can persevere with much-needed strategic reform.

"Time is a wasting asset. Most of us realize this truth too late to avoid spending a lot of time unwisely..." said Chief Justice William Rehnquist at George Mason University's 1992 commencement ceremony in Fairfax, Virginia. "Another way to look at life," the 68-year-old Supreme Court justice continued, "is as a shopping mall—not the usual kind where goods are purchased with money, but one where items such as worldly success, love of music, a strong backhand, close relationships with your family, a few good friends and countless other things are on sale. The commodity with which they are purchased is not money, but time. ...[E]very one of us has exactly the same amount of time in each hour, in each day, in each year. Bear in mind this message from the older generation to your younger one: The most priceless asset that can be accumulated in the course of any life is time well spent" (quoted in an Associated Press story).

Supporting community problem solving by protecting the COPS office from those in Congress who would wipe out the office and dump its funds into state block grants is not, incidentally, a partisan political cause. Confidence in community problem solving as the appropriate strategy for safeguarding America's neighborhoods and local business investments is expressed by police, public officials, and citizens of every political stripe. Even the *Wall Street Journal* ran a commentary in favor of community policing and its federal infrastructure. "[O]n this much there is agreement," the columnist declared:

> "Community policing works, and promoting it is one small thing Washington can

The Edmonton Police Service in Canada, in an in-house newsletter, By the Way, offers the following guidance on how to implement change:

IMPLEMENTING CHANGE: WHERE DO WE BEGIN?

Since change is inevitable, the first task of a leader or leadership team is to decide what kind of change will prevail. Then as a clearer sense of purpose and a vision for constructive change begin to emerge, the next question becomes, "where do we begin?" Of course, there is no sure-fire, guaranteed formula for conflict-free change. Nonetheless, here are some suggestions about how and where to begin implementing change.

1. **Sell the problem before attempting to sell the solution.** *Think creatively about how you can help people to understand the nature of the problem that you are trying to solve. Do not allow those opposed to the change to misunderstand or misrepresent the basic issue.*

2. **Give people a sense of ownership in the process.** *Hold the vision before them clearly and consistently. Define the problem that needs to be solved. Then invite their help in creating a solution. Say, "This is where we need to go; can you help us develop an effective plan for getting there?"*

3. **Keep the process people centered.** *Let people know that you care about them. Never give the impression that your dream or your agenda is more important to you than the people who have been entrusted to your care.*

4. **Remember that people adopt change at different paces.** *Don't regard the slow adopters as enemies. Keep in mind that resistance to change is generally more emotional than rational. A rational answer will not usually satisfy an emotional need.*

5. **Be willing to work through others.** *Mark Twain observed that it is amazing how much can be accomplished if no one cares who gets the credit. Know who your key influencers are and let them lead the way.*

6. **Do not attempt to ignore or suppress dissent.** *Establish clear communication channels so that people can express their resistance and opposition without fear of reprisal. Let them know that you regard their thoughts, feelings, and comments as important. Answer their questions clearly, patiently, and gently. Ask them directly, "How do you think we should handle this problem?"*

7. **Don't move too quickly.** *Move in steps. Don't overload people with change. When possible, implement only one change at a time. Establish "pilot projects." Say, "Let's try this for the next three months, then we will evaluate it using these specific criteria." For positive reinforcement, try to develop a strategy that builds in some early successes.*

8. **Always think "win/win"; never try to beat people.** *Wherever possible, avoid calling votes. Seek to develop a consensus in order to move on to the next stage in planning and implementing. At the very least, try to avoid voting on the issue during the early stages of discussion.*

9. **Keep repeating the vision.** *Say it, show it, say it again. When you are at the point where you can hardly bring yourself to repeat it again, many people are just beginning to hear you for the first time.*

10. **Whenever possible, seek to make changes by addition, rather than by division or subtraction.** *In other words, seek as much as possible to give one group what they want without taking away from another something that they value.*

11. **Don't be surprised** *that the immediate response of most people to proposed change is to ask, "How will this affect me?" Anticipate their questions and fears, and be prepared to respond to them.*

12. **Remember that there are three types of change.** *PARALLEL DEVELOPMENT seeks to build new structures or programs alongside those that are already in place, perhaps in a complementary manner. GRADUAL CHANGE seeks to implement a new strategy over time, giving those affected lots of room to adjust. RADICAL CHANGE, as the name implies, is like surgery that is required immediately to save a dying patient. Reflect carefully, together with the other members of your leadership group, about which of these is most appropriate to your particular situation (Percy 1995).*

"By far the greatest challenge facing any leader is the ability to create positive change."—John Maxwell.

do right in the fight against crime. Now Congress wants to end the kinds of grants Kansas City is getting [from the COPS Office to fund community policing officers] and turn the money into 'block grants' that states can spend as they see fit. But perhaps as it sends out tax dollars, Congress ought to ensure that they are at least directed to police programs that are known to prevent crime. It's cheaper than building prisons" (Seib 1995: A16).

Another situation in which senior police and governmental support may be necessary is when middle managers try to fly in the face of entrenched and sometimes ugly aspects of police organizational subcultures. We have in mind bigotry on the basis of race, gender, religion or other characteristics. A lesson extracted by Kelling and Bratton (1993: 5) from Dallas was that racism can be an obstacle to police strategic reform if the reform entails community empowerment and diversification of the workforce. The chief wanted to increase minority recruitment as part of his strategic reform, and his efforts were resisted mightily by some members of the organization. Diversification of the police workforce will be sought to aid many community problem-solving efforts today also. As a result, it is important for senior, influential people in the police department, the local government, and the community's established institutions to cultivate the external demand for minority recruitment. Some analysts would argue that much of the resistance to community policing is resistance to shifting power within the community and the police department along class and racial lines (compare some of the insights in Tonry 1995 concerning the nature, extent, and effects of racism in American criminal justice policy and institutions).

Just as middle managers must strive to create work settings in which failure is allowed, so long as it is treated as a learning opportunity, so too must the middle managers' superiors enable constructive mistakes at the mid-ranks. Not only must honest mistakes be allowed, but upper-level administrators will have to ensure that there are ample new opportunities for middle managers to *succeed* within the new organizational incentive system. The new opportunities to succeed and get thanked for succeeding should be in place *before* the old opportunities are jettisoned, lest there be huge transitional problems. Middle managers have legitimate *vested interests* in continuing to have *equal opportunities*—not guarantees—of winning organizational approval, for they have been promoted to positions of responsibility based on their ability in the past to capitalize on such opportunities (Kelling and Bratton 1993: 10).

A highly specialized skill that some successful police chiefs have developed, and that middle managers need them to exercise judiciously, is the know-how to capitalize on organizational crises to make change. *Huge* crises can topple even the best organizational change agents from the posts that afford them the opportunity to reorient their agencies. But building strategically and incrementally on a succession of *survivable* crises—the pitter patter of little defeats—could well accelerate the pace of significant strategic innovation. Successfully using small crises *seriatim* requires the talent to make "maximum use of minimal crises," a phrase popular among some business school professors and related by Moore and Stephens (1991a: 111; also see Sherman and Bouza 1991). Sherman (1978) has done some of the classic writing on this topic, under the rubric of "scandal and reform."

The minimal (or larger but still bearable) crises on which the savvy administrator knows how to build to accomplish pre-existing strategic reform agendas may include:

- ☐ crime waves
- ☐ fiscal or workload crises (Kelling and Bratton 1993: 8 describe this problem in Reno, Nevada; see also Glensor 1990)
- ☐ morale crises (Kelling and Bratton 1993: 8 discuss these difficulties in the New York City Transit Police)
- ☐ integrity scandals
- ☐ crises of manifest operational ineffectiveness (for instance, if a department's radios don't work in some high-risk areas—Kelling and Bratton 1993: 8; also see Moore and Stephens 1991a: 109)
- ☐ collective violence, as in the riots in various cities over the past several decades (Moore and Stephens 1991a: 109)
- ☐ civic dysfunction or erosion of tax bases or revenue streams (e.g., a ridership drop on the public transit system because of fear of crime—Kelling and Bratton 1993: 8-9)

"[M]ost important strategic changes in police departments," Moore and Stephens (1991a: 111) argue, "have occurred in the aftermath of dramatic performance failures that seemed to reveal an incompetent organization." Although the *organization* may have been shown to have glaring incompetencies, the *change agent*, to take good advantage of the window of opportunity for innovation, must have considerable competencies. A few leaders may simply get lucky and attain important reforms without much skill. But far more often, we believe, as Elmer Letterman observed, "luck is what happens when preparation meets opportunity" (Wall, et al. 1991: iv).

"Crises seem to be important in police reform precisely because they unsettle expectations about how the police should behave. In this sense, crises might be seen as the public sector equivalent of private sector bankruptcies. *** Often what happens is that the firm is 'restructured' into a profit-making enterprise. Old activities that were not profitable are sold off. Inefficient managerial and operational practices that have accumulated within the organization are rooted out" (Moore and Stephens 1991a: 109-10).

Despite the potential strategic *opportunities* that open to a police department being buffeted by "the gale of public outrage and concern" (Moore and Stephens 1991a: 111), such crises, except in the hands of masters, may be more likely to *preclude* positive strategic reforms. A "good" scandal almost certainly will be in the eyes of the beholder. Too many politically motivated influentials, including elected officials, may be ready for their own reasons to seize on a department's scandal as proof that "the department had better quit fooling around with unproven, social-workish fads and get back to the basics of good old-fashioned law enforcement." Thus, there remains to touch on here one additional, enormous challenge for senior administrators and community elites who have the power to influence the nature and extent of strategic opportunities and obstacles. That challenge, which will powerfully affect the capacities of mid-managers to move their organizations forward, is to protect community policing from the vicissitudes of political opportunism.

In particular, a community's opinion shapers—widely respected community leaders, commentators, activists, chambers of commerce, news media assignment editors, editorial writers, voters' groups, and the like—must help ensure that *long-term* police-community strategies are sheltered from the *short-term* timetables of electoral politics (see Skogan, et al. 1994). As Trojanowicz (1994: 262) put it, "Political leaders can both support long-term policies that are needed to prevent and control crime and provide job security for chiefs of police so that they are willing to be innovative, take risks, and be agents of change." As Neil Behan (1986: 5) sees things,

> "Too often police administrators, stimulated by political necessity or the demands of the budget cycle, look only for immediate successes. State or Federal funding usually lasts for two years or less; sometimes it seems that the public's attention can be held for only a few days. But the kinds of innovations needed in policing often take longer to mature. Police managers must be ready to take risks, to sacrifice short-term gains in favor of long-term gains."

Community problem solving entails planting sequoias, and somebody has to keep the tourists from trampling the saplings.

* *

A genuine expert maintains expertise by constantly keeping "a beginner's mind," as in the epigraph: "In the beginner's mind, there are many possibilities, but in the expert's mind, few" (Rev. Ed Harris).

We began this discussion by detailing a host of reasons underlying the experts' prognostications that middle managers would thwart community problem solving if the reformers didn't find a way to remove them from the game. We weren't prepared to accept the experts' views at face value when we commenced. And we're even less inclined to accept their views now, after compiling these materials and being forced in the process to think about the issues in more depth. Experts undoubtedly will continue to amass data about the roles and potential contributions of middle managers and to dispute the data's implications, as well they should. But suppose we momentarily put aside the many living "data" we know personally who, from their posts at the mid-ranks of American policing, are contributing enormously to the implementation of community problem solving. Suppose we discounted the civilian and sworn police middle managers who, as Sensenbrenner (1991: 75) nicely phrased it, are "liberating human ingenuity and the potential pleasure in good work that lie at least dormant in every organization." Still, we would be left with a *logical* problem with the expert prognostications: Isn't it often true that someone with the power to *subvert* also has the capacity to *help*—if only by refraining from subversive tactics? If so, then the question, as numerous police leaders have suggested to us in the course of our writing, is not only about middle management *know-how* but about their *motivation* to do the right thing. Motivational questions put the ball back in the leadership court.

We end with quotes from people—Herman Goldstein, George Kelling and Bill Bratton—who have thought long and hard about two central issues: What is at stake in the life or death of community problem solving? And what are the prospects for police middle managers to be part of the solution rather than part of the problem? First, Goldstein:

> "By building on past progress and capitalizing on current momentum, change [in policing strategy] that is deeper and more lasting can be achieved. But there is an even more compelling, overriding incentive to struggle with these complexities. We are being challenged today to commit ourselves anew to our unique character as a democracy, to the high value we as a nation place on diversity, ensuring

equality, protecting individual rights, and guaranteeing that all citizens can move about freely and enjoy tranquil lives. The social problems that threaten the character of the Nation are increasing, not decreasing. It will take major changes—apart from those in the police—to reduce these problems. In this turbulent period it is more important than ever that we have a police capacity that is sensitive, effective, and responsive to the country's unique needs, and that, above all else, is committed to protecting and extending democratic values. That is a high calling indeed" (Goldstein 1993: 6).

So can middle managers help answer the call? Kelling and Bratton (1993: 11) conclude their essay, and ours, thusly:

"The idea that mid-managers are spoilers, that they thwart project or strategic innovation, has some basis in fact. Mid-managers improperly directed can significantly impede innovation. Yet, ample evidence exists that when a clear vision of the business of the organization—its purpose or objective—is put forward, when mid-managers are included in planning, when their legitimate self-interests are acknowledged, and when they are properly trained, mid-managers can be the leading edge of innovation and creativity."

Amen. Now let's get back to work!

References and Bibliography

Adams, Lorraine (1995) "Simpson Jurors Cite Weak Case, Not 'Race Card': Police Handling of Evidence Was Major Concern for Panel." *Washington Post* (October 5): A1, A26.

Alpert, Geoffrey P., and Roger G. Dunham (1989) "Community Policing." In Roger G. Dunham and Geoffrey P. Alpert (eds.), *Critical Issues in Policing: Contemporary Readings*. Prospect Heights, IL: Waveland Press.

American Bar Association (1979) "The Urban Police Function Standards." In American Bar Association, *Standards for Criminal Justice*. Washington, D.C.: American Bar Association.

Angell, John E. (1971) "Toward an Alternative to the Classic Police Organizational Arrangement: A Democratic Model." *Criminology* 8: 185-206.

Armstrong, David M. (1992) *Managing by Storying Around*. New York: Currency/Doubleday.

Associated Press (1995) "'Legalized Extortion' Targets Peoria 'Johns'." *Chicago Sun-Times* (October 4): 20.

Baker, Russell (1995) "Those Vital Paupers: Welfare is Part of Capitalism." *New York Times* (January 17): A15.

Barlett, Donald L., and James B. Steele (1992) *America: What Went Wrong?*. Kansas City, MO: Andrews and McMeel, A Universal Press Syndicate Company.

Barthel, Joan (1992) *For Children's Sake: The Promise of Family Preservation*. New York: Edna McConnell Clark Foundation.

Bayley, David H. (1988) "Community Policing: A Report from the Devil's Advocate." In Jack R. Greene and Steven D. Mastrofski (eds.), *Community Policing: Rhetoric or Reality?* New York: Praeger.

_____ (1994) "International Differences in Community Policing." In Dennis P. Rosenbaum (ed.), *The Challenge of Community Policing: Testing the Promises*. Thousand Oaks, CA: Sage.

Behan, Cornelius (1986) "Foreword" In Philip B. Taft, Jr., *Fighting Fear: The Baltimore County C.O.P.E. Project*. Washington, D.C.: Police Executive Research Forum.

Bennett, Trevor (1994) "Community Policing on the Ground: Developments in Britain." In Dennis P. Rosenbaum (ed.), *The Challenge of Community Policing: Testing the Promises*. Thousand Oaks, CA: Sage.

Berry, Rynn (1993) *The New Vegetarians*. New York and Los Angeles: Pythagorean Publishers.

Bieck, William H., William Spelman, and Thomas J. Sweeney (1991) "The Patrol Function." In William A. Geller (ed.), *Local Government Police Management*. Washington, D.C.: International City/County Management Association.

Bigham, Steve (1993) *Attitude and Public Opinion Survey: Reno Police Department—April 1993*. Reno, NV: Reno Police Department (May 18).

Bittner, Egon (1970) *The Functions of the Police in Modern Society*. Washington, D.C.: U.S. Government Printing Office.

_____ (1975) "The Capacity to Use Force as the Core of the Police Role." In Jerome H. Skolnick and T.C. Gray (eds.), *Police in America*. Boston: Little, Brown and Company.

_____ (1980) "The Capacity to Use Force as the Core of the Police Role." In *The Functions of the Police in Modern Society: A Review of Background Factors, Current Practices, and Possible Role Models*. Cambridge, MA: Oelgeschlager, Gunn and Hain.

_____ (1983) "Legality and Workmanship: Introduction to Control in the Police Organization." In Maurice Punch (ed.), *Control in the Police Organization*. Cambridge, MA: MIT Press.

_____ (1995) "Staffing and Training Problem-Oriented Policing." In Thomas G. Blomberg and Stanley Cohen (eds.), *Punishment and Social Control: Essays in Honor of Sheldon L. Messinger*. Hawthorne, NY: Aldine de Gruyter Publishers.

Block, Peter (1987) *The Empowered Manager: Positive Political Skills at Work*. San Francisco: Jossey-Bass Publishers.

Block, Wally (no date) "Briefing Memo: What Great Sergeants *DO* Differently." Oakland, CA: Author (2-page newsletter).

Boone, J. Allen (1954) *Kinship with All Life*. San Francisco: Harper San Francisco, a division of

HarperCollins Publishers.

Bracey, Dorothy L. (1992) "Police Corruption and Community Relations: Community Policing." *Police Studies* 15 (4, Winter): 179-83.

Bradford, David L., and Allan R. Cohen (1984) *Managing for Excellence*. New York: John Wiley and Sons.

Braiden, Chris (1985, 1986) "Bank Robberies and Stolen Bikes: Thoughts of a Street Cop." *Canadian Police College Journal* 10 (1) (1986). (Also available through Chris Braiden Consulting, St. Albert, Alberta, Canada).

_____ (1987) "Community Policing: Nothing New Under the Sun." (Unpublished paper available through Chris Braiden Consulting, St. Albert, Alberta, Canada).

_____ (1990a) "Nothing New Under the Sun." *Problem-Solving Quarterly* (summer). Washington, D.C.: Police Executive Research Forum. Adapted and republished in Daniel E. Lungren (ed.), *Community Oriented Policing and Problem Solving*. Sacramento, CA: California Department of Justice (1992).

_____ (1990b) "Community Based Policing: A Process for Change—A Position Paper Written for the Executive Officers' Team." (Unpublished paper available through Chris Braiden Consulting, St. Albert, Alberta, Canada).

_____ (1995) Personal communication with William A. Geller with former Edmonton, Canada, Police Superintendent Braiden (June 22).

_____ (undated) "Policing—From the Belly of the Whale." (Unpublished paper available through Chris Braiden Consulting, St. Albert, Alberta, Canada).

_____ (undated) "Leadership: It's Not What—Or Where—We Think It Is" (Unpublished paper available through Chris Braiden Consulting, St. Albert, Alberta, Canada).

_____ (undated) "Moments of Truth—What Are They?" (Unpublished paper available through Chris Braiden Consulting, St. Albert, Alberta, Canada).

_____ (undated) "Monopoly: The Congenital Disease of Policing." (Unpublished paper available through Chris Braiden Consulting, St. Albert, Alberta, Canada).

_____ (undated) "Ownership: Who Paints A Rented House?" (Unpublished paper available through Chris Braiden Consulting, St. Albert, Alberta, Canada).

_____ (undated) "Ownership II: Who Washes A Rented Car?" (Unpublished paper available through Chris Braiden Consulting, St. Albert, Alberta, Canada).

_____ (undated) "Plato's Cave." (Unpublished paper available through Chris Braiden Consulting, St. Albert, Alberta, Canada).

_____ (undated) "Policing: The 'Stuff' Is Doing More Harm Than Good." (Unpublished paper available through Chris Braiden Consulting, St. Albert, Alberta, Canada).

_____ (undated) "Policing: Time for A New Winejug." (Unpublished paper available through Chris Braiden Consulting, St. Albert, Alberta, Canada).

_____ (undated) "Thinking About Justice." (Unpublished paper available through Chris Braiden Consulting, St. Albert, Alberta, Canada).

_____ (undated) "Why Change?" (Unpublished paper available through Chris Braiden Consulting, St. Albert, Alberta, Canada).

Brann, Joseph E. (1995a) Personal conversation between William A. Geller and the Director of the Office of Community Policing Services, U.S. Department of Justice (June 28).

_____ (1995b) Personal communication between William A. Geller and the Director of the Office of Community Policing Services, U.S. Department of Justice (October 5).

Brann, Joseph E., Craig Calhoun, and Paul Wallace (1992) "A Change in Policing Philosophy." In Daniel E. Lungren (ed.), *Community Oriented Policing and Problem Solving*. Sacramento, CA: California Department of Justice.

Brann, Joseph E., and Suzanne Whalley (1992) "COPPS: The Transformation of Police Organizations." In Daniel E. Lungren (ed.), *Community Oriented Policing and Problem Solving*. Sacramento, CA: California Department of Justice.

Bratton, William J. (1994) "Reengineering the New York City Police Department." Paper presented at the Major City Chief's Meeting (October) (available through the NYPD).

Briggs, Gary (1995) "Remarks to the Panel on Community Policing." In Community Relations Service, U.S. Department of Justice, *Workshop Summaries: Fifth Annual Regional Police Chiefs'*

Conference—"Policing in the Nineties IV," Des Moines, IA. Washington, D.C.: Community Relations Service.

Broder, David S. (1995) "Less and Less for the Poor." *Washington Post* (October 1): C7.

Brown, Lee P. (1985) "Police-Community Power Sharing." In William A. Geller (ed.), *Police Leadership in America: Crisis and Opportunity*. New York: Praeger.

_____ (1989) "Community Policing: A Practical Guide for Police Officials." *Perspectives on Policing*, No. 12. Washington, D.C.: National Institute of Justice.

_____ (1991) *Policing New York City in the 1990s: The Strategy for Community Policing*. New York: New York City Police Department.

Brown, Lee P., and Mary Ann Wycoff (1987) "Policing Houston: Reducing Fear and Improving Service." *Crime and Delinquency* 33: 71-89.

Bryson, Bill (1995) "On Language: Say What?" *The New York Times Magazine* (September 3): 18.

Buerger, Michael E. (1994) "The Limits of Community." In Dennis P. Rosenbaum (ed.), *The Challenge of Community Policing: Testing the Promises*. Thousand Oaks, CA: Sage.

Burgreen, Bob, and Nancy McPherson (1990, 1992) "Implementing POP (Problem-Oriented Policing): The San Diego Experience." *Police Chief* (October 1990). Reprinted in Daniel E. Lungren (ed.), *Community Oriented Policing and Problem Solving*. Sacramento, CA: California Department of Justice (1992).

Byham, William C., and Jeff Cox (1988) *Zapp! The Lightning of Empowerment: How to Improve Quality, Productivity, and Employee Satisfaction*. New York: Fawcett Columbine.

Capowich, George E., and Janice A. Roehl (1994) "Problem-Oriented Policing: Actions and Effectiveness in San Diego." In Dennis P. Rosenbaum (ed.), *The Challenge of Community Policing: Testing the Promises*. Thousand Oaks, CA: Sage.

Chamberlin, Bruce D. (1995a) Letter to William A. Geller (May 9).

_____ (1995b) Personal communication between William A. Geller and Chief Chamberlain of the Cheektowaga, New York, Police Department (June 12).

Charlotte-Mecklenburg Police Department, Police Academy In-Service Training Staff (1995) *Advanced Law Enforcement Readiness Training (ALERT): Building Partnerships to Prevent the Next Crime*. Charlotte, North Carolina: Author.

Cheh, Mary (1995) "Are Law Suits an Answer to Police Brutality?" In William A. Geller and Hans Toch (eds.), *And Justice for All: Understanding and Controlling Police Abuse of Force*. Washington, D.C.: Police Executive Research Forum.

Chicago Police Department (1993) *Together We Can: A Strategic Plan for Reinventing The Chicago Police Department*. Chicago: Chicago Police Department.

Chicago Police Department, Research and Development Division (1994) *CAPS [Chicago Alternative Policing Strategy] Management Seminar: CAPS Training for Sergeants, Lieutenants, and Captains—Instructor's Guide*. Chicago: Author (unpublished).

Coch, L., and J.R.P. French, Jr. (1948) "Overcoming Resistance to Change." *Human Relations* 1: 512-33.

Cohen, Steven, and William Eimicke (1995) *The New Effective Public Manager*. San Francisco: Jossey-Bass.

Comer, James P. (1988) *Maggie's American Dream: The Life and Times of a Black Family*. New York: Plume/New American Library.

Community Policing Consortium (1995) "Giving Voice: Interviews Conducted Across Ranks." *Community Policing Exchange* (May/June): 3.

Cordery, John L., and Toby D. Wall (1985) "Work Design and Supervisory Practice: A Model." *Human Relations* 38 (5): 425-41.

Cordner, Gary (1985) "Police Research and Police Policy: Some Propositions about the Production and Use of Knowledge." In William A. Geller (ed.), *Police Leadership in America: Crisis and Opportunity*. New York: Praeger.

_____ (1986) "Fear of Crime and the Police: An Evaluation of a Fear-Reduction Strategy." *Journal of Police Science and Administration* 14: 223-33.

_____ (1988) "A Problem-Oriented Approach to Community-Oriented Policing." In Jack R. Greene and Stephen D. Mastrofski (eds.), *Community Policing: Rhetoric or Reality?* New York: Praeger.

_____ (1994) "Foot Patrol Without Community Policing: Law and Order in Public Housing." In Dennis P. Rosenbaum (ed.), *The Challenge of Community Policing: Testing the Promises*. Thousand Oaks, CA: Sage.

Cosgrove, Colleen A., and Jerome E. McElroy (1986) *The Fixed Tour Experiment in the 115th Precinct: Its Effects on Police Officer Stress, Community Perceptions, and Precinct Management*. New York: Vera Institute of Justice.

Couper, David C., and Sabine H. Lobitz (1991) *Quality Policing: The Madison Experience*. Washington, D.C.: Police Executive Research Forum.

Crawford, Robert (1992) "Beat Health and Crack House Abatement (in Oakland, California)." In Daniel E. Lungren (ed.), *Community Oriented Policing and Problem Solving*. Sacramento, CA: California Department of Justice (1992).

Cresap Associates (1991) "Houston Police Department: Draft Final Report." Washington, D.C.: Author.

Crime Control Digest (1995) "Corruption: Six Atlanta Officers Charged." *Crime Control Digest* (September 15): 7.

Davis, Raymond (1985) "Organizing the Community for Improved Policing." In William A. Geller (ed.), *Police Leadership in America: Crisis and Opportunity*. New York: Praeger.

Dean, James W., and Daniel J. Brass (1985) "Social Interaction and the Perception of Job Characteristics in an Organization." *Human Relations* 38 (6): 571-82.

Delattre, Edwin J. (1994) *Character and Cops: Ethics in Policing*, 2nd ed. Washington, D.C.: American Enterprise Institute Press.

Delattre, Edwin J., and Cornelius J. Behan (1991) "Practical Ideals for Managing in the Nineties: A Perspective." In William A. Geller (ed.), *Local Government Police Management*. Washington, D.C.: International City/County Management Association.

Deming, W. Edwards (1986) *Out of the Crisis*. Cambridge, MA: MIT Press.

Drucker, Peter (1964) *Managing for Results*. New York: Harper and Row.

_____ (1974) *Management: Tasks, Responsibilities, Practices*. New York: Harper and Row.

_____ (1986) *The Frontiers of Management*. New York: Truman Talley Books.

Duck, Jeanie Daniel (1994) "Managing Change: The Art of Balancing." *Harvard Business Review* (November-December): 109-18.

Eck, John E. (1983) *Solving Crimes: The Investigation of Burglary and Robbery*. Washington, D.C.: Police Executive Research Forum.

_____ (1992) "Helpful Hints for the Tradition-Bound Chief: Ten Things You Can Do to Undermine Community Policing." *Fresh Perspectives* series. Washington, D.C.: Police Executive Research Forum (June).

_____ (1993) "Alternative Futures for Policing." In David Weisburd and Craig Uchida (eds.), *Police Innovation and Control of the Police: Problems of Law, Order and Community*. New York: Springer-Verlag.

Eck, John E., and William Spelman, with Diane Hill, Darrel W. Stephens, John R. Stedman, and Gerard R. Murphy (1987) *Problem solving: Problem-Oriented Policing in Newport News*. Washington, D.C.: Police Executive Research Forum.

Faiola, Anthony (1995) "At Upscale D.C. Hotels, Suite Deals for Celebrities." *Washington Post* (October 2): A1, A10.

Farmer, Michael T. (ed.) (1981) *Differential Police Response Strategies*. Washington, D.C.: Police Executive Research Forum.

Farrell, Michael J. (1988) "The Development of the Community Patrol Officer Program: Community-Oriented Policing in the New York City Police Department." In Jack R. Greene and Stephen D. Mastrofski (eds.), *Community Policing: Rhetoric or Reality?* New York: Praeger.

Farrell, Michael, Doug Young, and Alex Wright (1993a) *Disorderly Groups: Problem Solving Annual for Community Police Officers and Supervisors (of the New York City Police Department)*. New York: NYPD (Summer).

_____ (1993b) *Drugs: Problem Solving Annual for Community Police Officers and Supervisors (of the New York City Police Department)*. New York: NYPD (Summer).

Feder, Barnaby J. (1993) "At Motorola, Quality Is a Team Sport." *New York Times* (January 21): D1.

Federal Judicial Center (1981) *Experimentation in the Law: Report of the Federal Judicial Center Advisory Committee on Experimentation in the Law.* Washington, D.C.: U.S. Government Printing Office.

Fischer, Bill (1995) Personal communication between William A. Geller and Chicago-area corporate employee (and former minister) Bill Fischer (June 29).

Flanagan, Timothy J., and Michael S. Vaughn (1995) "Public Opinion About Police Abuse of Force." In William A. Geller and Hans Toch (eds.) *And Justice for All: Understanding and Controlling Police Abuse of Force.* Washington, D.C.: Police Executive Research Forum.

Friedman, Warren (1994) "The Community Role in Community Policing." In Dennis P. Rosenbaum (ed.), *The Challenge of Community Policing: Testing the Promises.* Thousand Oaks, CA: Sage.

Fyfe, James J. (ed.) (1985) *Police Management Today: Issues and Case Studies.* Washington, D.C.: International City/County Management Association.

_____ (1989) "The Split-Second Syndrome and Other Determinants of Police Violence." In Roger G. Dunham and Geoffrey P. Alpert (eds.), *Critical Issues in Policing: Contemporary Readings.* Prospect Heights, IL: Waveland Press. Reprinted from Anne Campbell and John Gibbs (eds.), *Violent Transactions.* New York: Basil Blackwell (1986).

_____ (1995) "Training to Reduce Police-Civilian Violence." In William A. Geller and Hans Toch (eds.), *And Justice for All: Understanding and Controlling Police Abuse of Force.* Washington, D.C.: Police Executive Research Forum (Yale University Press version forthcoming).

Galvin, Gerald T. (1992) "Community Policing: Focus on Youth, Graffiti and Drugs (in Vallejo, California)." In Daniel E. Lungren (ed.), *Community Oriented Policing and Problem Solving.* Sacramento, CA: California Department of Justice.

Gates, Henry Louis, Jr. (1995) "The Political Scene: [Colin] Powell and the Black Elite." *The New Yorker* (September 25): 64-80.

Geller, William A. (1985) "Officer Restraint in the Use of Deadly Force: The Next Frontier in Police Shooting Research." *Journal of Police Science and Administration* 13 (2): 153-71.

_____, and Michael S. Scott (1992) *Deadly Force: What We Know—A Practitioner's Desk-Reference on Police-Involved Shootings.* Washington, D.C.: Police Executive Research Forum.

Geller, William A., and Hans Toch (1995) "Improving Our Understanding and Control of Police Abuse of Force: Recommendations for Research and Action." In William A. Geller and Hans Toch (eds.), *And Justice for All: Understanding and Controlling Police Abuse of Force.* Washington, D.C.: Police Executive Research Forum (Yale University Press version forthcoming).

Glensor, Ronald W. (1990) *Community Oriented Policing-Plus.* Reno, NV: Reno Police Department.

_____ (1994) "The Sergeant's Role as a Change Agent." *Problem Solving Quarterly* (Winter/Spring): 3, 8.

Goldberg, Debbie (1995) "For Many in North Philadelphia, Police Corruption is No Surprise." *Washington Post* (October 5): A3.

Goldstein, Herman (1979) "Improving Policing: A Problem-Oriented Approach." *Crime and Delinquency* 23 (2): 236-58.

_____ (1987) "Toward Community-Oriented Policing: Potential, Basic Requirements, and Threshold Questions." *Crime and Delinquency* 33 (1): 6-30.

_____ (1990) *Problem-Oriented Policing.* New York: McGraw-Hill.

_____ (1993) "The New Policing: Confronting Complexity." *National Institute of Justice Research in Brief.* Washington, D.C.: NIJ (December).

_____ (1995) Personal communication between William A. Geller and Goldstein (October 8).

Goodbody, William L. (1995) "A Square Peg in Bureaucracy's Round Hole: Community Policing—The View from the Sergeant's Desk" (fourth article in a series). *Law Enforcement News* (June 30): 12, 14.

Goodmeasure, Inc. (1982) "99 Propositions on Innovation from the Research Literature." In *Stimulating Innovation in Middle Management.* Cambridge, MA: Author.

Gordon, Thomas (1977) *Leader Effectiveness Training.* New York: Bantam Books.

Greene, Jack R., William T. Bergman, and Edward J. McLaughlin (1994) "Implementing Community Policing." In Dennis P. Rosenbaum (ed.), *The Challenge of Community Policing: Testing the Promises.* Thousand Oaks, CA: Sage.

Greene, Jack R., and Stephen D. Mastrofski (eds.) (1988) *Community Policing: Rhetoric or Reality?* New York: Praeger.

Greene, Jack R., and Ralph B. Taylor (1988) "Community-Based Policing and Foot Patrol: Issues of Theory and Evaluation." In Jack R. Greene and Stephen D. Mastrofski (eds.), *Community Policing: Rhetoric or Reality?* New York: Praeger.

Greenwood, Peter W., and John Petersilia (1975) "The Criminal Investigation Process." In Peter W. Greenwood and John Petersilia, *Summary and Policy Implications*, vol. 1. Santa Monica, CA: RAND.

Guth, William D., and Ian C. MacMillan (1986) "Strategy Implementation Versus Middle Management Self-Interest." *Strategic Management Journal* 7: 313-27.

Guyot, Dorothy (1979) "Bending Granite: Attempts to Change the Rank Structure of American Police Departments." *Journal of Police Science and Administration* 7: 253-84.

_____ (1991) *Policing as Though People Matter*. Philadelphia: Temple University Press.

Hansberry, Lorraine (1958) *A Raisin in the Sun*. New York: Signet/New American Library.

Harris, W. Edward (1995a) *How You Can Have a Good Day Everyday (Even If You Made Other Plans)*. Evanston, IL: Stonework Press.

_____ (1995b) "What Cannot Be Changed." Sermon at Unitarian Church of Evanston, Illinois (April 30).

Hartmann, Frank X. (ed.) (1988) "Debating the Evolution of American Policing." *Perspectives on Policing*, No. 5. Washington, D.C.: National Institute of Justice.

Hayward Police Department (1990) "Community Oriented Policing and Problem Solving (COPPS) Implementation Plan." Hayward, CA: Hayward Police Department.

Herman, Susan (1995) Personal communication between William A. Geller and the Director of Community Services for the Columbia, Maryland-based Enterprise Foundation (October 1).

Herbert, Bob (1995a) "In America: Cops Off the Pedestal." *New York Times* (September 8): A15.

_____ (1995b) "In America: Disgracing the Badge." *New York Times* (September 18): A11.

Hickman, Craig, and Michael Silva (1977) *Creating Excellence*. New York: New American Library.

Hornick, Joseph P., P.J. Keith Duggan, and Denise LeClaire (1993) "Community Policing in Edmonton." (Unpublished paper, available from Edmonton, Alberta, Canada Police Department) (December).

Howley, J. Patrick (1995) Personal communication between William A. Geller and Yale Child Study Center school reform specialist Howley (October 3).

Hughes, Langston (1959) "Harlem" in Langston Hughes, *Selected Poems of Langston Hughes*. New York: Vintage Books/Random House.

Hunsaker, Phillip L., and Anthony J. Alessandra (1980) *The Art of Managing People*. New York: Simon and Schuster.

Joachimstaler, Roy (1995) Unpublished internal St. Louis Metropolitan Police Department memorandum from Major Joachimstaler (Special Assistant for C.O.P.S.) to Chief Clarence Harmon re: "Continuous Implementation Strategies for Command Staff and Supervisors of the Districts and the Communications Division" (February 23).

Johnson, John (1995) "LAPD at Crossroads of Old, New: Ranks Torn Between Aggressive Past, Diplomatic Present." *Los Angeles Times* (July 30): A1, A22-A23.

Jordon, S.M. (1992) *Developing Officer Performance Evaluation Systems in Community Policing Agencies by the Year 2002*. Sacramento, CA: California Commission on Peace Officer Standards and Training.

Judge, Mark Gauvreau (1995) "Dance of Democracy: The Cheek-to-Cheek Cure for the Alienation That Ails Us." *Washington Post* (October 1): C1.

Kanter, Rosabeth Moss (1979) "Power Failure in Management Circuits." *Harvard Business Review* (July-August): 65.

_____ (1982) "The Middle Manager as Innovator." *Harvard Business Review* (July-August): 92-105.

_____ (1983) *The Change Masters: Innovation for Productivity in the American Mode*. New York: Simon and Schuster.

Kauffman, Draper L. (1980) *Systems One: An Introduction to Systems Thinking*. Minneapolis: Future Systems, Inc.

Kelling, George L. (1985) "Order Maintenance, the Quality of Life, and Police: A Line of Argument." In

William A. Geller (ed.), *Police Leadership in America: Crisis and Opportunity.* New York: Praeger.

_____ (1988) "Police and Communities: The Quiet Revolution." *Perspectives on Policing*, No. 1. Washington, D.C.: National Institute of Justice.

Kelling, George L., and William J. Bratton (1993) "Implementing Community Policing: The Administrative Problem." *Perspectives on Policing* No. 17. Washington, D.C.: National Institute of Justice.

Kelling, George L., and Robert Kliesmet (1995) "Police Unions, Police Culture, The Friday Crab Club, and Police Use of Force." In William A. Geller and Hans Toch (eds.), *And Justice for All: Understanding and Controlling Police Abuse of Force.* Washington, D.C.: Police Executive Research Forum.

Kelling, George L., and Mark H. Moore (1988) "The Evolving Strategy of Policing." *Perspectives on Policing*, No. 4. Washington, D.C.: National Institute of Justice.

Kelling, George L., Robert Wasserman, and Hubert Williams (1988) "Police Accountability and Community Policing." *Perspectives on Policing*, No. 7. Washington, D.C.: National Institute of Justice.

Kelling, George L., and Mary Ann Wycoff (1991) "New Roles for Mid-Managers." In William A. Geller (ed.), *Local Government Police Management.* Washington, D.C.: International City/County Management Association, p. 292.

Kennedy, David M. (1993) "Strategic Management of Police Resources." (paper prepared for the National Institute of Justice, Washington, D.C.; available through NIJ's National Criminal Justice Reference Service, accession number 139565).

Kimberly, John (1981) "Managerial Innovation." In W.H. Starbuck (ed.), *Handbook of Organizational Design.* New York: Oxford.

Klockars, Carl (1988) "The Rhetoric of Community Policing." In Jack R. Greene and Stephen D. Mastrofski (eds.), *Community Policing: Rhetoric or Reality?* New York: Praeger.

_____ (1995) "A Theory of Excessive Force and Its Control." In William A. Geller and Hans Toch (eds.) *And Justice for All: Understanding and Controlling Police Abuse of Force.* Washington, D.C.: Police Executive Research Forum.

Koenig, David, J., John H. Blahna, and Richard L. Petrick (1979) *Team Policing in St. Paul, Minnesota: An Evaluation of Two Years of Implementation.* St. Paul, MN: Team Police Evaluation Unit, St. Paul Police Department.

Koller, K. (1990) *Working the Beat: The Edmonton Neighborhood Foot Patrol.* Edmonton, Alberta, Canada: Edmonton Police Service.

Kupcinet, Irv (1995) "Kup's Column." *Chicago Sun-Times* (October 11): 60.

Kouzes, James M., and Barry Z. Posner (1987) *The Leadership Challenge: How to Get Extraordinary Things Done in Organizations.* San Francisco: Jossey-Bass.

Langworthy, Robert H. (1986) *The Structure of Police Organizations.* New York: Praeger.

Lavrakas, Paul J. (1995) "Community-Based Crime Prevention: Citizens, Community Organizations, and the Police." In Lawrence B. Joseph (ed.), *Crime, Communities, and Public Policy.* Chicago: Center for Urban Research and Policy Studies, The University of Chicago (distributed by University of Illinois Press).

Leighton, Barry N. (1994) "Community Policing in Canada: An Overview of Experience and Evaluations." In Dennis P. Rosenbaum (ed.), *The Challenge of Community Policing: Testing the Promises.* Thousand Oaks, CA: Sage.

Leo, John (1992) "The Broken-Window Theory of Urban Decay." *This World* (March 15). Reprinted in Daniel E. Lungren (ed.), *Community Oriented Policing and Problem Solving.* Sacramento, CA: California Department of Justice (1992).

Leonard, V.A., and Harry W. More (1971) *Police Organization and Management*, 3rd rev. ed. Mineola, N.Y.: The Foundation Press.

Locke, Hubert G. (1995) "The Color of Law and the Issue of Color: Race and the Abuse of Police Power." In William A. Geller and Hans Toch (eds.) *And Justice for All: Understanding and Controlling Police Abuse of Force.* Washington, D.C.: Police Executive Research Forum.

Longfellow, Michael R. (1995) "Community Oriented Policing in Ormand Beach, Florida." (unpublished paper by Ormand Beach Commander Longfellow).

Lungren, Daniel E. (ed.) (1992) *Community Oriented Policing and Problem Solving.* Sacramento, CA:

California Department of Justice, Attorney General's Office, Crime Prevention Center.

Lurigio, Arthur J., and Dennis P. Rosenbaum (1994) "The Impact of Community Policing on Police Personnel: A Review of the Literature." In Dennis P. Rosenbaum (ed.), *The Challenge of Community Policing: Testing the Promises*. Thousand Oaks, CA: Sage.

Lurigio, Arthur J., and Wesley G. Skogan (1994) "Winning the Hearts and Minds of Police Officers: An Assessment of Staff Perceptions of Community Policing in Chicago." *Crime and Delinquency* 40 (3): 315-30.

Maclean, Norman (1992) *Young Men and Fire: The True Story of the Mann Gulch Fire*. Chicago: University of Chicago Press.

Margolick, David (1995) "Jury Clears Simpson in Double Murder; Spellbound Nation Divides on Verdict." *New York Times* (October 4): A1, A10.

Major, Clarence (1994) *Jubba to Jive: A Dictionary of African-American Slang*. New York: Penguin Books.

Marsh, Anne (1995) "A Prayer at Fifty." A sermon presented at the Unitarian Church of Evanston, Illinois (September 24).

Martin, Hugo (1994) "City Panel Urges Award in LAPD Failure to Inform Man of Threat: North Hollywood Theatre Manager, Witness in Robbery Case, Was Shot in 1985; Police Knew of Possible Death Contract." *Los Angeles Times* (January 5): A15.

Mastrofski, Stephen D. (1988) "Community Policing As Reform: A Cautionary Tale." In Jack R. Greene and Stephen D. Mastrofski (eds.), *Community Policing: Rhetoric or Reality?* New York: Praeger.

_____ (1993) "Eying the Doughnut: Community Policing and Progressive Reform—Book Review Essay of *Beyond 911: A New Era for Policing*, by Malcolm K. Sparrow, Mark H. Moore, and David M. Kennedy." *American Journal of Police* 12 (4): 1-17.

McCrary, Charles (1995) "Remarks to the Panel on Community Policing." In Community Relations Service, U.S. Department of Justice, *Workshop Summaries: Fifth Annual Regional Police Chiefs' Conference—"Policing in the Nineties IV," Des Moines, IA*. Washington, D.C.: Community Relations Service.

McElroy, Jerome E., Colleen A. Cosgrove, and Susan Sadd (1993) *Community Policing: The CPOP (Community Patrol Officer Program) in New York*. Newbury Park, CA: Sage.

McEwen, Tom (1995) "National Assessment Program: 1994 Survey Results." *National Institute of Justice Research in Brief* (May). Washington, D.C.: National Institute of Justice.

McEwen, J. Thomas, Edward F. Connors III, and Marcia I. Cohen (1984) *Evaluation of the Differential Police Response Field Test: Executive Summary*. Alexandria, VA: Research Management Associates.

McNally, D.D. (1991) "Community Based Policing: Organizational Review Recommendations." *By the Way...: A Bi-weekly Publication from the Chief of Police (of Edmonton, Alberta, Canada)*. Edmonton: Edmonton Police Service (April 8).

Meese, Edwin III (1993) "Community Policing and the Police Officer." *Perspectives on Policing*, No. 15. Washington, D.C.: National Institute of Justice.

Melrose, Ken (1995) *Making the Grass Greener on Your Side: A CEO's Journey to Leading by Serving*. New York: Berrett-Koehler Publishers.

Meyer, Josh (1994a) "LAPD Unit on Trial for Allowing Sunland Robbery: Court Battle Pits Safeguarding the Public Against the Need to Gather Evidence, Experts Say." *Los Angeles Times* (January 5): A1, A15.

_____ (1994b) "Lawyers Debate Police Actions in '90 Restaurant Holdup." *Los Angeles Times* (January 6): B8.

Michigan State University School of Criminal Justice (1992) "Basics of Community Policing." *Footprints* 4 (2, Fall-Winter): complete issue (six articles).

Miller, Bill (1995) Personal communication between William A. Geller and Skokie Police Chief Miller (June 21).

Milloy, Courtland (1995) "Washington, Capital of Hypocrisy." *Washington Post* (October 1): B1, B5.

Mintzberg, Henry (1980) *The Nature of Managerial Work*. Englewood Cliffs, N.J.: Prentice-Hall.

Moody, John (1995) "Crime: Safe? You Bet Your Life—New York Can Still be Murder, But Your Chances of Surviving in the Big Apple Have Just Improved." *Time* (July 24): 35.

Moore, Mark H. (1990) "Police Leadership: The Impossible Dream?" In E.C. Hargrove, and J.C. Glidewell (eds.), *Impossible Jobs in Public Management*. Lawrence: University Press of Kansas.

_____ (1992) "Problem Solving and Community Policing." In Michael Tonry and Norval Morris (eds.), *Modern Policing*. Chicago: University of Chicago Press.

_____ (1994) "Research Synthesis and Policy Implications." In Dennis P. Rosenbaum (ed.), *The Challenge of Community Policing: Testing the Promises*. Thousand Oaks, CA: Sage.

_____, and Darrel W. Stephens (1991a) *Beyond Command and Control: The Strategic Management of Police Departments*. Washington, D.C.: Police Executive Research Forum.

_____ (1991b) "Organization and Management." In William A. Geller (ed.), *Local Government Police Management*. Washington, D.C.: International City/County Management Association.

Munro, James L. (1974) *Administrative Behavior and Police Organization*. Cincinnati: W.H. Anderson Co.

Murphy, C., and G. Muir (1985) "Community-Based Policing: A Review of the Critical Issues." Ottawa, Canada: Communications Group of the Solicitor General.

Muwakkil, Salim (1995) "Finding Ways to Stop Police From Crossing That Thin Blue Line." *Chicago Sun-Times* (October 2): 27.

Naisbitt, John, and Patricia Aburdene (1985) *Re-inventing the Corporation*. New York: Warner Books.

Newsweek Magazine (1968) "The King Richard Version." *Newsweek* (September 23): 35.

Nowicki, Dennis E., Gary W. Sykes, and Terry Eisenberg (1991) "Human Resource Management." In William A. Geller (ed.), *Local Government Police Management*. Washington, D.C.: International City/County Management Association.

Nunn, James (1995) "Remarks to the Panel on Community Policing." In Community Relations Service, U.S. Department of Justice, *Workshop Summaries: Fifth Annual Regional Police Chiefs' Conference—"Policing in the Nineties IV," Des Moines, IA*. Washington, D.C.: Community Relations Service.

Oclander, Jorge (1995a) "Gangs Move Into Police Ranks: At Least 15 Officers Tied to Crime Groups." *Chicago Sun-Times* (October 8): 1, 22-23.

_____ (1995b) "'Something Fishy Going On': Neighborhood Wary of Gangs' Link to Cops." *Chicago Sun-Times* (October 9): 1, 8.

_____ (1995c) "Top Cop Shakes Up Gang-Linked District: New Commander Only First Change." *Chicago Sun-Times* (October 11): 1, 12.

Ogle, Dan (no date) "Detectives and Community Policing: Learning, Leading, Managing—A Case Analysis." (unpublished paper available through the Edmonton, Alberta, Canada, Police Service).

Osborne, David, and Ted Gaebler (1993) *Reinventing Government: How the Entrepreneurial Spirit Is Transforming the Public Sector*. New York: Penguin.

Pate, Antony M., Mary Ann Wycoff, Wesley G. Skogan, and Lawrence W. Sherman (1986) *Reducing Fear of Crime in Houston and Newark: A Summary Report*. Washington, D.C.: Police Foundation.

Peak, K, Robert V. Bradshaw, and Ronald W. Glensor (1992) "Improving Citizen Perceptions of the Police: 'Back to the Basics' with a Community Policing Strategy." *Journal of Criminal Justice* 20: 25-40.

Percy, Harold (1995) "Implementing Change: Where Do We Begin?" *By the Way...: A Bi-weekly Publication for Edmonton Police Service Employees* (June 20): 14.

Peters, Thomas J. (1987) *Thriving on Chaos*. New York: Alfred Knopf.

_____ (date unknown) "We Can Learn from Military by Adopting Nine Battlefield Traits." *Chicago Tribune* (included in Chicago Police Department 1994 and Ramsey, et al. 1994).

_____, and Jane Austin (1985) *A Passion for Excellence*. New York: Random House.

_____, and Robert H. Waterman, Jr. (1982) *In Search of Excellence: Lessons from America's Best-Run Companies*. New York: Harper and Row.

Portland Police Bureau (1990) "Community Policing Transition Plan." Portland, OR: Portland Police Bureau.

Potter, Tom (1992) "Strategic Planning and Community Policing." In Daniel E. Lungren (ed.), *Community Oriented Policing and Problem Solving*. Sacramento, CA: California Department of Justice.

Pritchett, Price, and Ron Pound (1995) *A Survival Guide to The Stress of Organizational Change*. Dallas, TX: Pritchett and Associates.

Punch, Maurice (ed.) (1983) *Control in the Police Organization*. Cambridge, MA: MIT Press.

Ramsey Charles H., Barbara B. McDonald, Nola Joyce, Kevin P. Morrison, Margaret J. Poethig, and Tim

Oettmeier (1994) *CAPS Management Seminar: CAPS Training for Sergeants, Lieutenants, and Captains*. Chicago: Chicago Police Department, Research and Development Division.

Reiner, Robert (1992) "Police Research in the United Kingdom: A Critical Review." In Michael Tonry and Norval Morris (eds.), *Modern Policing*. Chicago: University of Chicago Press.

Reiss, Albert J., Jr. (1985) "Policing a City's Central District: The Oakland Story." Washington, D.C.: National Institute of Justice.

_____ (1991) "What is 'R&D' Really?" In William A. Geller (ed.), *Local Government Police Management*. Washington, D.C.: International City/County Management Association, p. 339.

_____ (1992) "Police Organization in the Twentieth Century." In Michael Tonry and Norval Morris (eds.), *Modern Policing*. Chicago: University of Chicago Press.

Reuss-Ianni, Elizabeth (1983) *Two Cultures of Policing: Street Cops and Management Cops*. New Brunswick, N.J.: Transaction Books.

Reynolds, Dan (1994) "Problem Oriented Policing Mid-Level Supervisor Survey." Savannah, GA: Savannah Police Department.

Rich, Thomas F. (1995) "The Use of Computerized Mapping in Crime Control and Prevention Programs." *National Institute of Justice Research in Action* (July). Washington, D.C.: National Institute of Justice.

Riechers, L.M., and Roy R. Roberg (1990) "Community Policing: A Critical Review of Underlying Assumptions." *Journal of Police Science and Administration* 17: 105-14.

Roberg, Roy R. (1994) "Can Today's Police Organizations Effectively Implement Community Policing?" In Dennis P. Rosenbaum (ed.), *The Challenge of Community Policing: Testing the Promises*. Thousand Oaks, CA: Sage.

Robert, Michael (1995) *Product Innovation Strategy Pure and Simple: How Winning Companies Outpace Their Competitors*. New York: McGraw-Hill.

Roberts, Lane J. (1995) "Performance Appraisal in Reverse." *FBI Law Enforcement Bulletin* (September): 21-25.

Rosenbaum, Dennis (ed.) (1994) *The Challenge of Community Policing: Testing the Promises*. Thousand Oaks, CA: Sage.

Rossi, Rosalind (1995) "Steak an Saunas at School Seminars: While City System Battled Big Deficit, Posh Retreats Cost Half Million Dollars." *Chicago Sun-Times* (September 26): 1, 14-15.

Sadd, Susan, and Randolph Grinc (1994) "Innovative Neighborhood Oriented Policing: An Evaluation of Community Policing Programs in Eight Cities." In Dennis P. Rosenbaum (ed.), *The Challenge of Community Policing: Testing the Promises*. Thousand Oaks, CA: Sage.

St. Louis Metropolitan Police Department (1993a) "Minutes from Chief's Meeting with Police Officers Regarding C.O.P.S. Implementation." (unpublished memorandum on file in Chief's Office) (May 5).

St. Louis Metropolitan Police Department (1993b) "Minutes from Chief's Meeting with Lieutenants." (unpublished memorandum on file in Chief's Office) (June 21).

San Diego Police Department (1994) *Problem Oriented Policing Training Guide*. San Diego: San Diego Police Department (May).

Santora, Joyce E. (1992) "Rating the Boss at Chrysler." *Personnel Journal* May: 38.

Sawyer, Forrest (1995) ABC-TV news reporter, reporting during ABC TV's *Nightline* on the inventiveness under pressure of the Apollo 13 Space Shuttle flight and ground crews during 1970 (July 14).

Sayles, Leonard R. (1993) "Middle Managers Can Rescue Business." *New York Times* (February 14): sec. 3, p. 11.

Scharf, Peter, and Arnold Binder (1983) *The Badge and the Bullet: Police Use of Deadly Force*. New York: Praeger.

Scharm, George L. (1994) Memorandum to William A. Geller on things police supervisors do that either help or hinder a department's implementation of community policing (March 28).

Schorr, Lisbeth B., with Daniel Schorr (1988) *Within Our Reach: Breaking the Cycle of Disadvantage*. New York: Anchor/Doubleday.

Schwartz, Alfred I., and Sumner N. Clarren (1977) *The Cincinnati Team Policing Experiment: A Summary Report*. Washington, D.C.: Police Foundation.

Schwartz, Tony (1973) *The Responsive Chord: How Radio and TV Manipulate You...Who You Vote For..What You Buy...And How You Think.* Garden City, NY: Anchor Press/Doubleday.

_____ (1983) *Media: The Second God.* Garden City, NY: Anchor Press/Doubleday.

Seattle Police Department (1995) "Mission, Vision, Core Values." Seattle: Author.

Seib, Gerald F. (1995) "Capital Journal: What the Feds Can Really Do To Fight Crime." *The Wall Street Journal* (September 13): A16.

Sensenbrenner, Joseph (1991) "Quality Comes to City Hall." *Harvard Business Review* (March-April): 64-75.

Shadish, William R., Jr., Thomas D. Cook, and Laura C. Leviton (1991) *Foundations of Program Evaluation: Theories of Practice.* Newbury Park, CA: Sage.

Shanahan, Michael G. (1985) "Private Enterprise and the Public Police: The Professionalizing Effects of a New Partnership." In William A. Geller (ed.), *Police Leadership in America: Crisis and Opportunity.* New York: Praeger.

Sherman, Lawrence W. (1975) "Middle Management and Police Democratization: A Reply to John E. Angell." *Criminology* 12: 363-77.

_____ (1978) *Scandal and Reform: Controlling Police Corruption.* Berkeley and Los Angeles: University of California Press.

_____ (1980) "Causes of Police Behavior: The Current State of Quantitative Research." *Journal of Research in Crime and Delinquency* 17(1): 69-100.

_____ (1986) "Policing Communities: What Works?" In Albert J. Reiss, Jr., and Michael Tonry (eds.), *Communities and Crime*, vol. 8 of *Crime and Justice: An Annual Review of Research* (series edited by Michael Tonry and Norval Morris). Chicago: University of Chicago Press.

Sherman, Lawrence W., Catherine Milton, and Thomas Kelly (1973) *Team Policing: Seven Case Studies.* Washington, D.C.: Police Foundation.

Sherman, Lawrence W., and Anthony V. Bouza (1991) "Seizing Opportunities for Reform." In William A. Geller (ed.), *Local Government Police Management.* Washington, D.C.: International City/County Management Association, pp. 358-61.

Skogan, Wesley G. (1990) *Disorder and Decline: Crime and the Spiral of Decay in American Neighborhoods.* New York: The Free Press.

_____ (1994) "The Impact of Community Policing on Neighborhood Residents: A Cross-Site Analysis." In Dennis P. Rosenbaum (ed.), *The Challenge of Community Policing: Testing the Promises.* Thousand Oaks, CA: Sage.

Skogan, Wesley G., Susan M. Hartnett, Jill DuBois, Justine H. Lovig, Lynn Higgins, Susan F. Bennett, Paul J. Lavrakas, Arthur Lurigio, Richard L. Block, Dennis P. Rosenbaum, and Gail Dantzker (1994) *Community Policing in Chicago, Year One: An Interim Report.* Chicago, IL: Illinois Criminal Justice Information Authority.

Skogan, Wesley G., Susan M. Hartnett, Justine H. Lovig, Jill DuBois, Sheila Houmes, Sirgulina Davidsdottir, Robert VanStedum, Marianne Kaiser, Dana Cole, Noele Gonzalez, Susan F. Bennett, Paul J. Lavrakas, Arthur Lurigio, Richard L. Block, Dennis P. Rosenbaum, Scott Althaus, Dominique Whelan, Tabatha R. Johnson, and Lynn Higgins (1995) *Community Policing in Chicago, Year Two: An Interim Report.* Chicago, IL: Illinois Criminal Justice Information Authority.

Skolnick, Jerome H., and David H. Bayley (1986) *The New Blue Line: Police Innovation in Six American Cities.* New York: The Free Press.

_____ (1988) *Community Policing: Issues and Practices Around the World.* Washington, D.C.: National Institute of Justice.

Smith, Doug (1994) "L.A. Cleared of Liability: Judge Rules Against the Former Sunland Manager Who Said Officers Should Not Have Waited to Intervene After Robbers Broke In." *Los Angeles Times* (January 13): B1, B8.

Smith, Hedrick (1995) "Address to the National Press Club Luncheon" (Washington, D.C., July 12, moderated by Monroe Karmin). Transcribed by Federal News Service, Washington, D.C.

Smitherman, Geneva (1977) *Talkin' and Testifying: The Language of Black America.* Detroit: Wayne State University Press.

Sonenclar, Robert J. (1993) "Case Study: Ben & Jerry's—Management with a Human Flavor." *Hemispheres*

Magazine (March): 25-26.

Sparrow, Malcolm (1988, 1992) "Implementing Community Policing." *Perspectives on Policing.* Washington, D.C.: National Institute of Justice (November 1988). Reprinted in Daniel E. Lungren (ed.), *Community Oriented Policing and Problem Solving.* Sacramento, CA: California Department of Justice (1992).

Sparrow, Malcolm, Mark H. Moore, and David M. Kennedy (1990) *Beyond 911: The New Era of Policing.* New York: Basic Books.

_____ (1993) "A Response to Mastrofski." *American Journal of Police* 12 (4): 19-21.

Spelman, William, and John E. Eck (1987) "Problem Oriented Policing." *National Institute of Justice Research in Brief* (January).

Spiotto, Michael (no date) Comment made by former First Deputy Superintendent, Chicago Police Department and reported to William A. Geller by Dennis Nowicki.

Spitzer, Dean R. (1995) *Super Motivation: A Blueprint for Energizing Your Organization from Top to Bottom.* New York: AMACOM Books.

Stamper, Norman H. (1976) *San Diego's Community-Oriented Policing: A Case Study in Organizational Change.* San Diego: San Diego Police Department.

_____ (1992) *Removing Managerial Barriers to Effective Police Leadership: A Study of Executive Leadership and Executive Management in Big-City Police Departments.* Washington, D.C.: Police Executive Research Forum.

_____ (1995a) Personal communication between William A. Geller and Settle Chief Norman Stamper (April 20).

_____ (1995b) Personal communication between William A. Geller and Seattle Chief Norman Stamper (September 18).

Stephens, Darrel W. (1993) "Meeting the Challenges of Tomorrow Today: Community Policing in St. Petersburg." St. Petersburg, FL: St. Petersburg Police Department.

_____ (1995a) Letter to William A. Geller (September 11).

_____ (1995b) "Fuhrman Tapes Cast Undue Shadow on Police Nationwide." *St. Petersburg Times* (September 29): 2.

Stewart, James K. (1985) "Research and the Police Administrator: Working Smarter, Not Harder." In William A. Geller (ed.), *Police Leadership in America: Crisis and Opportunity.* New York: Praeger.

Strandberg, K.W. (1992) "Community Policing: Is It Working?" *Law Enforcement Technology* 19 (10, October): 34-35, 70-72.

Sulton, Anne Thomas (1992) "East Dallas Community-Police and Refugee Affairs Office." In Daniel E. Lungren (ed.), *Community Oriented Policing and Problem Solving.* Sacramento, CA: California Department of Justice.

Swan, William S. (1991) *How to Do a Superior Performance Appraisal: A Guide for Managers and Professionals.* New York: Wiley.

Sweeney, Albert (1995) Memorandum to William A. Geller from Captain Sweeney, Commanding Officer of the Boston Police Department Training Academy (July 21).

Szanton, Peter (1981) *Not Well Advised: The City as Client—An Illuminating Analysis of Urban Governments and Their Consultants.* New York: Russell Sage Foundation and The Ford Foundation.

Taft, Philip B., Jr. (1986) *Fighting Fear: The Baltimore County C.O.P.E. Project.* Washington, D.C.: Police Executive Research Forum.

Taylor, Frederick W. (1947) *Scientific Management.* New York: Harper and Brothers.

Thomas-Lester, Avis (1995) "Search for Chief Should Stop at Soulsby, Many in D.C. Say." *Washington Post* (October 1): A1, A24.

Thurman, Q., P. Bogen, and A. Giacomazzi (1993) "Program Monitoring and Community Policing: A Process Evaluation of Community Policing in Spokane, Washington." *American Journal of Police* 12: 89-114.

Toch, Hans (1995a) "The Violence-Prone Police Officer." In William A. Geller and Hans Toch (eds.) *And Justice for All: Understanding and Controlling Police Abuse of Force.* Washington, D.C.: Police Executive Research Forum.

_____ (1995b) "Research and Reform in Community Policing." *American Journal of Police* 14 (1): 1-10.

Toch, Hans, and J. Douglas Grant (1991) *Police as Problem Solvers*. New York: Plenum Press.

Toch, Hans, J. Douglas Grant, and Raymond T. Galvin (1975) *Agents of Change: A Study in Police Reform*. New York: John Wiley and Sons.

Toch, Hans, and John Klofas (1994) "Pluralistic Ignorance, Revisited." In G.M. Stephenson and J.H. Davis (eds.), *Progress in Applied Social Psychology*, Vol. 2. Chichester, England: John Wiley and Sons.

Tonry, Michael (1995) *Malign Neglect: Race, Crime, and Punishment in America*. New York: Oxford University Press.

Townsend, Robert (1984) *Further Up the Organization: How to Stop Management from Stifling People and Strangling Productivity*. New York: Alfred A. Knopf.

Travis, Jeremy (1995) "National Institute of Justice Solicitation: NIJ Invites Proposals for Policing Research and Evaluation." Washington, D.C.: NIJ (May).

Travis, Jeremy, Gerald Lynch, and Ellen Schall (1993) *Rethinking School Safety: The Report of the [New York City School] Chancellor's Advisory Panel on School Safety*. New York: New York City School Chancellor.

Trojanowicz, Robert C. (1992) "Building Support for Community Policing: An Effective Strategy." *FBI Law Enforcement Bulletin* 61 (5, May): 7-12.

_____ (1994) "The Future of Community Policing." In Dennis P. Rosenbaum (ed.), *The Challenge of Community Policing: Testing the Promises*. Thousand Oaks, CA: Sage.

_____, and Bonnie Bucqueroux (1990) *Community Policing: A Contemporary Perspective*. Cincinnati: Anderson Publishing.

_____ (1992) "Toward Development of Meaningful and Effective Performance Evaluations." East Lansing, MI: Michigan State University, School of Criminal Justice.

Utterback, James (1974) "Innovation in Industry." *Science* (February): 620-26.

Vernon, R.L., and J.P. Lasley (1992) "Police/Citizen Partnerships in the Inner City (Los Angeles)." *FBI Law Enforcement Bulletin* 61 (5, May): 18-22.

Vogl, A.J. (1993/1994) "The Age of Reengineering" (an interview with Michael Hammer and James Champy, authors of *Reengineering the Corporation: A Manifesto for Business Revolution*). *Acumen* (December 1993/January 1994): 50-57 (reprinted from *Across the Board*—June 1993—published by The Conference Board.

Vonnegut, Kurt, Jr. (1961) "Harrison Bergeron." In Kurt Vonnegut, Jr., *Welcome to the Monkey House*. New York: Delacorte Press/Seymour Lawrence. Originally published in *Fantasy and Science Fiction*.

Walker, Sam (1993) "Does Anyone Remember Team Policing? Lessons of the Team Policing Experience for Community Policing." *American Journal of Police* 12: 33-55.

Wall, Jim, William DeLano, and Cary DeLano (1991) *Ropes Course Procedural Manual*. Pittsboro, North Carolina: Outdoor Institute.

Wasserman, Robert, and Mark H. Moore (1988) "Values in Policing." *Perspectives on Policing*, No. 8. Washington, D.C.: National Institute of Justice.

Watson, Elizabeth M., and Gerald L. Williams (1991) "Community Policing and Law Enforcement Accreditation: Emerging Issues." In William A. Geller (ed.), *Local Government Police Management*. Washington, D.C.: International City/County Management Association, pp. 392-93.

Webber, Alan M. (1991, 1992) "Crime and Management: An Interview with New York City Police Commissioner Lee P. Brown." *Harvard Business Review* (May-June). Reprinted in Daniel E. Lungren (ed.), *Community Oriented Policing and Problem Solving*. Sacramento, CA: California Department of Justice.

Weisburd, David (1994) "Evaluating Community Policing: Role Tensions Between Practitioners and Evaluators." In Dennis P. Rosenbaum (ed.), *The Challenge of Community Policing: Testing the Promises*. Thousand Oaks, CA: Sage.

_____, Jerome McElroy, and Patricia Hardyman (1988) "Challenges to Supervision in Community Policing: Observations on a Pilot Project." *American Journal of Police* 7 (2): 29-50.

Weisel, Deborah Lamm (1990, 1992) "Playing the Home Field: A Problem-Oriented Approach to Drug Control." *American Journal of Police* 9 (1) (1990). Reprinted in Daniel E. Lungren (ed.), *Community Oriented Policing and Problem Solving*. Sacramento, CA: California Department of Justice (1992).

_____ (1994) "Toward a Practical Approach to Organizational Change: Community Policing Initiatives in Six Cities." In Dennis P. Rosenbaum (ed.), *The Challenge of Community Policing: Testing the Promises*. Thousand Oaks, CA: Sage.

Wheelis, Allen (1973) *How People Change*. New York: Harper and Row.

Whitney, John O. (1994) *The Trust Factor: Liberating Profits and Restoring Corporate Vitality*. New York: McGraw Hill.

Wilkinson, Deanna L., and Dennis P. Rosenbaum (1994) "The Effects of Organizational Structure on Community Policing." In Dennis P. Rosenbaum (ed.), *The Challenge of Community Policing: Testing the Promises*. Thousand Oaks, CA: Sage.

Williams, Gerald, and Ronald Sloan (1990) *Turning Concept Into Practice: The Aurora, Colorado Story*. Aurora, CO: Aurora Police Department.

Williams, Hubert (1985) "External Resources." In William A. Geller (ed.), *Local Government Police Management*. Washington, D.C.: International City/County Management Association.

_____, and Patrick V. Murphy (1990) "The Evolving Strategy of Police: A Minority View." *Perspectives on Policing*, No. 13. Washington, D.C.: National Institute of Justice.

Wilson, Dot (1995) Interview on National Public Radio by Debbie Elliot with New Orleans public housing resident Dot Wilson (broadcast September 16).

Wilson, James Q. (1968) *Varieties of Police Behavior*. Cambridge, MA: Harvard University Press.

_____ (1989) *Bureaucracy: What Government Agencies Do and Why They Do It*. New York: Basic Books.

_____, and George L. Kelling (1983) "Broken Windows: The Police and Neighborhood Safety." *The Atlantic Monthly* (March): 29-38.

_____ (1989) "Making Neighborhoods Safe." *The Atlantic Monthly* (February): 46-52.

Wilson, Orlando W., and Roy C. McLaren (1972) *Police Administration*, 3rd ed. New York: McGraw-Hill.

Wycoff, Mary Ann (1988) "The Benefits of Community Policing: Evidence and Conjecture." In Jack R. Greene and Stephen D. Mastrofski (eds.), *Community Policing: Rhetoric or Reality?* New York: Praeger.

Wycoff, Mary Ann, and Tim N. Oettmeier (1993) *Evaluating Patrol Officer Performance Under Community Policing: The Houston Experiment*. Washington, D.C.: Police Foundation.

Wycoff, Mary Ann, and Wesley G. Skogan (1993) *Community Policing in Madison: Quality From the Inside Out*. Washington, D.C.: National Institute of Justice (December).

_____ (1994) "Community Policing in Madison: An Analysis of Implementation and Impact." In Dennis P. Rosenbaum (ed.), *The Challenge of Community Policing: Testing the Promises*. Thousand Oaks, CA: Sage.

X, Poet (aka Derek Jennings) (1995) "Talkin' That Talk: There's More to African American English Than Just Slang—It's History and Culture." *YSB [Young Sisters and Brothers]* Magazine 5 (2, October): 57-70.

Yates, Ronald E. (1994) "Building Trust Means Tearing Down Old Business Ways." *Chicago Tribune*.

Zhao, Jihong, Quint C. Thurman, and Nicholas P. Lovrich (1995) "Community-Oriented Policing Across the U.S.: Facilitators and Impediments to Implementation." *American Journal of Police* 14 (1): 11-28.

Police Executive Research Forum

The Police Executive Research Forum is the national professional association of chief executives of large city, county, and state police departments. The Forum's purpose is to improve the delivery of police services and the effectiveness of crime control through several means:

- the exercise of strong national leadership;
- public debate of police and criminal justice issues;
- research and policy development;
- the provision of vital management and leadership services to police agencies.

Forum members are selected on the basis of their commitment to the Forum's purpose and principles. The principles which guide the Police Executive Research Forum are that:

- research, experimentation, and exchange of ideas through public discussion and debate are paths for development of a professional body of knowledge about policing;
- substantial and purposeful academic study is a prerequisite for acquiring, understanding, and adding to the body of knowledge of professional police management;
- maintenance of the highest standards of ethics and integrity is imperative in the improvement of policing;
- the police must, within the limits of the law, be responsible and accountable to citizens as the ultimate source of police authority;
- the principles embodied in the Constitution are the foundation of policing.